ARTHUR ROSENBERG

FORMERLY PROFESSOR OF HISTORY AT
THE UNIVERSITY OF BERLIN

∽

DEMOCRACY AND

SOCIALISM

*A Contribution to the Political History
of the Past 150 Years*

D1197700

BEACON PRESS   BOSTON

Originally published as
DEMOKRATIE UND SOZIALISMUS: ZUR POLITISCHEN
GESCHICHTE DER LETZTEN 150 JAHRE

Copyright 1938 by Verlag Allert de Lange, Amsterdam

Copyright 1939 by Alfred A. Knopf, Inc.

First published as a Beacon Paperback in 1965 by arrangement with
Alfred A. Knopf, Inc.

Published simultaneously in Canada by S. J. Reginald Saunders
and Company, Ltd., Toronto

I dedicate
the American Edition of this book
to my friend
JESSE D. CLARKSON
Brooklyn College, New York

PREFACE

The present book is a historical contribution to the present discussion of democracy. As in my former works I have not hidden my personal point of view, but at the same time I have written entirely independently of every party or group interest. The book is intended to present primarily the practical political work of Marx and Engels during the period of 1845–95. For these two socialist leaders their practical policy was a continual controversy with democracy, so that, seen historically, the entire problem of " democracy and socialism " belongs to the history of these fifty years.

The concept and the general estimate of democracy have changed completely from 1845 to the present. It was therefore necessary, in order to make the political beginnings of Marx and Engels comprehensible, to present the early history of modern democracy up to 1845 in a short sketch. Finally the reader can justly demand that the threads of development should not be dropped in 1895, but that he should be assisted in constructing the connexion between 1895 and the present. The concluding part of the book is intended to serve this purpose.

How Marx and Engels thought at a particular moment of their political lives, and what purpose their actions pursued, can only be gathered from their contemporary utterances. What they wrote during the later periods of their lives concerning the past is sometimes one-sided, because it arises out of a changed political situation. Thus, for instance, one

would run into gross misunderstandings if one should infer
the attitude of Marx and Engels towards revolutionary democracy during the years 1845 to 1849 only from their writings after the miscarriage of the revolution.

Thus the chief source for this book is the correspondence
between Marx and Engels, as it has now been published in
the exemplary four-volume edition of the Marx-Engels Institute. A rich source for the history of early democracy is Vol-
ume VI of the first section of the great complete edition of
the works of Marx and Engels, which contains the writings
of both men from May 1846 to March 1848. Besides this,
the other writings and collected letters of Marx and Engels
were used as far as they belong within the bounds of this
book. Of the copious literature on Marx and Engels the
works of Karl Korsch and Gustav Mayer were especially
valuable to me. The following authorities were important
for my understanding of these topics: Mathiez for the great
French Revolution; Beard for Jefferson and the older American democracy; Seignobos for the history of the French
parties during the nineteenth century; Bergsträsser and Veit
Valentin for German revolutionary and party history. I have
substantiated my own conception of the Russian Revolution
and the German Republic more fully in the books *History of
Bolshevism, Origin of the German Republic,* and *History of
the German Republic.*

I wrote the greatest part of my book in Liverpool and received the most cordial assistance from the Liverpool University Library while doing so. While at work on the conclusion of the book I received the same friendly aid from
the International Institute of Social Research in New York.
Finally I must thank my friend Dr. Franz Neumann, especially for his co-operation in procuring the literature.

ARTHUR ROSENBERG

New York, November 1937

PREFACE

FOR THE AMERICAN EDITION

ى

The text of the American edition follows that of the German edition without any change. Only the Notes have been added especially for the American edition.

The recent events which culminated in the so-called Peace of Munich brought about a big defeat for European democracy. The breakdown of the French Popular Front has been stressed in the text of this book. Now it is clear that the defeat of the French Popular Front is a historical event of first-class importance, for it wholly paralysed the democratic force in France. Only because the French government was ready to capitulate at any moment after the beginning of the Czechoslovak crisis did the endeavours of the Labour Party and Tory democracy in England also become useless, enabling the governing Right wing of the Conservative Party to follow its own tendencies and co-operate with the French will to retreat. Once more France has been proved to be the centre of the social struggle in Europe. As in 1871, so in 1938 the failure of French democracy became the failure of democracy throughout Europe. Czechoslovak democracy, isolated and abandoned by all its " friends," has now to share the fate of the workers of Vienna.

During the last weeks international public opinion has been speaking again of the " weakness " of democracy. But people forget that the commonwealth which is not ready at any moment to make the supreme sacrifice for its freedom and existence is no democracy at all.

ARTHUR ROSENBERG

New York, October 16, 1938

CONTENTS

PART III

From 1895 to the Present [*1937*]

PART I

MODERN DEMOCRACY BEFORE MARX

MODERN DEMOCRACY
BEFORE MARX

1. *What is Democracy?*

The first consciously socialist statesman of the great French Revolution, Babeuf, developed his program in a significant letter to his friend Bodson early in 1796. In this letter Babeuf acknowledges that he is an absolute follower of Robespierre. He represents the reawakening of Robespierre as his task. Babeuf writes: " To awaken Robespierre again means to reawaken all the energetic patriots of the Republic and with them the People. . . . Robespierrism lives in the whole Republic, it lives in the entire class of clear-thinking people who are competent to judge, and naturally in the People. The cause for this is simple: Robespierrism is democracy, and both of these words are absolutely identical. Therefore if one reawakens Robespierrism, one can be certain to awaken democracy again."

Today if one were to ask an average politician, or for that matter any educated person, whom he considered as the historical personification of democracy, it is very improbable that one would receive the answer " Robespierre." The man of the Terror, the head of the bloody dictatorial government of 1793, is not exactly a democrat for the present generation. For Babeuf, however, the system of Robespierre and democracy are absolutely identical. The passage

3

in the above letter shows us still another thing. It shows us that Babeuf in the year 1796 considered not only Robespierre but likewise himself as a democrat. At that time Babeuf was preparing a violent uprising of the poor French people, in order to overthrow the corrupt capitalistic government of the Directory and to replace it by a new political organization based upon the principle of community of property. For Babeuf and his period such efforts were democratic.

Half a century later Marx and Engels published their *Communist Manifesto*. In this document Marx and Engels did not wish to erect any learned theories, but they wanted to express themselves in such a manner that every worker would understand them. In the *Communist Manifesto* of 1848 they say: "We have seen above that the first step in the revolution by the working class is to raise the proletariat to the position of the ruling class, to establish democracy. The proletariat will use its political power to wrest all capital gradually from the bourgeoisie." According to this, "the elevation of the proletariat to the position of the ruling class" is identical for the authors of the *Communist Manifesto* with the struggle to obtain democracy. At that time Marx and Engels could write thus without having to fear that they would excite any misunderstanding or any confusion among the masses of the people. Democracy is the conquest of political power by the proletariat. Babeuf would have subscribed to this without any hesitation.

Nevertheless democracy and communism were not completely identical for Marx and Engels around 1848. For the proletariat can indeed exercise political power in the state, but it does not therefore have to carry out a consistent community of property. Despite this, democracy and communism were closely related to each other for the generation of 1848. In October 1847 Engels wrote in an article in the *Deutsche Brüsseler Zeitung:* "The Communists are far removed under present conditions from starting useless arguments with the Democrats; on the contrary, at present they themselves proceed as Democrats in all practical party questions. In all civilized countries the necessary result of democracy is the political rule of the proletariat, and the political rule of the proletariat is the first condition for all communistic measures. As long as democracy is not yet won, so long do Communists and Democrats fight together, and so long are the interests of the Democrats likewise those of the Communists. Until then the differences between both parties are of a purely theoretical nature, and can be discussed very well theoretically without disturbing their common action in any way. It will even be possible to agree on some measures which are to be undertaken in the interest of the previously oppressed classes immediately after the achievement of democracy, for instance, the management of the large industries and the railroads by the state, the education of all children at the expense of the state, etc."

The differences between democracy and communism as the revolutionary fighters of 1848 saw them will be discussed in greater detail below. Here it is sufficient to emphasize the close relationship and the community of interests between both tendencies as they existed for the general public in 1847. For the *Deutsche Brüsseler Zeitung* certainly did not want to print lectures on political science, but only to use and to clarify the political concepts which were commonly employed. Now compare with this the relations between democracy and communism in our own generation. After the Revolution of November 1918 a "Democratic Party" arose in Germany. It was the party of the bourgeois republicans. The industrialist and subsequent Minister Rathenau belonged to it. The German Democratic Party had nothing in common with the Communists and always considered itself as the mortal enemy of the German Communist Party. At the same time in the United States, President Wilson, who certainly considered himself a good democrat, was the most violent opponent of all communistic efforts among the working classes.

Now let us listen to a voice from the opposing camp during the Revolution of 1848-9. In November 1849 the conservative deputy von Bismarck declared in the Prussian Landtag: " Landed property is desired not only by those who already have a temporary use of land, but also by those who do not have it. Throughout the whole of last year the numerous class of day labourers in the eastern provinces — for instance, in Pomerania and Prussia — has been stirred up to such demands by the promises of the Democrats. In the loyal provinces at that time the elections of Deputy Bucher and his political friends, for example, were made possible by promises of land. . . . It is a deplorable fact that the envy of the day labourer towards the landed peasant is rising, for he sees that the fruits of the revolution are being harvested only by the wealthy, without benefiting him. The demands of the day labourers are by no means restricted to this: that the plots of land whose use forms a part of their wages should be bestowed upon them, for no one can exist on that alone. They go further: they demand complete division, not only of the manor estates, but also of the farms."

Nor did the deputy von Bismarck desire to proclaim any political discoveries from the platform of the Prussian Landtag; but he used the political expressions that everyone understood. To the Prussian junkers at that time the democrats were the men of the agrarian revolution, the Red agitators, who summoned the agrarian labourers to divide not only the manor estates but also the larger farms. At that time the deputy Lothar Bucher was the type of this agrarian rebel to the junker von Bismarck. As a result of historical circumstances the junker von Bismarck later became the Reich Chancellor Prince Bismarck and the communist Bucher the Royal Prussian Privy Councillor Bucher, the most loyal and most valuable collaborator of Bismarck.

A generation later, in December 1884, Friedrich Engels wrote in a letter: " As far as pure democracy and its role in the future are concerned, I am of the opinion that it plays a far more subordinate part in Germany than in countries with an older industrial development. That would not prevent it, however, from achieving a momentary significance at the moment of revolution as the extreme middle-class party, as which it set itself up in Frankfurt [that is, in the German Parliament at Frankfurt in 1848–9], and as the last sheet-anchor of the entire bourgeois and even feudal economy. At such a moment the entire reactionary mass steps behind it and strengthens it. Everything which was reactionary behaves democratically. . . . At any rate our only opponent on the day of the crisis and on the following day is the collective reaction which gathers around pure democracy, and that, I believe, should not be forgotten."

It is important that Engels does not speak about " democracy " here, but always about " pure " democracy. Quite obviously he means a bourgeois state, in which indeed general suffrage prevails, but private property is not touched. It could be said that Engels had already called attention to the difference between democracy and communism in 1847. Nevertheless the change of the political concept from the time of the Brussels newspaper article to the letter of 1884 is entirely obvious. To express it very simply, in 1847 the socialist workers and democracy are on the same side of the barricades, but no longer in 1884. Engels in 1884 no longer writes that democracy, even non-communistic democracy, necessarily coincides with the political rule of the proletariat. Now Engels considers the possibility that pure democracy may be the barrier from behind which all the combined groups and tendencies of the bourgeoisie and even of feudalism will ward off the rule of the proletariat. As his letters show, Engels occupied himself in detail, during the eighties, with the question of what a revolution in Germany at some future day would look like, whether it would be

possible to erect a socialist state directly after the overthrow
of the feudal and military monarchy of the Hohenzollerns,
or whether pure democracy — that is, the bourgeois-capitalistic republic — would first come into power. Engels believed that the decision would lie with the Prussian army.
The Socialists would have to attempt to win the rural proletariat with the slogan of an expropriation of large estates
and their transfer to co-operatives of the rural workers. The
recruits for the Prussian guard regiments came from the
rural districts east of the Elbe. The regiments on which
Prussianism and the rule of the house of Hohenzollern
rested could be disrupted by the slogan of an expropriation
of landed property. Then it would perhaps be possible in
Germany to avoid the intermediate stage of pure democracy. This measure is extremely noteworthy; " expropriation of landed property and transfer of the land to the rural
workers " was considered typically democratic in 1848, and
now this same slogan should serve the purpose of making
" pure democracy " dispensable in Germany!

During the World War the Entente powers, America and
President Wilson at their head, affirmed that they fought
for the victory of democracy. At that time people had already long become accustomed to understand by a democratic state a bourgeois state governed by the method of
general suffrage. The path of reform, which might be
achieved peacefully by persuading the majority of the people, was considered as the democratic form of action, in
contrast to all attempts of revolutionary violence. It is likewise known that in all countries after 1918 the radical and
activistic elements who were dissatisfied with existing conditions began to disregard democracy. We recall only the
bolshevist and fascist propaganda against democracy.

In 1923 in Hamburg the Communist workers revolted
against the then existent German state, the bourgeois-democratic Republic. Subsequently the Communist Party secretary Urbahns was tried on the indictment that he had insti-

gated the revolt. Urbahns defended himself in an impressive speech, which ended with the words: " The masses will say with us: we will rather burn in the fire of revolution than perish on the dung-heap of democracy."

What a change in the opinion of democracy from Babeuf to Urbahns! Then the self-evident supposition that a violent socialist revolution would be a democratic affair, no matter how much blood and terror accompanied it; and now the deep contempt and hate of the radical socialist for democracy, which appears to him as the personification of the existing capitalist order with all its inadequacies. It is evident that in the course of the past hundred and forty years the concept of democracy had changed fundamentally, and that the turning-point must lie somewhere in the period between 1850 and 1880.

The present inquiry is intended to explain the relation of democracy to Marxism. There are very many and contradictory definitions of Marxism. For the purpose of this book the simplest and most indisputable definition has been taken as a basis — namely, as the political theory and practice of Marx and Engels themselves. Both men started their political activity approximately about 1845. Engels died twelve years after Marx, in 1895. The problem lies therefore in the relations between democracy and Marxism in the fifty years from 1845 to 1895.

It will later be shown in detail that the labour policies of Marx and Engels were an incessant controversy with democracy. At all times the democratic movements furnished the basis upon which Marx and Engels had to construct their policy, and on the other hand Marx and Engels sought constantly to influence and to transform the democratic parties and tendencies in accordance with their own ideas. Therefore it will be necessary to trace the history of the democratic movement from 1845 to 1895 briefly, and at the same time to examine repeatedly the attitude of Marxism to the single phases of democracy. The most important battlefield of the European classes during the nineteenth century was France. Again and again Marx expected France to furnish the impulse for decisive revolutionary action. Therefore, in agreement with the conception of Marx, the history of the French class struggles during these fifty years will be traced in somewhat greater detail.

2. *Robespierre and Jefferson*

When Marx began his political activity he already found democracy a great international movement. The history of European democracy extended back two and a half millennia. In the republics of ancient Greece the political form of democracy was the contrast to aristocracy or oligarchy, to the rule of the " best," or of the " minority " of the rich or noble. In contrast to this, democracy was the rule of the majority, of the masses in general, whereby the owners of property or the bearers of nobility had no privileges to claim. Greek political science already occupied itself with the question, whether every state in which the will of the majority of the citizens decides is a democracy, no matter what the composition of this majority is and how it arises, or whether a definite class character belongs to a democracy. Aristotle, the greatest political thinker of antiquity, answered the question thus: that democracy is nothing more than the rule of the poor in the state, just as oligarchy is the rule of the rich!

The ancient democracies came to an end together with the civil society of antiquity. In the Middle Ages democratic forms showed themselves in the urban communes. During the transition to modern times the radical religious sects became the bearers of democratic ideas. Modern bourgeois society developed in the Dutch Revolution of the sixteenth century and in the English Revolution of the seventeenth century. In both revolutions, however, the democratic movements of the broad working masses were suppressed early. The rich bourgeoisie retained power. However, the two great revolutions at the close of the eighteenth century ran a different course. In France the first wave of the Revolution in 1789 brought the victory of the rich bourgeoisie; but after four stormy years the power passed to the working people in 1793. In North America the new federal state was likewise governed at first by the wealthy upper class, but the presidential election of 1800 brought the party of the working farmers into power.

The movements that are connected with the name of Robespierre in France and with the name of Jefferson in America both opposed the mass of the people to a privileged aristocracy. In France it immediately became manifest at the outbreak of the Revolution of 1789 that the interests of the peasants and of the poorer townspeople were not identical with those of the rich bourgeoisie. Consequently after 1789 a political movement developed in France which differed completely from the political propaganda and the political goals of the wealthy bourgeoisie. It can likewise be determined that in America after 1765 the form and method of political struggle against the English government was different among the farmers and the poorer townspeople from among the rich merchants and landowners. During the Revolutionary War itself the differences between the classes in America receded in the face of the common national task. After that, however, class antagonism flared up again during the struggles which centred on the new federal Constitution, and after 1793 Jefferson organized the " Republican " Party, which was determined to oppose the will of the people to the ruling capitalistic alignment.

The faction of the French " Patriots " which had entrusted itself to the leadership of Robespierre was not satisfied with the overthrow of the King and the nobility of birth, but likewise considered the nobility of money its enemy. The Republicans of America would not have had any object at all to oppose if they had only wanted to fight against a non-existent hereditary monarchy or aristocracy; the right of the Republicans to exist lay only in their opposition to financial capital. Just as classic democracy aimed at the erection of a class government of the poorer citizens within the state in opposition to the rich, so did both modern movements in America and in France. Thus the ancient name of democracy justly celebrated its resurrection in both countries. It was entirely common in the daily political life of America to designate the adherents of the Republican Party as democrats, and the patriots of Robespierre's group likewise felt themselves to be democrats, since they opposed the rights of the " people " to the privileges of the aristocracy. Instead of further evidence here, it is only necessary to recall the words of Babeuf cited above.

The often misused and falsely applied concept of the so-called Renaissance of Antiquity is fixed around 1500 in Italy in the ordinary text-books. Actually the political and social renaissance of antiquity in modern Europe belongs to the eighteenth century, when with the growing power of bourgeois society the political and social forms of antiquity again became possible. It was not only the objective agreement of social facts that created the similarity between the revolutionary movements of the eighteenth century and of antiquity. The leading popular politicians and political philosophers of the eighteenth century were completely conscious of the connexion. They had not spent their schooldays studying the classics of antiquity in vain. Even for educated people who had already left their school years far behind them, antiquity played a much greater role than it does today.

The republicans of the eighteenth century usually began their historical controversy with the monarchy with the Tarquins and Tiberius. The revolutionary mind was inspired by the deeds of the enemies of the tyrants and the tyrannicides of antiquity. All this had now suddenly stepped out of the dusty school-books and had taken on new life. Robespierre's thoughts lived entirely in the Roman

Republic, and when he had to fight against his Catilines, he felt like a second Cicero. The American statesmen of the revolutionary period reflected with acumen on the characteristics common to their own period and to antiquity, on patricians and plebeians, on the agrarian laws, on speculation, and on the struggle of debtors against creditors.

Thus it is comprehensible that the use of the word " democrats " as the name of a party also took on new life, and indeed entirely in the genuine, classic sense of a struggle of the masses against the aristocrats, and not in the attenuated sense of formal democracy, which wants nothing more than equal suffrage, the rule of the majority, no matter how it is achieved, and political activity only by peaceful means within the bounds of the law. Equal suffrage also belonged to the political demands of modern democracy, but it was not the essence of political democracy itself. Robespierre's party had indeed erected its Constitution for France in 1793 on the principle of general suffrage, but it was not intended to put this Constitution into effect until after the termination of the war, with no elections to be held during the period of armed struggle. Jefferson was likewise fundamentally in favour of general suffrage, but he was not angry when individual American states withheld the franchise from artisans who had no property. Similarly in antiquity the democracy of Athens had indeed granted equal suffrage to all citizens, but no one thought of extending it to the aliens and slaves living there.

For Robespierre, as for Jefferson, the foundation of democratic politics was not a statistical computation, but rather the active participation of the reliable and enlightened part of the mass of the people. In America, Jefferson's party looked above all to the politically active farmers, and in France, Robespierre looked primarily to those patriots who took part in the work of the Parisian sections. It is clear that such a principle of selection signifies a certain danger for the actual self-government of the masses. Jefferson selected the farmers from the masses and did not think very highly of the urban proletariat. Robespierre, on the other hand, trusted his Parisian workers rather than any backward agrarians. In this way the concept of the people could easily be misused and be interpreted anew according to the interests of the particular ruling party. Lamartine relates a fine anecdote about the February Revolution of 1848 in Paris. After the victory of the revolt in the streets of Paris, the Parliament of the monarchy had gathered for its last session. The republican journalists waited eagerly in the gallery for the appearance of the first band of armed workers so that Louis Philippe's Parliament would be dispersed. Finally the first troop of victorious rebels appeared on the floor of Parliament, but being shy, as workers sometimes are, in unaccustomed surroundings, they did nothing harmful, but stood around and listened to the speeches of the representatives. At this point a republican journalist exclaimed: " This is the wrong ' People,' I will go for the right one! " The temptation is only too great for every ruling party, in revolutionary periods, to consider only its adherents as the " right people " or the " right proletariat."

The way in which Jefferson and Robespierre regarded general suffrage may or may not be dubious; at any rate there was no talk of any formal democracy with them. Just as little did they respect any incidentally existing legality when the higher interests of the revolution were concerned. Robespierre rebelled without any ado against the decisions of the Convention as long as the Girondins controlled it, and the American Republicans had the reactionary laws of the federal government declared invalid by the assemblies of the single states that they controlled.

The democracy of the great French Revolution is in agreement with the democracy of America and of antiquity, in that it does not concede any privileges at all to the industrial employee. It has already been emphasized repeatedly that Jefferson's tendency was frankly the contrary. But Robespierre too does not differentiate between peasants, artisans, and workers in his theoretical considerations. All three forms of democracy are likewise characterized by the fact that they are not socialistic. The American Republicans favored private property at all times, and among the French patriots socialist ideas first became pre-eminent after the death of Robespierre, under the influence of Babeuf. The Athenian democrats, exactly like the American Republicans and the French patriots under Robespierre's leadership, wanted to lead the fight for the poor manual labourers against capital while maintaining private property.

If one wants to appreciate correctly the historical position of modern democracy in its beginnings, one must have a clear understanding of the period during which modern democracy was born. The first period of modern democracy could be dated from 1765 to 1815. The beginning would be the appearance of Patrick Henry in the Assembly of Virginia, and the end the peace between America and England. Embedded in these fifty years of American development lie the few great years of the French democratic movement, starting with the storming of the Bastille and ending with the execution of Babeuf. This period of fifty years is characterized by the greatest technological revolution which has occurred in the history of mankind up to the present.

For five thousand years mankind knew the essential achievements of civilization: living in cities, the working of metals, writing and reading and theoretical thinking. During the entire five thousand years the human hand had produced the essential objects of daily life, and man had travelled on land with the help of animals and on water by means of oar and sail. Light had been spread by candles and oil, and books had first been written by hand and then later multiplied with the cumbersome hand printing press. Now all this was in the process of being revolutionized; machines began to replace the working hand in the production of commodities necessary for life, mechanical means of transportation entered upon their triumphal march on land and sea. Illumination and the production of books and newspapers took place in a completely new way. Finally mankind had realized the age-old dream of flying, though the invention of the balloon did not acquire a considerable practical significance at first. This entire revolution of the technical bases of human life took place in closest connexion with bourgeois-capitalistic production, first of all directly for the needs of capitalistic commodity production.

This same enormous energy which got under way in the technical revolution also showed itself at the same time in the entire political and economic life of the leading bourgeois nations. What gigantic energy was developed by the French bourgeoisie in all fields after 1789! Everywhere the French bourgeoisie pushed forward beyond its frontiers and sought to expand its basis, its export markets, and its social sphere of power. The Girondins, and later Carnot and the Directory, founded the modern French army and the French policy of conquest. Later Napoleon Bonaparte took possession of these finished instruments and employed them with extraordinary mastery. The French policy of conquest went as far as Moscow in 1812. During the same period of the French Revolution and Napoleon the English bourgeoisie multiplied its achievements in industry, commerce, and navigation. England obtained control of the seas, expanded her empire in India, gained a footing in South Africa, and began the colonization of Australia. At the same time in the United States a bourgeois-capitalistic impulse to expand paralleled the democratic expansion of the farmers, who opened up the interior of the continent. Both movements, however, ultimately served the same goal. In uninterrupted conquest the United States expanded its sphere of power from the Atlantic to the Pacific Ocean, and the population of the U.S.A. grew from 4,000,000 in 1790 to 10,000,000 in 1810.

Approximately until 1812 the bearers of modern bourgeois development, England, France, and America, had progressed uniformly, each in its own sphere and in its own way. Those countries which suffered as a result of this development were the small capitalistic nation of the Dutch, which could not keep step with the great nations, and further the large partially or totally feudal countries of Europe: Germany, Austria, Russia, Spain, Italy, as well as the native peoples of the transoceanic continents. A certain turning-point in the distribution of the political forces among the powers began after 1813. France, under the leadership of Napoleon, had overestimated and overstrained its forces immoderately. Assisted tardily and inadequately by America, France had entered into a struggle with England and at the same time with the old powers of the European continent, which had to lead to catastrophe. After 1815 France was restricted to her original borders, while the German powers and Russia, on the other hand, could again strengthen themselves.

What was the attitude of the French and American democracies towards the fundamental social facts of the period from 1765 to 1815? If a statesman wants to transform his age by leading his people to new goals, he must first of all understand his own time. The most important thing during the period with which we are dealing here was the enormous revolution in industrial production and at the same time the immense increase of bourgeois-capitalistic energies. The typical country of the social revolution then was England. It is correct that at that time France and America were yet far behind the tempo of British development, that French industry still employed the methods of the hand manufacturing period, and that in America industry on the whole was in its first beginnings. Nevertheless a far-sighted statesman would already have been able to understand in 1793, even in France and America, in what direction the wind was blowing. Even in the age of the sailing ship the passage from Paris to London was not far, and anyone in France who wanted to orient himself concerning English conditions had opportunity enough to do so. The journey over the Atlantic Ocean was, to be sure, still a long adventure at that time. Yet the economic and social relations between America and the mother country were so close at all times that in the United States, too, all the facts concerning the English development were known.

Nevertheless democracy in America at that time, as well as in France, had failed completely when faced with the problems of modern times. Jefferson and the other leaders of the American Republicans persuaded themselves that modern capitalism could be kept away from America and that the United States could be fixed permanently at the stage of a snug little farm. In France Robespierre and his friends were indeed forced by the necessity of war to interfere with economic relations. But they, too, lacked all insight into the economic relations of their time. It was entirely correct that they wanted to solve the agrarian question in the interest of the small proprietor. Beyond that, however, they had no economic plan. Robespierre was ready to expropriate the so-called " Suspects " and to divide their property among the poor patriots. The division of heaps of paper at that time, however, would not have made anyone happy. Only a few large industrial plants existed in France, and they could not be divided. Practically therefore, nothing of economic significance would have remained but to divide a number of large estates and to equip the new proprietors with furniture, and so forth. Even if Robespierre did not share the agrarian prejudice of Jefferson, still his social ideals likewise revolved around the independent and satisfied small farmer, and it is no accident that in France during the Great Revolution, socialism and communism hide behind the slogan of the " agrarian law " — that is, of division of the land.

One can attempt to imagine what would have happened in France if Robespierre had remained the victor on the 9th of Thermidor. Soon thereafter he would have concluded a moderate peace abroad, he would have reduced the terror at home and the democratic Constitution would have come into operation. He would have expropriated the Suspects, but the property of the patriots would have remained holy for the government. And where would better patriots have been found than among the purveyors of war supplies and the bankers of the state? In peace France, under a government of Robespierre would have looked approximately like America under the rule of Jefferson. On the whole, one can only obtain a correct standard for the great French Revolution by comparing it with the corresponding development in America. The French democrats are always seen only in the fiery glow of the bloody year 1793–4, while under peaceful conditions they might not have shown any heroism, but instead the same honourable narrowness as their American partisans. Robespierre as the ruler of France would have had enormous difficulties in time of peace to defend republican simplicity and honesty against the advances of capital. It remains doubtful whether he, together with his friends, would have been capable of achieving greater clarity in economic matters.

Democracy in the eighteenth century was the protest of the labouring masses against the encroachment of the monarchy and the nobility, and at the same time against the disturbance of the accustomed modes of life by an overwhelming capitalism. The peasants wanted to free themselves from excessive taxes and debts, the artisans wanted to find favourable market possibilities again, and the workers wanted to return to the " good old times," when skilled hand-labour still received a corresponding wage. It is the same period in which the embittered workers demonstrated against the appearance of modern industry by breaking machines and demolishing factories. People could not yet come to terms with the irrevocability of modern technology and modern large-scale industry. The leaders of the democratic movement had schooled themselves in the philosophy of the eighteenth century. The leading thinkers of the eighteenth century all fought for freedom and progress, but while some greeted the flourishing of commerce and industry with joy and thus arrayed themselves in the front of the forward-marching bourgeoisie, critical voices were not lacking. It was asked whether the progress of technology and capital actually makes men happier, whether growing wealth does not destroy all moral values, and whether men, instead of seeking happiness in a life of metropolitan business and pleasure, shouldn't rather return to nature and the country-side.

Thus the democratic masses and their leaders were united in a distrust of modern development, and their view that both the Republic and democracy were primarily a moral matter, a moral renewal of the human race, already contained a condemnation of modern economic and social development. The democratic movement in France as well as in America was filled with passionate enthusiasm. The leaders could arouse in the masses that enthusiasm for a better world order without which nothing important can be changed. The early democratic movement, however, drew its strength and its weakness from the same sources. It had traits of moralizing seclusion from the world and petty-bourgeois romanticism, and it is amazing how little under-standing its leaders had for the actual social processes of their time.

The democrats had to swim against the current of social development, and they were defeated. In this respect the course of events in America is even more important than the events of the French Revolution, for there was no 9th of Thermidor in America. The Republican Party was not ex-pelled by any counter-revolution. It ruled the state, even after 1815, and won elections, and yet it was mercilessly un-dermined by the bourgeois-capitalistic spirit of the age; the struggle which had begun so hopefully in 1793 had com-pletely lost its purpose twenty-five years later. One can ask oneself whose fate contains a greater tragedy, the destiny of Robespierre, who fell in open warfare on the battlefield of the Revolution and counter-revolution, or the fate of Jefferson, who died as a peaceful old man and as a universally honoured father of his country, who in the last years of his life could only delude himself with difficulty concerning the wreck of his work. Jefferson lived just long enough to see, for instance, what dimensions the slave question had assumed and how uncertain it made the existence of the Union.

After 1815 America went its own way in its social development. In Europe, however, democracy also spread farther and farther outside of France, until it was finally able, in 1848, to challenge the collective ruling forces to a struggle. Nevertheless France still remained the chief country of European democracy, where all the problems were seen most clearly and where all the conclusions were drawn most completely.

3. *From Napoleon I to Louis Philippe*

With the death of Babeuf and the destruction of his party, democracy as a political movement in France was eliminated for a time. After the short transitional period of the Directory, the bourgeois-capitalistic state consolidated itself under the dictatorship of Napoleon I. The Emperor Napoleon was the brilliant representative of the advancing French bourgeoisie, which was eager for conquest, and of the new French army, which arose during the Revolution. At the same time, however, Napoleon enjoyed an amazing popularity among the broad labouring masses of the people. The French peasants saw in the Emperor the protector of their free possessions, acquired during the Revolution. The Emperor provided a correct and punctual administration. In the general economic rise the peasant could sell his products favourably, and every peasant boy who had made good as a soldier saw immeasurable possibilities of rising in the world and dreamed of himself, according to well-known models, as a future marshal or duke.

Although Napoleon, like a genuine upstart, hated every kind of democracy, he also enjoyed the sympathy of the largest part of the French workers for similar reasons. Here, too, the rise of industry, the order and justice of the administration, and the possibilities of advancing in the army acted together. It must also be considered that Napoleon's wars, compared with the World War, claimed only a small part of the French people, and that the losses, even when all the campaigns are taken together, comprise only a moderate percentage of the victims of 1914–18. Napoleon actually appeared like a good king out of a fairy-tale to the great masses of the French people. Even in 1815, when everything was lost, particularly many Parisian workers wanted to fight to the end for the Emperor, and Napoleon asked himself with astonishment how he had earned the loyalty of these people for whom he had hardly done so much!

The enchantment of the masses of the French people by Bonapartism is one of the most important facts for the understanding of the history of France in the nineteenth century. After the destruction of genuine French democracy, after the 9th of Thermidor, and after the catastrophe of Babeuf, the Empire became a kind of substitute democracy for the French people. It became the form of capitalistic rule which appeared most bearable to the masses and which apparently offered the peasants and the workers as much as could be expected at all in a capitalistic state at that time. To this was added the connexion of the masses with the imperial army. Even the poorest Frenchman felt that the Emperor's victorious battles also elevated him. Dictators who cannot carry on any wars work on the national emotions of the people through military pageants and solemn orations, and the success that they obtain is by no means small. The effect which the actually incessant victories of the Emperor must have exerted on the masses of the French people should be judged in accordance with this.

In 1815 the defeat of France brought the Bourbons back to the throne. Once again the feudal monarchy could continue from the point where it had left off in 1789. Actually, however, the revived feudalism in France lacked any real basis. The nobility had lost its property in the Revolution, and even the restored Bourbons didn't dare to force the French peasant back into the dependent condition which he had borne until 1789. Without its old economic power the nobility remained completely without influence. Among the people the feudal party could actually depend only on the small minority, which remained loyal to the Catholic King because of its devotion to the Catholic Church. The inability of the Bourbons to conquer the army morally, however, made their position completely untenable. Despite all attempts by the Bourbons to replace the Bonapartist tradition of the French army by a royal tradition, the average French officer and soldier endured the government of Louis XVIII and Charles X only with abashment. The only living force in the army was the memory of the Emperor, and the Bourbons had to be tolerated because France had lost the war. Thus the restored French monarchy of 1815 had the same fatal congenital defects as the German Republic of 1918.

The Bourbons would perhaps have been able to strengthen their throne if they had honestly abandoned the past and had openly combined with the French capitalistic bourgeoisie. The moderately liberal Constitution and the co-operation of the Parliament as Louis XVIII allowed them, seemed to present such a connecting link between the dynasty and the bourgeoisie. Nevertheless such a compromise proved to be impossible for any length of time. The Bourbons could not renounce their old feudal traditions, and after the vacillations under Louis XVIII, Charles X again set his foot on the path of absolutism, first disguised and then open, which led to the Revolution of 1830. On the other hand, even with the best intentions on both sides, the bourgeoisie would never have been able to reconcile itself to the foreign policy of the Bourbons, since the restored French Kingdom had to maintain peace with the powers of the Continent for reasons of self-preservation. It was impossible for the Bourbons to carry on the active foreign policy which was demanded by the leading groups of the French bourgeoisie. King Charles X sought to divert the national ambitions and shortly before the end he obtained Algiers for France.

Under the Bourbons after 1815 only a cautious bourgeois-liberal opposition was possible. Democratic and republican ideas were represented only by individuals and small groups. They could not act on the public. Nevertheless the more King Charles X turned towards open absolutism, the greater became the agitation among the people. In July 1830 the masses arose in Paris against the hated Bourbons. The army did not exhibit much fervour for royalty. Charles X was forced to flee, and with that the danger of feudal absolutism was removed. In Paris the street fights of July 1830 were fought by the workers and the students, but the wealthy bourgeoisie enjoyed the fruits of victory. The capitalists crowned as King the liberal Duke Louis Philippe of Orléans, a descendant of a collateral line of the house of Bourbon.

Louis Philippe is usually called the bourgeois King, but this designation is correct only to a very limited degree. If Louis Philippe had actually been a bourgeois King — that is, if his government had been identical with the rule of the class interests of the bourgeoisie — then he would not have had to fear a new revolution. Then Louis Philippe would never have been ousted from his throne again. The development of France from 1830 to 1848 was actually such that King Louis Philippe increasingly antagonized particularly the decisive and active strata of the bourgeoisie. The con-

flict between the so-called bourgeois King and the bourgeoisie permitted no stabilization of the political conditions in
France, and the struggle within the ruling class gave the
democrats new hope after 1830.

Since Napoleon France had constantly advanced in wealth,
the number of inhabitants, and economic activity. The 25,-
000,000 inhabitants at the time of the Great Revolution had
grown to 35,000,000 in 1846. Gradually French industry accommodated itself to modern technical conditions. During
that period, however, financial capitalism grew incompara-
bly more rapidly and energetically than industrial capitalism. The bankers utilized for their own purposes the impulse to save and the desire to speculate of large classes of
the population. Banking and stock-exchange transactions
flourished, while the manufacturers were not satisfied with
their position. The French industrialists complained that
foreign markets were closed to them by tariffs, and they demanded from the government that a strong foreign policy
should open new export markets. The large Parisian banks,
on the other hand, earned enough on government bonds,
railroad stocks, and other speculations, and they did not
want to let themselves be drawn into any policy of adventure. This uneven tempo in the growth of French banking
capitalism in relation to industrial capitalism led to a corresponding political separation of the interests of both.

It soon became evident after the July Revolution of 1830
that King Louis Philippe had no intention of becoming the
confidant of the French bourgeoisie, even though he was
very much the man of the people to all appearances. His
dynastic interests were always uppermost for Louis Philippe.
He wanted to defend the newly won throne for himself and
his family at any price. In peace he saw the most certain
guarantee for his throne, and thus his foreign policy became
even more cautious than that which the older line of the
Bourbons had carried on until 1830. The national growth
which the French bourgeoisie had expected as a result of the

July Revolution proved to be an illusion. From 1830 to
1848 France's foreign policy under Louis Philippe went
from bad to worse.

The King wanted peace because he feared that war might
bring him defeat and revolution. He was thus forced to a
passive foreign policy. At home Louis Philippe wanted to
keep the reins of government in his own hands. He did not
want to give the Parliament and its parties any leeway, because he feared that ambitious politicians might entangle
him in all kinds of experiments possible, which would ultimately result in his fall. Therefore Louis Philippe did not
desire any parliamentary government of the English type,
but he wanted to have a parliamentary majority and ministers upon whom he could rely personally. Under the social
conditions of France at that period, there resulted an alliance between the King and the bank and stock-exchange
capitalists. The financiers approved his peace policy, under
which the prices on the stock exchange flourished, and by
controlling the French home policy, financial interests found
numerous opportunities for successful subsidiary deals of
all kinds.

Now it became necessary for the King and his allied bankers to obtain a majority in Parliament in order to retain at
least the appearance of a liberal constitutional government.
The electoral franchise under the French July Kingdom was
construed in a very narrow-minded fashion. Only those who
paid large taxes were entitled to vote. Thus there were
only 200,000 voters among the 35,000,000 inhabitants of
France. Yet even this number was really too large for Louis
Philippe and his backers, for even among the 200,000 the
bankers and the stock-exchange operators, together with
their adherents, were only a minority. With honest elections
the manufacturers and the independent citizens would have
obtained a majority. Thus a system of refined bribery and
cunning frauds became necessary in order to influence the
elections in the right way and to collect a majority agree-

able to Louis Philippe's principles. However, a government whose political basis rested on bribery and sharp practices could maintain its existence only by similar means. Consequently the internal politics of Louis Philippe's system of government were characterized by cynical corruption and a long series of financial scandals. The Prime Minister, who led the financial party which was true to the King, was Guizot.

The national opposition of the French bourgeoisie to the system of Guizot embodied itself in the person of the brilliant journalist and historian Thiers. Gradually Louis Philippe's methods of government became unbearable for the manufacturers and for the majority of the bourgeoisie. It is not true that the policy of the large banks must always be the policy of bourgeois society too. Single great banks are historically older than bourgeois society. The Fuggers, for example, were powerful in Germany at a time when bourgeois society was still unknown. The power of the bourgeoisie as a class does not rest on single great banking houses or even on single industrial concerns, but on the broad middle class, on all the manufacturers, merchants, agents, higher-salaried employees, and the like, who together with the intellectual professions make up educated urban society. As a rule the interests of the large capitalists will also be decisive for the average bourgeoisie. If, however, a separation arises at any time, under special historical circumstances, then the large banks are not capable of procuring a useful substitute for the missing help of the bourgeois centre.

If Louis Philippe had united with the majority of the French bourgeoisie, then he would have had public opinion on his side. His cause would have been identical with the principles of order and private property. The bourgeois government would have obtained the help of the peasants without any trouble, and the army would have remained absolutely reliable. Then the isolated radical workers of Paris would never have been able to endanger the Kingdom. Now,

however, the system of Louis Philippe and Guizot was opposed by independent public opinion and all the national
bourgeois forces. Even in the ranks of the democrats the
formula could be heard that the French manufacturers were
forced to pay their workers poorly because foreign countries
were closed to French goods, and because at home financial
capitalism exacted tribute from industry. Only the overthrow of the ruling system would introduce a new era of development and prosperity for the entire French people.

The bourgeois-liberal opposition, led by Thiers, did not
turn against the King personally and against the legal monarchy, but it protested against the foreign policy of renuncia-
tion and the internal policy of corruption. In 1840 Thiers
had had a transitory majority in Parliament, and Louis
Philippe had been forced to appoint him Prime Minister.
Thiers had immediately attempted to restore the French
position as a major power in the Mediterranean and to bring
Egypt and Syria under his influence. Thereupon the four
other major European powers united against France. When
war threatened, the King dismissed the inconvenient Prime
Minister. France retreated again, peace was preserved, and
Guizot became Minister. Since that time the break between
the system of Louis Philippe and the national industrial
bourgeoisie had become incurable.

The more difficult the position of Louis Philippe became,
and the sharper the differences within the ranks of the
wealthy bourgeoisie defined themselves, the greater grew the
courage of the democrats. The Revolution of 1830 had
brought the political resurrection of the French democratic
movement. The tradition of Robespierre and Babeuf had
indeed never perished entirely in the Parisian working-class
quarters. On purely physical grounds alone it was impossible, since a Parisian worker who was fifty-six years old in
the year of the July Revolution had experienced the 9th of
Thermidor at the age of twenty. The period from the death
of Robespierre to Louis Philippe's accession to the throne

appears so long only because in the meantime infinitely many
and contradictory events had taken place. The living bond
between the first and the second period of European democracy was Buonarrotti, the friend and collaborator of Babeuf,
whom the executioners of the Directory had spared, and who
in the twenties had written his famous history of Babeuf
in Geneva. Buonarrotti's book was well known among the
Parisian workers after 1830. It belonged to the popular literature of the Revolution, together with the new editions of
Robespierre's speeches and Marat's articles.

The tradition of the great years 1793 and 1794 furnished
the French workers and democrats not only with a sublime
example, but at the same time with the proof that their political goals were no empty Utopia. The events of 1789 to
1793 proved that the people can conquer if they unite, take
up arms, and oppose their foes courageously in the street.
The July days of 1830 appeared to show anew the correctness
of this lesson. Furthermore the democratic poor people in
France had actually had power in 1793 and 1794. What had
happened once could repeat itself, if the democrats took the
lesson of the past to heart and avoided unnecessary mistakes.

The class significance of the events of 1793 and 1794 was
still clear at that time to every person who was acquainted in
some degree with political conditions. Thus, for example,
Heinrich Heine wrote in one of his Parisian letters of November 1840, at a time when war threatened to break
out between France and the other great powers: " Through
the threat of a war with the new coalition, not only will
the throne of the King be endangered, but also the rule of the
bourgeoisie, whom Louis Philippe represents legally. The
bourgeoisie, not the people, began the Revolution of 1789
and finished it in 1830. It is the bourgeoisie that now rules,
although many of their deputies are of distinguished lineage,
and it is they who have kept in check the people, who press
forward and who demand not only equality of the laws but
also equality of possessions. The bourgeoisie, which must

defend its toilsome work, the new political establishment, against the pressure of the people who desire a radical transformation of society, is certainly too weak, granted that foreign countries would attack them with forces that were four times as strong, and the bourgeoisie would abdicate even before it would come to an invasion. The lower classes would again take their place, just as in the terrible nineties."

In 1847 in a newspaper article Friedrich Engels discussed the question of centralization. He remarked: " The democratic proletariat not only needs centralization as it has been started by the bourgeoisie, but it will even have to extend it very much further. During the short period of the French Revolution, while the proletariat was at the helm of the state, during the rule of the Mountain, it carried out a policy of centralization with all the means at its disposal with grapeshot and the guillotine."

If the French workers as a group were actually deeply agitated, it was not at all difficult to urge them on to an armed revolt, because they constantly had the memories of 1789, 1792, 1793, and more recently of July 1830. A revolt was not considered a fantastic wonder, but as something that had frequently succeeded and could succeed again. A characteristic event was the uprising of the workers in Lyons in 1831. A general strike developed out of a purely economic conflict between the manufacturers and the silk-weavers. When the workers collided with the organs of the state, the proletariat advanced with such energy that it soon controlled the entire city. At the same time this revolt lacked all political leadership, for the republican-democratic organizations were still so weak at that time, that they could neither lead the Lyons movement nor bring help to the workers from outside. Thus the revolt of Lyons remained isolated and was suppressed by Louis Philippe without much trouble.

The organizations of the French democrats developed slowly after July 1830. They were sometimes legal and sometimes illegal, always depending on the momentary situation.

Dissolved by the police, they were always reconstituted under new names, and thus the societies of the revolutionary democrats maintained themselves throughout the entire period of Louis Philippe's government up to the victorious revolt of February 1848. The chief democratic society first called itself the Society of the Friends of the People, with reference to the title of Marat's famous newspaper: *Ami du peuple*. Then came the Society of the Rights of Man, and finally, under a harmless name, the Society of Families. Lamartine called these fighting organizations a democratic Freemasonry against the capitalistic monarchy.

The strongest personality among the revolutionary democrats during the period of Louis Philippe was Blanqui. He was the leader of several unsuccessful revolts of the thirties. When he appeared at court in 1836, the presiding judge questioned him as to his occupation, as is usual during a trial. Blanqui declared: " Proletarian." The judge stated that this was no occupation. Blanqui replied: " What, it is no occupation? It is the occupation of thirty million Frenchmen, who live from their labour and are robbed of their political rights." One sees from this answer that Blanqui still belonged completely to the older school of democracy. For him the proletarians are nine tenths of the French people, and not only the minority of factory workers. The concept of the proletariat appears here completely in the classic sense of the word. In the Roman Republic the " proletarians " were the poor citizens, whose franchise was inferior to that of the wealthy " classes." Blanqui strove for the union, the arming, and the victorious revolt of the entire enormous mass of the working people. Among the proletarians he counted the peasants, the artisans, the industrial workers, and also the pauperized intellectuals, such as he himself was. This grand feeling of the unity of the " people," in contrast to a privileged minority, was the strength and at the same time the weakness of the older democracy.

The government of Louis Philippe appeared to offer absolutely ideal prospects for the success of a revolt. For the ruling system was rejected by ninety per cent of the people, and it could by no means rely on the army as soon as the conflict became more serious. No one admitted that the King and his ministers had any moral right to rule France. Louis Philippe had occupied the throne by deluding the July fighters, and everyone waited for the next wave of revolution to overthrow him again. It is therefore not astonishing that under such conditions Blanqui and his friends attempted repeatedly to revolt. At most it is a wonder that Louis Philippe could still maintain himself for eighteen years. Apparently two causes contributed to the failure of the revolutionary attempts of the democrats in the thirties.

First of all, the bourgeois middle classes were indeed dissatisfied with the ruling system, but at the same time they asked themselves worriedly what would follow. A new revolution would obviously bring about the assumption of power by the republicans, and perhaps the Terror of 1793 would reappear, combined with communistic experiments like that of Babeuf. Thus the middle classes wavered as to what they should consider the lesser evil, the banker King Louis Philippe or a Red republic. After the July Revolution a National Guard, similar to that of 1789, had been re-established in France. In Paris, as in the provinces, it was composed of the wealthy middle classes, small business people, and the like. As a voluntary militia to maintain order these National Guards were intended to defend peace and bourgeois property by force of arms.

The amazing thing is that under the system of Louis Philippe most of the soldiers of the National Guard did not even possess the franchise. Nevertheless during the thirties in Paris they fired upon the revolting republicans, and the attitude of the National Guard gave the regular army its cue. After 1848 the policy of the government increased the anger and the feeling of shame of the lower middle class to such an extent that they preferred any change to the continuation of Louis Philippe's system. Secondly, the political consciousness of the working masses developed very slowly after 1830, and the peasants were even more backward in their political development. In July 1830 the people of Paris were still obliging enough to allow themselves to be misused for the purposes of the large capitalists. In 1831 the workers in Lyons attacked without any political plan. It required infinite labour before the consciously democratic organizations were capable of actually embracing the broad masses of the people.

At the same time the popular disease of Bonapartism was also a serious hindrance for the progress of the idea of a democratic republic. In 1832 a small band of revolting republicans sacrificed themselves in vain in the streets of Paris. An expert observer of the events was of the opinion, however, that the masses of the workers would have come to the help of the rebels if they had not cried: " Long live the Republic! " but rather: " Long live the Emperor! " After the death of the great Napoleon the hopes of the masses of the French people attached themselves to other members of his family.

4. *Early Socialism*

The democratic opinions of the French workers combined more and more with certain hopes for a social upheaval which would have to come with the political revolution. The tradition of Babeuf and Buonarrotti already supplied the connexion between the popular Republic and a naïve communism. The radical worker wanted the general right to work, and with that the elimination of the horrible crises with their periods of unemployment and hunger which interrupted the capitalistic development regularly from time to time. From the bitter inequality of daily life the proletariat fled to dreams of complete equality of all mankind, in property and pleasures, in a future world.

Philosophical systems which rejected private property and

wanted to replace it with another form of social organization had been erected in great numbers in Europe since the sixteenth century. Since the turn of the eighteenth and nineteenth centuries the interest of the public in social questions and social criticism constantly increased. Torn into the whirlpool of the modern technological revolution and observing the progressive dissolution of the old economic forms and modes of life, men felt impelled to seek some means of delivering mankind from the evils of capitalism. These philosophic critics of property generally had nothing to do with politics. They preached socialism and communism approximately like a new religion or a new form of life. They hoped that, outside all politics, men would become converted to the new gospels. Or these theoretical socialists founded model institutions, co-operatives, settlements, in Europe or in transoceanic countries, in order to furnish practical proof of the correctness of their teaching.

The adherents of philosophical socialism formed groups and societies where they discussed their ideas and also considered practical foundations of the kind mentioned. Thus there were in France, at the time of Louis Philippe, societies of the adherents of the older socialists Saint-Simon and Fourier. In addition there were the adherents of the more recent theories of Cabet and Proudhon, groups of religious socialists, and so forth. This theoretical occupation with socialism and communism was hardly disturbed by the authorities in France. In all countries before 1848 the word " socialism " sounded entirely harmless in people's ears. For everyone called himself a socialist, who in any way discussed the social question critically. The concept of communism already sounded somewhat more unpleasant, for it was generally considered the equivalent of radical equalitarianism. Nevertheless at that time a philosophical and unpolitical communist did not have much to fear from the police. Even the notorious German censorship at the time of Metternich permitted communistic publications, particularly when the

capitalistic bourgeoisie was criticized in them, since the ruling feudal bureaucrats considered that as their chief political
enemy. Only democracy smelt of blood and barricades at
that time, but neither simple socialism nor communism.
The ruling gentlemen professed the principle: " Only soldiers help against democrats," while they did not pay the
socialists a corresponding honour.

It was another thing, to be sure, if a revolutionary democrat also consciously advocated a socialistic transformation
of property relations. In Paris under Louis Philippe the
democratic movement was already more or less interspersed
with socialistic ideas. There were the greatest differences of
opinion among the French democrats concerning the type
and manner of the future new organization of society, corresponding to the many socialist and communist sects that opposed each other. In France at that time the philosophical
societies of the socialists and communists existed alongside of
the political organizations of the democrats approximately
as in modern Europe the clubs for workers' culture and
sports exist alongside of the political parties of the Social
Democrats and the Communists. The socialistic societies
and the democratic associations interlocked at many points.
Many people belonged to both groups of organizations simultaneously. Ideas were exchanged back and forth. Nevertheless one must differentiate political democracy from socialism and communism, which were not necessarily political at
that time.

After the failure of the republican revolts in the thirties,
another group of democrats was formed in France who
agreed entirely with Blanqui in their views and aims, but
who considered cautious tactics more correct under given
conditions. This school of democrats wanted first of all to
avoid hopeless armed revolts and to keep as far as possible
within the bounds of the law; to carry on their agitation with
the help of the press, of meetings, and, if possible, by entering
Parliament. They wanted to prepare the ground by means

of a skilful republican and democratic propaganda, so that the revolution would then have a better chance to succeed. The leader of the French democrats, who in the forties worked primarily with legal means, was Ledru-Rollin. He was an outstanding speaker and agitator, and he even found an election district where the citizens were so angry with Louis Philippe that the wealthy electors, as the strongest protest, sent the Red republican to Parliament. In Paris Ledru-Rollin's party founded the newspaper *Réforme,* which as the organ of the extreme Left soon procured considerable authority and in a certain sense was considered in all Europe as the central organ of democracy.

The most important party friend and collaborator of Ledru-Rollin was the outstanding socialist theoretician Louis Blanc. Blanc's historical significance lies in the fact that he personified the connexion between revolutionary democracy and socialism and thus continued successfully the tradition of Babeuf. Blanc understood his own period so far that he recognized the central significance of modern industry and of the industrial proletariat much better than most of the other democrats. Blanc too had as his ultimate aim both a popular republic, based on general suffrage, and a socialist society with the abolition of capitalistic property. The chief problem for him was to find a connexion between the inadequate present and the ideal future. In the field of politics in the narrower sense the correct tactics were present: propaganda with all means for general suffrage and the republic, and at a suitable moment the transition from peaceful agitation to victorious revolution. All the more difficult appeared the construction of the right road which should lead from capitalism to socialism.

In the centre of his social doctrines Blanc placed the theory of the co-operative. The workers should form free co-operatives, to which the state would give the necessary working capital if it could not be obtained from other sources. The co-operatives would then develop, slowly surpass and displace the capitalists, and so capture socialism. Such a triumphal march of the workers' co-operatives would be possible, however, only if the workers ruled the state and utilized it for their purposes; therefore the democratic republic is an absolute prerequisite for the creation of socialism.

The co-operative idea was extremely popular among the workers at that time, and the great success which the ideas of Louis Blanc had is explained by the fact that he reproduced in clear formulations that which slumbered in the masses themselves. It was its agreement with the prevailing currents of thought among the proletarian masses that gave the system of Blanc at the same time both its strength and its weakness. It is certainly correct that the co-operative presents a valuable means of social progress. Consumers' co-operatives have successfully asserted themselves today in almost all civilized countries, and producing co-operatives of working people have also achieved significant successes. We need only mention the agrarian co-operatives of the Jewish workers in Palestine. In Germany, for instance, until 1933 the Free Trade Unions had building and settlement co-operatives, their own bank, their own factories, etc. Further examples can be procured from other countries that producing co-operatives of workers — correctly organized and expertly managed — can be entirely successful. It is a childish illusion, however, which no practically working co-operative advocate will support today, to think that capitalism could be overcome with the help of co-operatives.

If, for instance, one hundred capitalistically managed furniture factories existed in a country, then it would be entirely possible to organize a co-operative of furniture workers, together with the necessary employees, to operate the hundred and first factory. The co-operative factory would hold its ground especially well within the framework of capitalistic competition if the state or the community would cover the losses of the enterprise in periods of crisis. None the less such a co-operative factory, even a successful one, would not

threaten the capitalistic social order. To reach this goal it
would be necessary to have at least fifty co-operative factories
instead of one, and how should the capital for the many new
organizations be procured? Indeed, only through expropriation of the private capitalists. Simultaneously, in order
to create a market for the new co-operative factories, a corresponding number of old capitalistic factories would have to
be closed. That means, in order for the co-operatives to be in
a position to conquer private, capitalistic competition, private capitalism must first be violently destroyed by the democratic workers' state. It is just this, however, that the co-
operative idea wishes to avoid. It depends on one's own
Weltanschauung whether one considers private capitalism
useful or harmful, and according to it one will recommend
or reject a definite policy. In no case, however, can the productive co-operatives of the workers conquer private capitalism within the frame of capitalistic society.

Nevertheless the co-operative idea as a means towards the
overthrow of private capital was very popular among European workers before 1848 as well as in the generation that
followed. The cause for this can easily be determined. The
workers of that period, who came partly from peasant and
partly from artisan circles, were still entirely filled with
petty-bourgeois traditions. They had indeed slowly comprehended that the modern capitalistic factory could not be removed by demolishing the machines and that one could not
return to the good old times by employing such methods.
They understood, too, that the single small master could not
compete with the modern manufacturer. Now they clung to
their last sheet-anchor; perhaps a united group of artisans
would achieve what a single artisan could not do. If they
would unite and the state were to aid them in a paternal manner, then they would be in a position to regain the honour
and demand the wage of the former independent artisan.

Owing to these illusions of the democratic European
masses regarding the inevitability of large centralized facto-

ries, managed according to the principles of modern technics, every theoretician was successful who met such ideas of the masses half-way. A gay letter of the young Engels in 1846 shows how very receptive, for instance, German journeymen and workers who lived in Paris were to such ideas. The co-operative ideas, which Engels derides, were advocated among the Parisian journeymen by a German socialist named Grün. In a coarsened form and with misunderstandings, Grün spread certain theories of Proudhon. We are not so much concerned here with what Proudhon or Blanc actually wanted, but with the reflections of such plans of social reform in the minds of single workers.

Engels relates that, according to the propaganda of Grün, a workers' co-operative would be founded which would then open a few factories with the help of the members' savings. " As soon as the society's capital has increased through new members or through savings of the old stockholders, it will be used to establish new ateliers (workshops) and factories, and so on and on until all the proletarians are occupied, all the productive forces in the country have been bought up, and the capital in the hands of the bourgeoisie has lost its power, because of this fact, to command labour and to pro-duce profits. Thus capital is abolished, by ' finding an in-stance where capital — i.e., interest — . . . vanishes, so to say.' . . . The people have nothing more and nothing less in mind than to buy up all of France some day, later perhaps also the rest of the world, by means of proletarian savings and by renouncing the profits and the interest on their capital. Has such an excellent plan ever been invented before? . . . And the stupid fellows, the workers here, I mean the Ger-mans, believe this rubbish. They, who cannot keep 6 sous in their pockets in order to go to a *marchand de vin* (wine house) in the evening for their meetings, want to buy up *toute la belle France* (the whole of beautiful France) with their savings. Rothschild and Company are true bunglers alongside of these colossal *accapareurs* (speculators) ! "

Louis Blanc's popular book on the *Organization of Labour* had an extraordinary success under the conditions of that period. From 1839 to 1847 the book had five editions in Paris. In a few weeks six thousand copies of the fifth edition were sold among Parisian workers. Ledru-Rollin's party appropriated the basic ideas of Blanc and promised the workers a better organization of labour upon obtaining power. As it turned out in France during the great agitation for electoral reform in 1847, the democratic party already had a strong influence not only among the Parisian workers, but also among the peasants and inhabitants of the small towns in the provinces. Ledru-Rollin and his friends also organized mass meetings in the smaller cities with great success. It was entirely correct that the party avoided isolating the Parisian workers from the peasants and artisans in the provinces. The agitation of the democrats dared not use such slogans as might frighten and repel the peasants.

Even if all this is considered, it must nevertheless be said that the agitation of the French democratic movement before the Revolution of 1848 was amply unclear and sentimental. The democratic speakers used to praise the workers, emphasize their honesty and willingness to make sacrifices, picture their misery, and take the part of the poor people with great fervour. It was difficult, however, to gather from the speeches of Ledru-Rollin and his friends what the party actually would do upon obtaining power to help its " beloved, loyal workers." It would have been entirely possible objectively to devise a French workers' program which would likewise protect all the justified interests of the peasants and the lower middle class. For this, however, it would have been necessary to possess a better insight into the economic conditions of the period than Ledru-Rollin's party had. In the forties the party also called itself " Socialist Democratic," in order to express in this way, that it not only aimed at a political democracy, but also attributed the necessary significance to the social question. Thus the important combination of these names appears here for the first time before the great political public.

5. Social or Bourgeois Democracy?

In the France of Louis Philippe there were arrayed: the party of the feudal aristocracy, which strove for the return of the expelled legitimate line of the Bourbons; further, the various parties of the wealthy bourgeoisie, who put up with the government of Louis Philippe, but who came forward partly for and partly against the system of Guizot; and, finally, the party of the masses of the poor people, the adherents of the democratic Republic. Bonapartism, which represented more of a general feeling among the people than an organized party, is not considered here. Besides these, however, there was still another party which interposed itself between the bourgeois opposition, which was loyal to the Constitution, on the one side, and the republican democrats on the other. This was the party of the bourgeois republicans. The complicated party relations in France in 1847, on the eve of the new Revolution, are illustrated in the table on page 42.

The central organ of the bourgeois republicans was the Paris newspaper *National* under the editorship of Marrast. The distinguished opposition writer and politician Lamartine did not belong to the group of the *National* personally, but he agreed with them on basic political questions. While the genuine democrats saw their ideal in the party of the Mountain of the Great Revolution, Lamartine and the *National* rejected everything that in any way resembled Jacobinism and the methods of 1793. In his widely read *History of the Girondins* Lamartine nevertheless made an important criticism of the tactics of the bourgeois-liberal majority in the French National Assembly of 1789–91. In Lamartine's opinion the liberal French bourgeoisie had made a decisive mistake at the beginning of the Revolution by remaining satisfied with a constitutional restriction of the

Workers and Peasants	Petty Bourgeoisie	Industry	Bank Capital	Aristocracy
Revolutionary Democracy	Moderate Democracy	Monarchist Opposition	Government Party	Church
legal illegal	*National*	*Thiers*	Guizot	Legitimists
Réforme				
Ledru-Rollin				
L. Blanc				
Blanqui				

(Socialists and Communists)

(Bonapartists)

monarchy. Instead the Republic should immediately have been proclaimed, openly and consistently. Then the French Republic would have arisen in a lawful and orderly manner and not by revolt and terror. An orderly republic, arising from a majority decision of the National Assembly, would not have found it necessary to execute the King. Such a republic would either have avoided the war with foreign countries or would have conducted it very differently. Then the 10th of August 1792 would never have occurred, nor the entire embitterment of the masses of the poor people, which finally ended with the fall of the Girondins and the rule of the Terror.

Fundamentally, Lamartine was right, and the theory of France's political past and future, as the *National* advocated it, was likewise entirely comprehensible, particularly from the point of view of the wealthy bourgeoisie. The combination of the interests of the liberal bourgeoisie with monarchist and feudal remnants did not strengthen them, but, on the contrary, weakened them extraordinarily. Monarchies with their antiquated methods had repeatedly aroused the exasperation of the masses, endangered the stability of the political order, prepared the way for revolutions, and thus had also endangered bourgeois society. Out of fear for the Republic the French bourgeoisie had accepted Louis Philippe as King in 1830, but had experienced the most bitter disillusionment as a result. The Bourbons of the older line were even more impossible, and who knew how a new Bonapartist adventure would end? Therefore it would be best if particularly the wealthy and educated classes declared themselves openly and unreservedly for the Republic.

The broader the base of the existing political order is, the stronger will it be. If the agitators of proletarian dissatisfaction are not concerned with a king, a group of aristocrats, or a reactionary ministry, but are dealing with bourgeois society itself, without any disguise, then the revolutionary danger is much smaller. Nevertheless the rich upper class in France could not rise to such bold realism. If a republic existed, general suffrage, too, could not be avoided, and since there are many more poor people than rich ones, as is well known, and Parliament is all-powerful, the rule of the state would fall into the hands of the exasperated poor masses. They would never be satisfied with political reforms, however, but would expose the social question with all its terrible consequences. Therefore it is indeed better to rely upon certain traditional authorities in the state, to retain a constitutional monarchy and a restricted franchise, and not enter upon the dangerous experiment of a republic and its consequences.

Because of such considerations the overwhelming majority of the wealthy bourgeoisie in France remained in the constitutional and monarchist opposition of Thiers. In general the party of the *National* was composed of intellectuals and small business men, who wanted to have the franchise and expected a better tax policy and similar things from the republic. In quieter times the party of the *National* would not have had any special significance, despite the attention which the splendidly written newspaper received. For neither the decisive capitalist groups nor the workers adhered to this party. In a revolutionary situation, however, the party of the bourgeois republicans could become extraordinarily important, as the extreme Left wing among all the defenders of private property. All the wealthy groups could then marshal themselves behind the party of the *National,* as behind a protective shield, in order to intercept the assault of the radical masses.

In 1847 the party of the *National* carried on an intense discussion with the followers of the *Réforme*. In the course of this discussion the group of the *National,* like Lamartine, laid claim to the name of " Democrats." They declared that they themselves were the true democrats, the representatives of an orderly and reasonable democracy, while only the " demagogues " and the " ultra-democrats " gathered around the *Réforme*. The argument between the two republican newspapers of Paris is extraordinarily important historically. For it initiates in Europe the separation of the younger bourgeois-liberal democratic movement from the older democratic tradition of the poor people. The fight of the two newspapers and their parties revolved around two subjects primarily, around tactics and the social question. While the *Réforme* in its struggle against the government rejected any alliance with the monarchist opposition, refusing even to consider it, the adherents of the *National* sought as far as possible to support Thiers. The *National* advocated further the absolute maintenance of private property, while the *Réforme,* without tying itself down too much, sympathized with the modern socialist endeavours. Thus in an article written at the end of 1847 and aimed at the *Réforme,* the *National* said:

"You speak of indefinite aspirations, of theories and systems, that arise among the people. You blame us because we openly attack these — to speak bluntly — communist endeavours. Now, declare yourselves directly, either for or against communism. We declare it aloud: we have nothing in common with the communists, with these people who deny property, family, and fatherland. On the day of the struggle we will not fight with, but against these detestable ideas. . . . And you believe the people would be with you? The people would give up the little property which it has acquired in the sweat of its brow, family, and fatherland? Do you believe the people would ever let themselves be convinced that it makes no difference whether Austria subjects us to its despotism or whether the powers partition France?"

Under "communism" no one in France then understood the theories of the young German writers Marx and Engels, but the older, naïve systems of Babeuf or Cabet. It was easy to fight against childlike theories of general equality and general division. Nevertheless for the *National* and for Lamartine, an aversion to any serious social change was hidden behind such polemics. In this sense the *Réforme* answered: " We are not communistic, and for the reason that communism does not consider the laws of production, because it does not care about seeing that enough is produced for all of society. But we are more sympathetic to the economic suggestions of the Communists than to those of the *National,* which accepts the present bourgeois economy without more ado. We will also further defend the Communists against the police and the *National,* because we concede them at least the right of discussion and because the doctrines which arise from the workers themselves always deserve consideration."

In the course of this same polemic between the two republican parties a discussion also took place on class antagonism and class struggle. A speaker of the *National* group, Garnier-Pagès, affirmed that no class antagonism exists between the bourgeoisie and the workers. For him there are only Frenchmen, all having equal rights. Class antagonism is only a vicious invention of the Prime Minister Guizot, for the purpose of dividing the French people. It is highly probable that Garnier-Pagès did not even know of the existence of Karl Marx when he made this speech in 1847, for then he would have been even less justified in accusing Guizot of having invented the wicked class struggle in order to incite the proletariat.

Actually in France all the serious political theoreticians of the bourgeoisie, who had learned from the Great Revolution and the developments which followed it, were completely clear on the class question. Such men, who openly defended the rule of the wealthy bourgeoisie, could have a complete understanding of the class question, just like their socialistic and democratic opponents. It is no accident, then, that in the nineteenth century particularly the conservative statesmen, such as Metternich and Bismarck, could deal with the class question extremely appropriately and clearly. On the other hand, the Left liberals could only regard the class question as a disturbing intrusion because bourgeois-liberal

" democracy " can only exist by denying the essential difference between the workers and the capitalists. Guizot, who was not only a bourgeois-conservative politician, but likewise a significant historian, understood the class struggle better than the editorial staff of the *National*.

No one can have the name of a political party patented, and just as there were a profusion of entirely different kinds of socialism in the course of the last century, the name of the democrats was also at everyone's disposal to be used freely. If therefore the republican Left wing of the bourgeoisie in France called themselves " democratic," they were fully within their rights. It is extremely significant historically, however, that at that time in large political circles of Europe the claim of the *National* group to the democratic name was felt to be presumptuous.

Ledru-Rollin challenged the *National* group publicly to submit to a common arbitration committee. It should be composed of an equal number of friends of the *Réforme* and of the adherents of the *National,* and it should decide which of the two groups had the correct democratic policy.

The *Deutsche Brüsseler Zeitung,* the organ of the revolutionary German democrats abroad, likewise entered the fray and wrote: " In its verdict of condemnation of the *National* the *Réforme* only expresses the verdict which the German, English, and Belgian democratic groups, in general all the democrats except the French, have long since pronounced." In the period before the outbreak of the Revolution of 1848 the democrats of the older tendency, the advocates of the poor people in their struggle against aristocracy and capitalism, did not want to recognize the Left wing of bourgeois liberalism as " democratic." Such was the vividness with which the idea of the revolutionary democratic movement of 1793 still existed at that time.

6. The English Chartists

While the democratic movement experienced a powerful development in France under the government of Louis Philippe and counted upon an imminent victorious revolution, a democratic mass party had also developed in England. It was the party of the Chartists, who, from 1837 on, won an ever increasing influence among the workers and soon represented a movement of millions. In its economic development England was then by far the most progressive country on earth. The great industrial revolution, which produced a modern machine industry and a large industrial proletariat for the first time, had taken place in England since 1760. Nevertheless the history of the English democratic movement during the century from 1760 to 1860 is entirely negative. During the course of this entire century there was enough bitter misery in England among the manually labouring masses in the city and the country. Outbursts of the furious dissatisfaction of the masses with the existing political and social order occurred often enough. The example of the great French Revolution had also influenced England and had strengthened the opposition to the ruling order among the workers as well as among the intellectuals. Individuals and whole groups had repeatedly called upon the English public for a radical democratic reform and yet all this was in vain. During the entire century the political power remained firm and unshaken in the hands of the wealthy bourgeois upper class and their aristocratic friends, and actually, despite all the agitation among the masses, and despite isolated bloody collisions, the prevailing political order was not really endangered for a moment.

It is not correct that a country which makes more rapid progress in economic and social matters also becomes " ripe " much sooner for a revolution. An upheaval of the political order does not take place when a country is especially progressive economically and socially, but only when a deep contradiction exists between the political order and the driv-ing social forces. In France the bourgeoisie had already had the economic leadership since the reign of Louis XIV, but they had to submit to the political tutelage of an inadequate and backward aristocracy for another century, until finally the contradiction between the political and the social or-ganization of France became so acute that it discharged itself in the Revolution of 1789. In America a new energetic bourgeois nation was developing in the thirteen colonies, but it saw itself hindered at every advance by a foreign gov-ernment whose interests were different from its own. Here too, therefore, the Revolution had to break the connexion which had become unbearable.

In England, on the other hand, the political rule of the wealthy bourgeoisie had been firmly established since the victorious Revolution of 1688. In England there was no longer any political antagonism between the feudal nobility and the monarchy on the one side, and the capitalistic bour-geoisie on the other, which shook the Continental states. In England the aristocracy was most closely allied with the bour-geoisie. The nobility took part in the business enterprises of the bourgeoisie, led the political parties of the bour-geoisie, and were, so to speak, at the head of bourgeois soci-ety. In England after 1688 a democratic mass movement could not direct itself against the king or the aristocracy alone. Everyone knew that the abdication of the king who happened to be reigning or even the abdication of the aris-tocratic upper house would not have changed the existing conditions much. The power of English political life lay in the lower house, in which many aristocrats sat, but which, as a body, represented the interests of the bourgeoisie. A political revolution in England would therefore not have been directed against an unpopular king, against privileges of the nobility, or against a reactionary minister, but against bourgeois society.

During the century from 1760 to 1860 it was still the bourgeoisie which personified social and technical progress in England. Despite the misery of large groups of the population, it was still seen every year that new factories were opened, new homes were built, England's foreign commerce grew. If a crisis did interrupt the economic development for a certain period, it was followed each time by a new period of increasing economic activity. The political institutions of the country were in complete harmony with social development, and where a disproportion resulted, it was soon corrected. The electoral reform of 1832 was such a correction; it gave the manufacturers the political influence which was their due, on the basis of their economic significance. On the other hand, this electoral reform did not represent any progress on the road to democracy. The great mass of the manually labouring population was just as much excluded from political rights after 1832 as before. The Chartist Party therefore set up general suffrage as the most important aim of its agitation.

The basic idea in doing so was the same as in the corresponding political movements by which France was shaken during the same years. The great majority of the people consists of the poor. General suffrage gives political power to the poor masses. When the poor first have political power in their hands, then they will use it in order to provide themselves with all that is necessary for their social needs. Because of these considerations the overwhelming majority of the English bourgeoisie absolutely rejected general suffrage and stuck stubbornly to the electoral system of 1832. The Chartists, in contrast to this, were essentially representatives of the interests of the industrial proletariat.

In their daily agitation the Chartists advocated the demands of the workers against the employers. They called attention to the miserable wages, the excessively long working hours, and the degrading working conditions under which the English proletariat then suffered. They pointed out the insolence of the ruling class, and they assured the masses that everything would change immediately as soon as the workers had the franchise. But what the new society would actually look like after the victory of the Chartists, on that subject not much clarity could be obtained from the Chartist propagandist speeches. In their merits as in their defects the Chartists were a genuine democratic party of the older type. Good-heartedness and love for the poor were supposed to take the place of a lack of economic clarity. The more indefinitely the situation was pictured, which would exist in England after the victory of the Chartists, the more terrible did it become in the imagination of their foes. Not only the capitalist class, but also the middle classes were convinced that the victory of the Chartists must lead to something like the irruption of the barbarians into the Roman Empire: chaos, robbery, and murder, and the confiscation of all property, large as well as small, by coarse, unrestrained elements. It was imagined approximately in the same manner as the Paris *National* described the victory of " communism " for the frightened average man at about the same time.

It is always extremely dangerous for a socialist or workers' party if no one knows exactly what it actually wants and if large classes of the population can arrive at the belief that it is not a matter of a better social organization of industry, but of barbaric anarchy. If the ordinary man convinces himself that the victorious revolution would break up his parlour and his piano, then the revolution cannot win at all. Then a democratic or socialistic revolution meets with such vehement resistance, not only among the upper class, but also among the entire middle class and from every person who has anything at all to defend in the way of domestic order and family habits, that victory becomes impossible. The worst enemies of any democratic or socialist movement are adventurous and demagogic elements which join it. Just as dangerous is the vague idea of a general decline of the world which could be connected with the victory of the radical movement.

In England bourgeois society was determined to defend itself to the end against Chartism, and the English workers were not equal, in either theory or organization, to the gigantic task of replacing bourgeois society, which was still in the ascendant, by a better order. Thus the Chartist Party made no positive progress, although it stirred millions of people for the new " Charter," the popular constitution with general suffrage. The social-reform plans of the Chartists, as far as they assumed a practical form, moved within the co-operative framework which was common at that time. Thus the chairman of the Chartist Party, Feargus O'Connor, founded a large agrarian co-operative. Out of the savings of its members land was to be bought, upon which unemployed workers would be settled. In this manner they wanted to reduce the reserve army of unemployed workers, whose existence depressed wages, from the industrial entrepreneurs, and at the same time a new class of democratic small farmers would be created in England.

This was certainly a sympathetic idea, but as a means towards the solution of the social question in the most progressive industrial country in the world it was pathetically ingenuous. How were the miserably paid English proletarians to obtain such sums from their savings, so that they could revolutionize industry and agriculture? In January 1848 the Chartists in London held a mass meeting where, among others, an authoritative leader of the party, Harney, expressed the aims of the movement in the following words: " Land for the people, a house for every man, a vote for every man, and a gun for every man." This is a powerful summary of the popular aims of traditional democracy, but it was a rather poor program for the workers' party of a major industrial country, because it did not consider the actual economic and social conditions. Today Harney's watchword would be a beautiful slogan for the conservative large farmers in Switzerland.

Before 1848 in Europe a democratic movement separated

from the capitalistic liberal bourgeoisie was only possible in countries where the bourgeoisie already had power. These were England, France, and, of the small countries, Belgium, Holland, and Switzerland. In a typical bourgeois revolution Belgium had broken away in 1830 from the Kingdom of Holland. After that a modern parliamentary monarchy had been established. With the extraordinary industrial development of Belgium the number of workers who possessed no political rights grew constantly, and they opposed the ruling capitalists with a democratic movement. In comparison to Belgium, its neighbour, Holland, had little industry. Here financial and banking capital ruled. Since the number of workers in Holland was small, no democratic movement worth mentioning developed there before 1848. The peculiar and important history of democracy in Switzerland will be discussed separately below.

In European countries where a feudal absolutism prevailed, there existed a natural union between the bourgeoisie and the poorer classes in opposition to the ruling feudal aristocracy and bureaucracy. Such, for instance, was the situation in Prussia and Austria. In countries which in addition had to bear a foreign rule, as for instance Poland, Italy, and Hungary, there was a still broader united front in the struggle for fatherland and freedom. It included the poorer classes, the bourgeoisie, and the patriotic nobility.

Where feudalism still ruled, a separate democratic movement developed most easily as a result of revolutions that had failed if the practice of the revolutionary struggle emphasized differences between the individual classes much more clearly. This took place in Poland during the great national revolt of 1830 against the rule of Russia. In Poland a bourgeoisie of the western-European type hardly existed as yet. Among thé patriots, however, there existed the party of the aristocracy, which defended all the historical privileges of the nobility, and a democratic movement which aimed at the emancipation of the peasants. During the revolt of Cracow in 1846 the Polish democratic party — that is, the party friendly to the peasants — had control. The attempt to free Poland from Cracow miscarried, however, and Austria destroyed the independent little Republic of Cracow at this opportunity.

In Italy the secret society of the Carbonari had led the movement for national liberation since the beginning of the century. The Carbonari were entirely a party of the educated bourgeoisie and the patriotic nobility. They had but little interest in the needs of the broad masses. The Carbonari led the revolutions in Naples and Piedmont in 1820 and 1821, as well as the revolt in central Italy in 1831. All these movements miscarried completely, and Italy, divided into many petty states, remained under the foreign rule of Austria. The notorious inadequacy of the Carbonari led to the formation of a new democratic party in Italy under the leadership of Mazzini after the failure of 1831. Mazzini's friends addressed themselves to the masses of the poor. A general revolt, with the general arming of the populace, would sweep away the foreign rule of Austria and the small dynasties, resulting in the establishment of a democratic republic. In his fanatical love for the simple people and in his religious and moral ideas Mazzini, too, was a genuine representative of the older democratic tradition. In the social field he advocated extremely unclear co-operative ideas, although in Italy the agrarian question, the conflict between the oppressed small tenant farmers and the ruling large landowners, would have demanded a clear solution.

In Germany political conditions were still entirely undeveloped. The German bourgeoisie had indeed adopted all the technical achievements of the Western countries — machine construction, railroads, steamships, and so forth. The industrial proletariat, especially in Prussia, was growing and occasionally it rebelled spontaneously against its miserable living-conditions, as in the famous revolt of the Silesian weavers. On the political stage in Germany, however, there was still only the struggle of the liberal bourgeoisie against the ruling feudal monarchy. The meeting of the united Prussian Diet in 1847 was regarded as a parallel to the convocation of the French General Estates in 1789, and therefore as a prelude to the German bourgeois revolution.

There were indeed differences of tactics and temperament within the great front of German liberalism. There were adherents of a republic and popular revolt, while in general the wealthy bourgeoisie preferred the constitutional path and a constitutional monarchy. How far an actually clear political division between the liberalism of the wealthy bourgeoisie and the democratic movement of the poor people would develop, however, depended on the course of a future revolution. The small group of German democratic communists who worked abroad before 1848 under the leadership of Marx and Engels also saw in Germany first of all only the possibility of a bourgeois-liberal revolution and gave their adherents the slogan to support the bourgeoisie with all means in the struggle against feudalism. The second act of a proletarian-democratic revolution in Germany was still very distant.

Consequently in 1847 a situation had developed all over Europe where either the democratic masses entered upon a struggle with the ruling liberal bourgeoisie, or the liberal bourgeoisie with the governing feudalism, or the oppressed nations against their foreign governments. It was a matter of uniting all these separate currents to an international European collective revolution. The future of European democracy depended on the victory or defeat of this coming European revolution.

PART II

DEMOCRACY AND MARXISM, 1845–95

§

DEMOCRACY AND MARXISM, 1845–95

1. Marx and Engels on the Eve of the Revolution of 1848

In 1846 and 1847 the international democratic movement was strengthened by two outstanding young revolutionaries from Germany, Karl Marx and Friedrich Engels. They had both fled from the persecution of the German police and now worked for their ideas abroad, in France, England, and Belgium. They called themselves Communists, since they wanted to replace the existing capitalistic form of property by a different, collective form of social economy; simultaneously, however, they also designated themselves as democrats, because they hoped to achieve their aims only as a result of the great democratic revolution. In July 1846 Marx and Engels, in the name of a group of German émigrés in Brussels, addressed an affirmative and encouraging declaration to O'Connor, the leader of the English Chartists. The address was printed in the Chartist newspaper, the *Northern Star*. It bears the signature: " For the German democratic Communists of Brussels, the committee: Engels, Ph. Gigot, Marx. Brussels, July 17, 1846." — " Democratic Communists " is a combination of words which appears very strange at present, but which was considered entirely proper by every revolutionary fighter of that period. Ph. Gigot, whose name so boldly interposes itself between Marx and Engels, was, to be sure, not a German, but a Belgian democrat.

For the first time Marx and Engels brought an actually comprehensive understanding of their own period to the democratic movement. The childlike and backward ideas concerning the social and political development of the world under which the democratic leaders in all countries laboured before 1848 have already been emphasized repeatedly. The most significant achievement which had been accomplished in the field of social criticism in the democratic camp until then is, without a doubt, Louis Blanc's book on the organization of labour. The writings of Louis Blanc are excellent as far as they describe the condition of the French workers during the author's time. Blanc is a master in describing the need of the French proletariat and conditions within the French state and French society. He becomes uncertain, however, as soon as he enters into foreign history or the history of past periods, and he becomes absolutely childish when he occupies himself with the general questions of economic and social development.

Louis Blanc sees the root of all evil in free competition, for it ruins both the worker and the bourgeois. The workers compete among themselves in the labour-market, and thus the employer can pick out the cheapest workmen, depress wages arbitrarily, and condemn the unemployed to misery. On the other hand, free competition allows the large entrepreneur to conquer the small one and thus finally to acquire monopolistic power. Furthermore, it is competition that increasingly intensifies the antagonism between nations and produces new wars. Thus competition with other nations had been the actual driving force of English politics during the last two centuries. Louis Blanc is convinced that only his co-operatives, organized and directed by the state, can do away with competition, this fundamental evil of mankind.

The criticism of free competition as Louis Blanc presents

it contains much that is correct. Owing to the fact, however, that Blanc was only concerned with the effects of competition, he was completely incapable of comprehending the nature of his own time as contrasted with earlier periods of human history. For free competition, and the contests of individuals and states that are connected with it, are as old as commerce itself. In antiquity competition already occasioned the rivalries of Athens and Corinth, of Rome and Carthage, during the Middle Ages of Genoa and Venice, of the Hanse towns and the Dutch, and so on. The condemnation of competition, when it is expressed as generally as Blanc does, is therefore nothing further than the condemnation of the will to power and the urge towards activity and gain as it exists in individuals or in human communities. It is nothing more than the old utopian criticism of private property and egoism as pernicious phenomena, which would have to be overcome by mankind in order to reach a higher moral form of life. Such propaganda for utopian socialism, which is also contained in Louis Blanc's philosophy of economics, immediately produces the counter-propaganda of the liberal defenders of private property — that the happiness of the individual, the existence of the family, of culture, and of the state, are dependent on private property, etc. This discussion had been carried on in Europe for about two thousand years, from the time of the Greek Sophists down into the nineteenth century, without any practical results.

There is one form of human association, however, where the evil of free competition is greatly restricted, if not entirely abolished. If one disregards the conditions of primitive times, then it is represented by the guild organization of handicrafts. The guild regulations took care that every artisan and small dealer worked and earned approximately as much as his confrere. When at the same time agriculture had its fine old traditional order, no one had to worry; one did his work in the manner of his fathers and then went quietly to sleep. The fight against competition as an evil in itself is therefore, if one looks at it closely, nothing more than a guild reaction. It is the protest of the ordinary man, who is frightened by modern developments, against the sinister convulsions of modern times.

The co-operatives which the democratic social critics of the nineteenth century endeavoured to establish were nothing more than a rebirth of the guilds in a modern form, a utopian experiment, which would never have been able to succeed. The agitation of Louis Blanc was approximately what the European worker of 1848 wanted to hear, but after the victory of the democratic revolution the greatest mischief could arise as soon as it was attempted to realize Louis Blanc's ideas. If the co-operatives which would be created failed, democracy and socialism would be seriously discredited. But there was still another and even greater danger. At the moment when the co-operative socialists and the democrats who were allied with them had attained power, they would first of all attempt to put their experiments into action. They would concentrate all their energies on this matter and would forget the actual conditions of political power, and also the bourgeoisie which should still continue to exist after the victory of the democrats, until the blows of the counter-revolution awakened them from their preoccupation with their playthings.

Marx and Engels were the first democrats who were completely free of all these illusions and of this desire to experiment without any foundation. They understood their age, because they had assimilated all that the leading thinkers of the bourgeoisie had to say concerning their own class. The English economists and the German philosophers had comprehended completely the nature of modern bourgeois society. By placing the doctrines of Ricardo and Hegel at the service of the democratic revolution, Marx and Engels had found the theoretical basis which Louis Blanc, O'Connor, or Mazzini lacked completely.

According to Marx and Engels, the most important fact

of modern development was the industrial revolution of the eighteenth century. The bourgeoisie of modern times had accumulated immense wealth through colonial politics, world commerce, modern banks, a system of state debts, and so forth. At the same time the dissolution of the feudal order and traditional agrarian conditions had uprooted large masses of people, had torn them loose from the soil, and had driven them into the cities. By overcoming the antiquated methods of production the rich bourgeoisie took possession of machine technics in the course of the eighteenth century. Thus the new means of production, which were decisive for society, were concentrated in the hands of a small minority, and the great mass of pauperized and expropriated people were forced to work at the machines of the capitalists.

This was the origin of the modern bourgeoisie. The industrial capitalists emerged as the decisive element of the modern period, and the old commercial and banking capitalists had to subordinate themselves to the tempo and the needs of modern industry. In the *Communist Manifesto,* which appeared in 1848, Marx and Engels speak of scarcely a century of modern bourgeois rule. They reckon therefore approximately from the victory of the industrial revolution in England between 1750 and 1760. In the course of this period the modern bourgeoisie had transformed the entire surface of the earth. Through the application of technology and organization it has accomplished wonders, in contrast to which all the achievements of older periods fade away. Of the great states which existed at the beginning of 1848, the modern bourgeoisie already had a decisive political influence in England, France, and America. In Germany the industrial bourgeoisie was on the verge of taking over power, and in the other countries its influence was also constantly increasing.

According to Marx and Engels, the modern bourgeoisie has the task of removing the remains of feudal, agrarian, and petty-bourgeois backwardness everywhere. In all the battles which the bourgeoisie has to fight, not only against the feudal nobility, monarchy, Church, and bureaucracy, but also against the traditional peasant and petty-bourgeois narrow-mindedness, Marx and Engels stand absolutely on the side of the bourgeoisie. Against such enemies the bourgeoisie represented social progress. According to the views of Marx and Engels, every country had to reach the stage of capitalism and the rule of the bourgeoisie first, before further progress became possible. Where feudalism still ruled, as for instance in Germany, the task of the Communists was to help the bourgeoisie in obtaining power. The democratic-proletarian revolution could only follow the bourgeois revolution as the second act of a great historical development.

While the modern bourgeoisie gathers the means of production into its hands to an increasing degree, expropriates the small owners, and depresses them to the level of propertyless wage workers, it nevertheless prepares its own fall. According to Marx, the bourgeoisie produces the proletariat as a natural necessity and with it its own grave-diggers. Marx and Engels no longer use the word "proletarian" in the general sense, as the older democrats had done, but especially for the employees of modern machine industry. The growing mass of expropriated, uprooted people who are torn loose from all historical connexions must see their only salvation in the revolution and in the overthrow of capitalism. Thus according to Marx and Engels the industrial proletarians become the actual bearers of the democratic revolution.

Marx and Engels do not even think of attacking private property on moral grounds in the manner of the utopian socialists. They do not bewail human egoism and the evils of free competition. They do not attack property as such at all, but only a definite historically developed form of private property peculiar to their own time. Just as feudal property in the hands of large landowners had gradually become an unbearable burden for the masses of dependent people, similarly the concentration of the means of industrial production in the hands of a few private individuals has become an evil of the worst kind for modern nations. All progress which modern capitalism produces is rendered questionable again and again by the crises which shake modern society with periodic regularity. Each crisis means infinite misery for the millions of workers and beyond them likewise for the middle classes. According to Marx, mankind can free itself from these evils only if capitalistic private ownership of the socially important means of production is abolished and the community manages its necessary means of production itself.

The acceptance of the teachings of Marx would have meant the liberation of the democratic movement from all petty-bourgeois illusions and backwardness. The democratic parties would have realized the necessity of modern centralized industry, and they would have renounced the doubtful petty-bourgeois and co-operative experiments upon the assumption of power. Marx and Engels never maintained that the abolition of modern capitalism would be possible at one blow. They themselves sketched programs for a gradual transition from a private to a collective economy. The starting-point of this entire development, however, could only be the victory of the democratic revolution.

Marx and Engels began their propaganda abroad among the German artisans who lived there. They organized a few hundred German journeymen and others in London, Paris, and Brussels. This was the foundation of the Communist League, which proclaimed its famous program, the *Communist Manifesto,* to the public at the beginning of 1848. It would have been simply laughable if Marx and Engels with their small band of organized Communists had wanted to undertake any kind of action in any country in the world. Marx and Engels were much too sober and realistic as statesmen to believe such a fantasy even for a moment. Nevertheless their writings before 1848 are filled with a firm belief in the coming revolution. The revolution should not be made, however, by a few Communist societies, but by the great mass movement of European democracy. The Communists should co-operate within the bounds of the democratic parties and should strive to influence the democratic revolution in the right direction.

For Marx and Engels too, the democratic movement, seen as a whole, was a coalition of the workers, the peasants, and the petty bourgeoisie. Within this coalition, however, the leadership must devolve upon the industrial proletariat as a natural necessity. For only the industrial workers, owing to their special class position, were capable of freeing themselves from all the vacillations and illusions from which the petty bourgeoisie suffered. The more advanced the democratic movement became, the more would it be compelled to submit to proletarian leadership. If the Communists were capable of giving the workers the correct slogans in the course of the revolution, then they could determine the tempo and the direction of the democratic revolution despite their small number. Without the democratic mass movement of 1846 and 1847, however, the entire Marxist theory of revolution loses its basis. It would then be in the same situation as someone speculating on the best form of navigation without having access to water.

Based upon the general situation of that period, the *Communist Manifesto* contains remarks on the tactics of the Communists which would be almost incomprehensible for the Social Democratic or Communist parties of the present. Thus Marx and Engels write in the *Communist Manifesto*: "The Communists do not form a separate party opposed to working-class parties. They have no interests separate and apart from those of the proletariat as a whole. . . . The Communists therefore are, on the one hand, practically the most advanced and resolute section of the working-class parties of every country, that section which pushes forward all others; on the other hand, theoretically, they have the advantage over the great mass of the proletariat of clearly understanding the conditions, the course, and the ultimate general results of the proletarian movement." The only actual workers' party which existed then in Europe was that of the democratic Chartists in England; Marx and Engels did not intend to oppose the Chartist Party in England with a competing party of their own, even if their propaganda developed favourably. The English Marxists, however, should work in the ranks of the Chartists.

The *Communist Manifesto* further says very clearly: " In France the Communists join the Socialist Democratic Party against the conservative and radical bourgeoisie, reserving, however, the right to maintain a critical attitude towards the phrases and illusions which derive from the revolutionary tradition." The Socialist Democratic Party is the party of Ledru-Rollin and Louis Blanc. In France, too, no attempt should be made to found a separate Communist party during the coming revolution, but the Marxists, like the mass of the French proletariat generally, should follow the party of Ledru-Rollin. The *Communist Manifesto* gives similar instructions for the other countries. It says then in summarizing: " Everywhere the Communists support every revolutionary movement against existing social and political conditions. In all these movements they call special attention to the property question as the basic question, no matter what its degree of development at that time." On the eve of the Revolution of 1848 Marx and Engels were far removed from splitting the democratic forces in any way. On the contrary, they recommended the greatest unity in the tactics of the revolutionaries everywhere, even beyond the ranks of the democrats in countries where it was still a matter of bourgeois and national revolutions.

Marx and Engels strove to enter into contact everywhere with the democratic movements abroad. Thus there existed in Brussels in 1847 a Democratic Union, where the leaders of Belgian democracy met with prominent émigrés. The honorary president of the union was an old radical Belgian general, Mellinet, the officiating president was the Belgian democratic lawyer Jottrand, and the vice-president was Karl Marx. Among the proclamations of the Brussels Democratic Union, which are composed entirely in the spirit of historical democracy, in the name of liberty, equality, fraternity, the name of Marx stands peacefully beside those of the local democratic leaders. Only the revolutionary movement as a whole was important for Marx, not the theoretical quality of each daily utterance.

When Engels came to Paris in October 1847, he looked up Louis Blanc and gave him a report on the situation in Germany. He told him: "You can consider Herr Marx as the leader of our party — that is, of the most advanced faction of the German democrats." Engels came to an agreement with Louis Blanc on co-operation in all international questions. Engels also became a collaborator on the *Réforme*, Ledru-Rollin's paper. The French Socialist Democratic Party, as may easily be understood, was a strong opponent of the non-political socialists, who aroused doubts among the workers as to the correctness of the democratic tactics. The most significant of the French non-political socialists at that time was Proudhon. Marx intervened directly in the quarrels of the French socialists and in 1847 he published in French his polemic against Proudhon: *The Misery of Philosophy*. The theoretical conceptions of Marx were just as far removed from those of Louis Blanc at that time as from those of Proudhon. Louis Blanc, however, belonged to the same party as Marx, in the broader sense of the word, and Proudhon opposed them. Marx and Engels already saw the personal inadequacy of Ledru-Rollin, Louis Blanc, and O'Connor very clearly in 1846–8, but before the public they carefully protected the Chartist and French democratic leaders. For at that time they were not concerned with this or that personality, but only with the democratic movement as a whole.

The most important service which Marx and Engels could

perform for the European democrats before 1848 was to unite the democratic forces on an international scale. The *Communist Manifesto* gives the Communists the direct task of working " everywhere for the union and agreement of the democratic parties of all countries." That, too, is a task which would appear very strange to the Communists today. The democratic International of 1848 had extraordinarily significant results historically, for the later socialist Internationals arose directly out of the democratic International. It is impossible to understand international socialism historically without taking the international democratic movement as a basis; just as revolutionary Marxism and socialism can only be understood as a development of revolutionary democracy.

The necessity of international co-operation was hammered into the democrats and also into the liberals of Europe by the activity of their enemies since 1815. The victors of 1815 had been the three feudal monarchies, Russia, Austria, and Prussia, who had allied themselves with the English ruling class. After Napoleon's fall the restored Bourbon monarchy in France had been added to them. The Holy Alliance, which was led intellectually by Metternich, advocated the solidarity of the conservative interests in all countries. Metternich regarded an international revolution as the greatest enemy of society. He would have preferred to see the wealthy bourgeoisie gathering around the throne and the nobility in order to beat off the assault of the radical masses. Metternich, by far the cleverest representative of the European counter-revolution, believed that the wealthy bourgeoisie thwarted their own interests by demanding liberal reforms; for as soon as the principle of popular sovereignty contained in every liberal constitution has once been recognized, the course of development inevitably proceeds leftward. One dike after another will be torn down by the radical flood, and finally general suffrage, democracy, and anarchy, destruction of property and culture, will be reached.

Metternich and the politically thinking conservatives of the European continent did not fight against liberalism as such, but only as a transitional stage towards democracy.

On the basis of his detailed studies on the French Revolution, Metternich concluded that all the dangers which menaced the social order in Europe were centred in Paris. Although as an Austrian statesman he necessarily opposed the policy of conquest of Napoleon I, yet he welcomed the fact that the Emperor had again established authority in France and prevented a social revolution. In the general interest of propertied Europe Metternich did not desire the fall of Napoleon at all, but only such restriction of his power as would have permitted the other states to exist peacefully alongside of France. It was not Metternich's fault that Napoleon did not want to compromise, but made his own fall inevitable. The collapse of the legitimate French Kingdom in 1830 was certainly a hard blow for the conservative interests of Europe. It was soon evident, however, that Louis Philippe also wanted to defend the existing social order and peace. Therefore Metternich and with him all of conservative Europe were satisfied if Louis Philippe maintained himself upon his throne and at least delayed a new outbreak of the Parisian volcano.

During the period of 1815–48 the collaboration of the five more or less conservative major powers of Europe was repeatedly disturbed by the clash of their special national interests, above all in the Orient and in America. Nevertheless, despite all diplomatic combinations and momentary subterfuges, the balance of power always allowed itself to be restored. The cautious and superior statesmanship of Prince Metternich, who kept the German powers away from disputable objects and waited quietly until the others again sought an alliance with Austria and Prussia, contributed towards the maintenance of this equilibrium. The conservative peace policy of the Holy Alliance served the political interests of Austria and the needs of Germany at the same time.

For as long as the system of Metternich existed, Austria and Prussia remained united, and both together led Germany. At the same time the rear of the large German bloc was protected by Russia and was therefore practically unassailable. Russia, for her part, could pursue her Oriental and Asiatic plans without being disturbed, and England likewise had a free hand in the transoceanic countries. The sufferer under the system of the Holy Alliance was France, whose impulse towards expansion in Europe as well as overseas was curbed by the agreement of the four other powers. Despite several escapades, Louis Philippe believed himself incapable of altering his course, because of internal political reasons. Consequently the weak and defensive foreign policy of the French King contributed essentially to his fall.

The conservative major European powers considered it their right and duty to oppose forcibly all disorders in any country. Together Russia, Austria, and Prussia prevented every uprising of the Poles, the Austrian army suppressed every revolution in Italy, and the agreement of the two major German powers suppressed German liberalism. During the twenties the armed intervention of France put down the revolution in Spain. Nevertheless, wherever new political organizations were achieved on a revolutionary basis, such as the Kingdom of Louis Philippe in France, and the kingdoms of Belgium and Greece, these new political structures had to fit themselves into the framework of an existent conservative Europe.

Every revolution in any European country, no matter whether it had liberal, democratic, or general national aims, had to reckon with the armed intervention of the conservative major powers. Consequently the international European counter-revolution spontaneously produced a revolutionary International. Since 1815 connexions had already existed between the French and Italian liberals. During the thirties and forties Mazzini worked for the international solidarity of all revolutionaries. Political émigrés from all possible countries met in Switzerland, Brussels, Paris, and London. It was above all the Polish revolt of 1830 that, despite its failure, aroused impassioned sympathies among all the liberal classes of central and western Europe. Polish émigrés were received everywhere with special affection, and the slogan of " Help for Poland " united the European revolutionary International. It was recognized as an absolute necessity that, in the event of a new revolt in a particular country, the democrats and revolutionaries of the other countries should do everything in their power to prevent the allied monarchs from intervening in the insurgent region. From this it followed that the revolution could not be allowed to remain isolated in one country, but that it would have to spread as quickly as possible to the rest of Europe. It was now necessary to draw the political and organizational consequences of these ideas. At the same time it must be considered that in the period around 1848 neither the counter-revolutionary nor the revolutionary front was uniform in Europe. Both camps were motley mixtures with respect to social status. Actually only accident decided which class or group was in power at a particular time in any country. The governing powers in Europe were united among themselves, and similarly the classes and groups who opposed them.

The counter-revolutionary front in Europe consisted primarily of the feudal monarchies, Russia, Austria, and Prussia, and of the remaining European feudalism, with its dynasties, aristocrats, bureaucrats, and ecclesiastical lords, who supported the three great rulers of eastern Europe. The wealthy bourgeoisie of England, Holland, and Belgium and the ruling faction of the financial capitalists in France, however, also belonged to the defenders of the existing order in Europe. To the revolutionary front belonged the poor democratic masses of England, France, and Belgium, and the other countries, the decisive part of the bourgeoisie, including most of the manufacturers, in France, and the entire politically interested bourgeoisie of Germany. In countries such as Italy, Hungary, and Poland all the nationalist elements — thus not only the poor masses, the bourgeoisie, and the intellectuals, but also the patriotic nobility — supported the revolutionary movement. An aristocrat, who would have been a loyal supporter of the Tsar in Russia and a conservative member of the upper house in England, was a fervent revolutionary in Poland or Hungary, ready to fight against his legitimate monarch. But what did such a man have in common with a communistic worker of Paris? Nevertheless both together were supposed to carry out the European revolution.

Marx and Engels recognized that the most important condition for the success of a democratic International was the co-operation of the French and English democrats. It was most important to create an alliance between the French Socialist Democratic Party and the English Chartists. It was therefore necessary that both parties should become more closely acquainted. For this purpose in 1847 and early in 1848 Engels wrote a series of excellent articles on the English labour movement and Chartism for the *Réforme,* and at the same time a corresponding series of articles on the French democratic movement for the *Northern Star.* Simultaneously Marx and Engels worked for the organ of the German democratic émigrés, the *Deutsche Brüsseler Zeitung,* and thus on the eve of the Revolution of 1848 they created at least a certain unity of the democratic press in western Europe.

In addition, however, direct organizational connexions were also necessary. In London there existed a Union of Fraternal Democrats. Its presiding committee contained Chartist leaders, German émigrés of Marx's group, besides Frenchmen, Poles, Swiss, and others. In November 1847 the Fraternal Democrats celebrated the anniversary of the Polish Revolution of 1830 with a large meeting in London. After the French and English speakers had finished, a German

Communist, Schapper, began to speak. At the close of his speech Schapper declared that he had a pleasant announcement to make: in Brussels a Society of Fraternal Democrats had likewise been formed, and they had sent a delegate, Dr. Marx, to represent them at this meeting. Schapper then read the following letter: "We the undersigned members of the presiding committee of the democratic society which has been formed in Brussels for the purpose of advancing the unity and fraternity of all peoples have the honour of delegating the vice-president of our committee, Dr. Karl Marx, to you for the purpose of creating conditions conducive to mutual correspondence and sympathy." Following this, Marx made a speech in German which was received with great applause. He said: "The Belgian democrats feel that the English Chartists are the true democrats, and when they have carried out the six points of their program, the path to freedom will be open for the entire world. Achieve this great goal, you workers of England, and you will be considered the saviours of all humanity."

Marx and Engels reckoned then that within a measurable period the democrats would achieve power in France and England. In fact, three months after the London meeting Ledru-Rollin and Louis Blanc were ministers of the French Republic. In England electoral reform had come in 1832 despite the resistance of the privileged classes. It was not at all impossible that under the increased pressure of the masses, in some form or other, an extension of the franchise would also be carried through in England. With that the Chartists would have entered into the English government. The firm alliance of an English labour movement with the French Republic would have furnished the basis for an international democratic policy. As things stood then, a democratic victory in England or France would immediately lead to a liberal revolution in Germany and national revolutions in Hungary, Italy, and Poland. It could be assumed that the German revolution, together with the revolts in Italy and other countries, would rapidly overrun Prussia and Austria. Then European democracy, together with its allies, would still have to carry on a war against the Russian Tsar, in order to destroy this strongest pillar of feudal reaction.

With a unified co-operation of the various revolutionary forces this entire program was by no means fantastic, and in the spring of 1848 not much was lacking for its completion. To be sure, a great deal of dexterity was necessary to prevent controversies between the individual national revolutionary movements. Marx and Engels paid special attention to the future national development of France. It was known that in France important groups of the bourgeoisie, especially many manufacturers, desired the fall of Louis Philippe and a break with the political system of 1815. These circles longed for a great war of conquest in the name of the French revolutionary tradition. It should lead French arms to and across the Rhine and again make France a major power of the Napoleonic type by opening a wide sphere of action for French business. It remained to be seen whether the French democrats would be strong enough to offer any resistance to such plans of conquest. In case the French army annexed the Rhineland in the name of the revolution, then the cause of democracy in Germany as well as in France would be seriously damaged. On the other hand, some liberal circles in Germany hoped again for a national revival as a result of their revolution and perhaps the reconquest of French Alsace-Lorraine.

Marx and Engels wanted to utilize the democratic International for the primary purpose of exerting pressure on the French democrats. In 1847 Marx and Engels as individuals were not entitled to give good advice to the powerful French democratic leaders. The English Chartists, however, had a greater right to do so. Thus in anonymous articles in the *Northern Star* Engels repeatedly rejected the nationalist deviations of Louis Blanc and others in friendly fashion. An international democratic congress had been planned for

1848, which was then frustrated by the storms of the Revolution. At the congress the Chartists together with the Germans would have formed a counterpoise to the French, and they would have been able to point out the dangers of the French plans for conquest.

Besides the Franco-German controversy, the democratic revolution, if victorious on a European scale, would have had to settle still other very difficult national questions. In restoring Poland it was necessary to draw the Polish-German boundary in such a manner that no ill feeling would arise, for a German-Polish alliance appeared an absolute necessity if it were actually desired to conquer the Russian Tsar. A future Italo-German frontier was another question which would arise once the Habsburg Empire had been destroyed. To whom should Trieste, for instance, belong? Marx and Engels demanded an absolute solidarity between the German and the Italian movements, which should not be disturbed by small questions of boundary. Besides this there existed another problem whose extraordinary significance for the success of the European revolution was hardly imagined as yet in 1847: namely, the relation of the Germans and the Hungarians to the Austrian Slavs. What should be the attitude of the Czechs and the South Slavs with respect to the German and Hungarian revolution? Thus, besides the deep social contrasts, the coming European revolution was also burdened with a number of almost insoluble national problems.

2. France, 1848

In 1848 the French workers were a small minority of the entire population. They had become so important, however, that every political movement had to take a stand on the questions of industry and of the proletariat, to a much greater degree than had been necessary in 1789. The condition of the French workers was generally very unfavourable. They did not have the right of association. The law did not allow them to organize for the purpose of bettering their condition by means of strikes. Working hours were extremely long. A working day of twelve to fourteen hours was very common; even longer hours were not unknown, especially for home workers. The hygienic conditions in the factories and likewise the living-conditions of the poor were extraordinarily unfavourable. The skilled worker could earn three to four francs a day in Paris, with which he could perhaps eke out an existence. The best trades suffered, however, even in normal times, from irregularity of employment. The skilled Parisian worker generally reckoned with three to four months of unemployment a year, during which time he received no unemployment relief. The wages of women and of all workers in the provinces were much lower and in most cases only permitted an existence which verged on starvation. It is therefore understandable that the masses of French workers were filled with profound dissatisfaction and that they demanded primarily an improvement of their material situation from a political revolution and a victory of democracy.

In France in 1847 and early in 1848 all groups of the opposition united under the slogan of electoral reform. First of all they wanted to overthrow the parliamentary majority, which the ruling clique, aided by the scandalous existing electoral law, had been able to maintain against the will of the overwhelming majority of the people. Demonstrations for electoral reform filled the French countryside in 1847. Early in 1848 the agitation also became more acute in the capital. Nevertheless Louis Philippe and Guizot did not grasp the gravity of the situation, and they refused any concession. When the government wanted to suppress the demonstrations for electoral reform in Paris, riots occurred, and on February 24 a regular revolt broke out, in which the workers and the students were primarily the active participants. The attitude of the National Guard was decisive. Under Louis

Philippe these troops were a citizen militia for the defence of peace and order, according to the model of 1789. The soldiers of the National Guard kept their uniforms and arms at home. They were mobilized for festivities and parades and likewise during disturbances of public order. It was a genuine representative body of the bourgeois middle class.

When Guizot called upon the National Guard in Paris, most of the soldiers went on strike and remained at home. The others, who were still on duty, did not fire upon the insurgents, but fraternized with the revolutionaries and joined in the cry: " Long live reform! Down with the ministers! " The example of the National Guard also acted in a paralysing manner on the regular army. The troops, who had little inclination anyway to sacrifice their lives for any line of the Bourbons, offered but little resistance to the revolt. In the course of twenty-four hours Louis Philippe's Kingdom collapsed. The King fled, the government of Guizot vanished from the scene, the soldiers evacuated Paris, the Republic had conquered.

The victorious revolt of February 24 had indeed been started and fought by the Parisian workers, but under the prevailing conditions the proletariat alone would never have been able to vanquish Louis Philippe. The decision had rather been brought about by the defection of the bourgeoisie from the so-called bourgeois King. Even though the army had left Paris for the present, still as a whole it was intact. After February 24 all the generals recognized the republican state and placed themselves at the disposal of the new government. The socialistic and democratic influence in the army was very insignificant. Furthermore the bourgeois National Guard also continued to exist after February 24 in Paris as well as in the provinces. They had their arms and their organization, while the revolutionary workers had obtained only a few rifles at first. The entire powerful centralized apparatus of the French state was likewise unshaken. This machine had been developed by Napoleon I and had been taken over afterwards by both royal lines. It extended from the central offices in Paris into the farthest villages. The administrative apparatus also placed itself at the disposal of the Republic after February 24, but in doing so it did not change its character.

After the collapse of the monarchy a provisional republican government was formed in Paris. It consisted of a coalition of both leading republican parties. The group of the *National* came to an understanding with the followers of the *Réforme*. It was to be the task of the provisional government to make the Republic secure against the danger of a monarchist counter-revolution and to permit the election of a National Assembly based on general suffrage as rapidly as possible. As the embodiment of French democracy the future National Assembly should present the country with a new republican constitution. Leading men of both parties formed the provisional government: Lamartine, Marrast, Garnier-Pagès of the moderate democrats, together with Ledru-Rollin and Louis Blanc. They also desired that the illegal republican societies of Paris should be represented in the new government together with the legal democratic politicians. Thus the socialist metal-worker Albert, who had played an important part in the illegal movement, likewise became a minister. A socialist worker as minister of a major power was something new and appeared to express the purpose of the Revolution of 1848.

At every opportunity the radical democrats of 1848 spoke of the tradition of 1793. Nevertheless their political practice proved that they had actually learned nothing from Robespierre. The example of the Great Revolution should have been an absolute warning against the entrance of the radical democrats into the government under the conditions of February 24. In the streets of Paris it appeared, indeed, as if the proletariat had captured power; for the army, the police, and the National Guard had all disappeared from the capital, and the Red workers were free to do as they pleased.

Yet any serious politician who examined the actual relation of the political forces could not let himself be deluded by the vivid picture of revolutionary Paris. All the actual instruments of power were still in the hands of the wealthy bourgeoisie. Any serious measure would necessarily uncover definite differences between the two parties within the provisional government. After February 25 all the groups of the bourgeoisie arrayed themselves under the flag of the *National,* declared for a moderate and peaceful democracy, and demanded severe measures against the "Terrorists, Communists, and Jacobins."

The situation after February 24, 1848 was much more unfavourable for the radical democrats than after August 10, 1792. At that time the royal army had been completely demolished and a new army was just developing. Furthermore, after August 10 the democrats had at least the city of Paris firmly in their hands. This time the old army was unbroken and the democrats did not even control the city of Paris, as will be shown immediately. Nevertheless Robespierre, after August 10, had not thought at all of entering into the government. But he left the power to the wealthy republican bourgeoisie, satisfied himself with consolidating his position in Paris, and waited until the Girondins had been completely discredited in the country. Besides this the Great Revolution also taught the following: although after the storming of the Bastille the wealthy liberal bourgeoisie had adopted an extremely reactionary course, opposed to the interests of the broad masses, it had lasted almost four years before the rule of liberalism was discredited in the eyes of the French people and ripe to be overthrown. Similarly in 1848 the democrats could by no means count upon obtaining political power by storm. Even under the most favourable conditions a considerable period had to elapse before the French people abandoned the illusions of Lamartine's group and espoused the cause of unwavering social democracy.

If all this was considered, it appeared very doubtful

whether the French Socialist Democratic Party could obtain any advantage by participating in the provisional government. Ledru-Rollin and Louis Blanc were convinced, however, that they could win positions of power within the government for the labouring masses and that they could improve the condition of the proletariat immediately. Nor was anything lost as long as the Socialist Democratic Party remained in close touch with the urban and rural masses, acted openly and clearly, didn't surrender any part of their program, and remained in the government only as long as the actual interests of the democrats permitted it.

The history of the months after February 24, 1848 in France is of extraordinary significance for an understanding of the democratic movement of the nineteenth century. For the first time during the nineteenth century both democratic tendencies had an opportunity to demonstrate their ability in the political arena. The older historical form of social democracy had to demonstrate what political freedom and general suffrage could accomplish for the poor masses under a republic and what practical advantages the modern industrial proletariat would be capable of deriving from democracy. Similarly the new form of bourgeois-liberal democracy had to pass its test. It had to show that freedom and general suffrage did not harm peace and order, that the masses of the poor were also basically peaceful and moderate and did not touch property — in short, that a republic with general suffrage presents the most convenient and most secure political form for capitalism and for the educated and wealthy classes generally. Both factions of French democracy stood the test of history very poorly. On the 24th of February they had all of France united behind them. Four months later they were both equally despised, used up, and impotent.

During the period of the provisional government from the end of February until the beginning of May 1848 a peculiar division of labour between the two ruling parties resulted. The bourgeois republicans practised power politics, and the socialists pursued social politics. The result was that the Socialist Democrats passed a series of extraordinarily important social laws within a very short time, but simultaneously lost all actual positions of power, so that finally their social policy remained isolated. This development was all the more peculiar since the Socialist Democrats had apparently obtained the most important positions of power during the first storm of the Revolution. For at the distribution of posts among the members of the provisional government Ledru-Rollin received the Ministry of the Interior. He honestly tried to influence the French administrative apparatus in a republican sense. He sent his commissaries into the provinces, issued energetic decrees, and sought to influence the coming elections according to the views of his party. But the result of his activity was entirely negative. It became evident that the Minister alone, even with the best of intentions, could not master the hostile giant machine.

The actions of the bourgeois republicans were all the more successful. It was their first thought on February 24 to seize the municipal administration of Paris, for they had actually learned from the Great Revolution and wanted to prevent the new party of the Mountain from again finding its centre in the city of Paris. While Ledru-Rollin struggled with the documents of his Ministry, the party of the *National* took possession of the city of Paris. First Garnier-Pagès became Mayor of Paris, and when he later took over the Ministry of Finance, Marrast himself took his place. The Minister of War, Arago, who likewise belonged to the bourgeois party, co-operated with the generals to avoid any disturbance of discipline in the army and to reconvert the troops into an instrument which would be ready to suppress any uprising of the workers. Under the eyes of the Minister Ledru-Rollin, the bourgeois party formed a new fighting organization for the event of a civil war in Paris itself. It was the so-called Mobile Guard, which was trained especially with an eye to a future revolt of the radical workers. The Mobile Guard was composed of young, unemployed Parisians who allowed themselves to be used against their class comrades for a handsome uniform and a secure daily wage.

An unusually felicitous combination could have given the radical democrats the possibility of arming the French proletariat in a completely legal way. For it was notorious after February 24 that the old exclusive method according to which the National Guard had been organized under the monarchy could no longer be maintained. The troops of the wealthy bourgeoisie had to become a general popular militia, to which the poor as well as the rich should have access. The principle of such a democratic transformation of the National Guard had been accepted by the government. Its execution was the business of the Minister of the Interior, therefore Ledru-Rollin's. Now, however, the sinister power with which the bureaucracy sabotaged developments that did not suit it became evident. Suddenly there were neither arms nor uniforms for the masses of the new soldiers of the National Guard, and the revolutionary Minister of the Interior was incapable of changing anything. Generally only such soldiers of the National Guard as the wealthy class trusted received arms and uniforms. Nevertheless the most unbelievable failure of the Socialist democrats lay in the fact that the party was not even capable of getting into its hands the organization of the unemployed which had formed around the national workshops as a result of the new social legislation.

Louis Blanc began an extraordinarily fruitful activity as minister in order to improve the condition of the working class in France. A state commission for labour questions was formed with Louis Blanc as chairman and Albert as vice-chairman. The Parisian workers were represented in the commission by delegates of each trade. The employers also sent a corresponding number of representatives, organized according to trades. This labour commission, which met in the Palais du Luxembourg, was a kind of economic council of Paris, or if only the workers' delegates were considered, a kind of trade-union congress. The commission discussed all the questions of economic reform and social policy which were under consideration at that time. In this way the French workers received for the first time the right of association, which was recognized by the state and of which the right to strike was an immediate corollary. The influence which Blanc himself exerted was extremely moderate. He lacked all malice towards the employers. In the name of the labour commission he sought to arbitrate the controversies between employers and workers and to create wage contracts.

At the suggestion of Louis Blanc the provisional government issued a law dealing with the hours of work. According to this the working day should not exceed ten hours in Paris and eleven hours in the provinces. For that period such a restriction of the working day was already a success for the workers. In the interest of the unemployed the government proclaimed the right to work. Practically this meant nothing more than a modest unemployment benefit. With this the state bound itself to pay for the support of each worker for whom the authorities could not find any work. The number of unemployed grew very rapidly after February 24, as a result of the intensified economic crisis, especially in Paris. The authorities instituted a program of work relief, which could only absorb a small part of the unemployed. The others, provided with the necessary identification cards, reported at the competent district office in Paris and received their benefits there.

The bourgeois members of the provisional government soon became worried over the daily gathering of unemployed groups at the relief offices. They therefore conceived the idea of organizing the unemployed in another manner, in order to render them politically innocuous. Work relief belonged to the province of the Minister for Public Works. This circumstance was used to concentrate all the questions dealing with the unemployed in the Ministry for Public Works, which was headed by the bourgeois republican Marie. Marie charged a very skilled organizer, Thomas, who understood how to treat the workers, with the task of organizing the unemployed. Now Thomas created the apparatus of the national workshops with extraordinary rapidity. At the same time Thomas's organization directed the public relief works and paid the unemployment benefits. The chief purpose of this arrangement was to create a kind of military organization of the unemployed, with a carefully contrived system of superior and subordinate officers. It may be compared with the German " Labour Service " after 1933.

Louis Blanc had not the slightest connexion with the national workshops. First of all, the relief jobs of the national workshops, which were usually entirely superfluous and were only invented to occupy the people, were not true productive co-operatives in the sense of Blanc's socialism. Secondly, the apparatus of the national workshops was created by Marie and Thomas for the very purpose of injuring Louis Blanc's party. The number of members of the national workshops, who partly performed relief work and partly drew monetary unemployment benefits, grew rapidly. In June the number exceeded a hundred thousand. The political purpose which the bourgeois republicans pursued with this organization had been completely attained. A political separation appeared between the employed and the unemployed. The employed, who sent their representatives to the Palais du Luxembourg, were generally on the side of the Socialist Democrats, while the unemployed, who were gathered into the organization of the national workshops, generally supported the bourgeois democrats.

One may wonder at the ease with which the French unemployed at that time allowed themselves to be won for the cause of the bourgeoisie. One must take into consideration, however, the general political confusion which had been produced by the democratic propaganda of the period. The

Republic and general suffrage had been obtained. Apparently therefore the " people " ruled in France, and the government showed that it was well disposed towards the unemployed and supported them in their need, a circumstance which was regarded as a great social achievement at that time. Why shouldn't the unemployed follow leaders like Marie and Thomas, who were apparently only concerned with their welfare? Louis Blanc and his friends, on the other hand, had lost contact with the unemployed. This was the worst sin of omission of the socialist republicans during the months after February 24. The fact that the party of the *National* was capable of organizing an unemployed army of a hundred thousand men in Paris made any revolutionary action by the Socialist Democrats impossible. That the bourgeois counter-revolution later turned with especial ferocity particularly against its loyal workers of the national workshops, and that just these economically peaceful workers were to wage the greatest revolutionary class struggle of the entire generation in June, changes nothing as far as the political fact itself is concerned.

Louis Blanc and his friends behaved extremely moderately towards the capitalists, and the dreaded productive co-operatives were not founded with the aid of the state, simply because the Republic had no money for them. Nevertheless the bankers and manufacturers followed the developments after February 24 with increasing dissatisfaction. The legal restriction of the hours of work and the new right of the workers to organize disturbed the manufacturers. Besides, the workers who were displeased with their working conditions could simply leave their factories and enter the national workshops. To be sure, the worker in a better factory in Paris earned three to four francs a day and only one to two francs in the national workshops. The wages received in the national workshops were therefore a kind of strike benefit which enabled the workers to hold out until the private em-

ployer yielded. The indignation of the manufacturers over
these conditions may be imagined.

Above all, the capitalists were extremely concerned over
the question: Would French social legislation actually be
satisfied with its present achievements? The victorious Revolution had brought the most diverse socialistic projects to
the surface. Everywhere people spoke and wrote of the new
socialist society, and as long as Louis Blanc was minister and
was permitted to deliver his socialistic speeches in the name
of the French Republic at the Palais du Luxembourg, every
French capitalist considered his wealth endangered. Consequently the moneyed elements fearfully withdrew their capital. As a result of the general distrust of the wealthy class
towards the new order of things and of the general nervous-
ness, business grew progressively worse, more and more
plants were closed, and unemployment increased constantly.
The capitalists circulated the slogan that the socialists and
communists would first have to be disposed of ruthlessly before trust and good business could return.

The government of Louis Philippe had bequeathed a
large deficit to the Republic. Under the monarchy the need
of the state for money had not been a misfortune, for the
bankers made money out of loans and advances to the state,
and so no one grew excited over a deficit. Now, however, the
republican government lacked money, and the growing crisis
decreased the revenues of the state. On the other hand, the
completely unproductive national workshops cost increasing sums, and the banks made no loans to the Republic. The
government was painfully embarrassed as to how it should
meet its financial obligations. Forceful measures against the
capitalists were highly unsympathetic to the bourgeois republicans. They desired neither a forced loan nor paper
money with a forced rate of exchange. They feared that
they might enter the path of economic dictatorship with such
measures as would necessarily lead to a political one and a

reign of terror in the manner of 1793. Nor did they dare on the other hand to suspend the payments to the unemployed, for they were the guarantee of internal peace.

The ruling party of the bourgeois republicans counted on the gratefulness of the wealthy class, for the policy of the *National* group had avoided civil war, protected private property, and suppressed all terroristic tendencies. As compensation for this the wealthy class would have to make other sacrifices. Therefore the Minister of Finance, Garnier-Pagès, proposed an addition of forty-five per cent to the land-tax as an extraordinary crisis levy. The Socialist Democratic ministers offered only weak resistance, and the fateful law was issued by the provisional government. Since there was no desire to touch the capitalists and at the same time expediency demanded that the workers be spared, the burden of the crisis was placed upon the class which at the moment could not make itself heard in Paris, on the farmers, above all on the mass of the small peasants. This was an act of political folly which was to have catastrophic consequences for both groups of the French democrats. The Republic, which had been called into life with so much acclaim, had as yet not produced anything positive for the rural population. Instead there came the tax increase.

Almost the entire French people had protested against Louis Philippe's methods of government. Now the same peasant who had had to pay 10 francs in taxes under the reviled monarchy was to give up 14.5 francs under the democratic Republic. In addition to this the reason which was offered for the tax increase was immensely harmful to the democratic policy. The money would be used primarily to maintain the unemployed of Paris. The mass of the small peasants of France — above all, the poor tenants and the agricultural labourers — would certainly have understood this if a popular program had united the demands of the rural and urban workers. However, an almost superhuman understanding would have been necessary for the hard-working peasant to have made voluntary sacrifices for the benefit of the idle city-dweller. Thus the democratic government, because it spared the capitalist, disrupted the united front between the urban and the rural masses, embittered the peasants against the workers and against the new system, and shook the foundations of the republican state.

During April the democratic socialists, and in general the politically active workers in Paris, gradually noticed that events were taking an unfavourable course. The reports which were received concerning the temper of the provincial population were unfavourable; Ledru-Rollin's commissaries achieved nothing, and uneasiness developed concerning the results of the imminent elections to the National Assembly. At this point the Socialist Democrats had the unhappy idea of demanding the postponement of the elections. A big propaganda campaign with street meetings was started in Paris, where demands were made for a later election date. It was declared that the counter-revolution had ruled in France for fifty years and had prevented all liberal propaganda. For this reason the rural and village masses had remained entirely unenlightened and would permit themselves to be misled by the reactionaries in the elections. It would therefore be necessary to allow a certain interval to elapse during which the republicans could enlighten the masses in all parts of France. Only then would elections which actually represented the uninfluenced opinion of the people be possible.

Had the socialistic republicans studied the lessons of the Great Revolution better, they would also have avoided a serious mistake this time. After August 10, 1792 Robespierre did not even think of demanding that the elections to the National Convention be postponed, although the conditions for the exercise of the franchise were much more unfavourable than under general suffrage in 1848. At the same time Robespierre, together with his friends, realized clearly that the elections would not turn out favourably for his party. After a victorious popular revolution in the name of democracy, it is psychologically impossible to agitate against the election of a National Assembly. The German Revolution after November 9, 1918, which on the whole shows some remarkable similarities to the French developments of 1848, produced the same mistake by the radical Socialists. Several weeks after the Revolution, when they already felt that the majority of the people were not on their side, they turned against the elections to the National Assembly. On the other hand Lenin in 1917 never opposed the convocation of the Russian Constituent National Assembly, but left the thankless task of delaying the elections to Kerenski's government.

The more the Socialist Democrats of Paris demanded a postponement of the elections, the more determined was the demand of the French bourgeoisie for an early election date. The Socialist Democrats achieved nothing more than a moral defeat and a further exasperation of the peasants and the petty bourgeoisie in the provinces. For the provincials now felt more than ever that the politicians in Paris were exploiting them and wanted to postpone the day of reckoning. The elections to the French National Assembly took place on April 23. In a purely technical sense, it was a spectacle of political democracy the like of which had not yet been seen. The number of eligible voters was 9,500,000. Almost 8,000,000 valid votes were cast. The result of the election was as unfavourable for the Socialist Democrats as could be expected. Of the 900 deputies only 100 were adherents of the party of the *Réforme*. On the other side approximately 100 deputies of the Catholic counter-revolution — that is, of the open adherents of the older line of the Bourbons — had been elected. To these were added 200 monarchists of Thiers's party. Thus after two months of the democratic Republic the monarchists had already won one third of all the mandates. This was the answer of the rural population to the forty-five-per-cent tax increase and the completely negative agrarian policy of the new rulers.

The majority of the new Parliament, about 500 deputies, were bourgeois republicans, who joined the party of the *National*. The result of the election would not have been so hopeless if these 500 deputies had actually been liberal democrats of the type of Lamartine — that is, at the same time supporters of private property, political liberty, and class conciliation. Actually the majority of these 500 alleged republican democrats consisted of rabid petty-bourgeois and agrarian reactionaries. They were the representatives of small manufacturers, who execrated Louis Blanc, and of exasperated peasants, who demanded an accounting with the Parisian idlers. These deputies — village lawyers, owners of estates, retired officers, and the like — called themselves republicans, to be sure, because they were not directly interested in a restoration of the Bourbons; they did not want any republic based on freedom of development and class conciliation, but rather the use of the mailed fist against everything that reminded them of the proletariat or socialism. It is clear that the 300 monarchists in the National Assembly incited the rabid Right wing of the bourgeois republicans more and more towards a struggle with the Parisian workers and socialism.

The Socialist Democrats were vanquished. During the last two months they had certainly made important mistakes in all questions of political power and election tactics. On the other hand, however, there were the outstanding achievements of Louis Blanc in the field of social policy. As matters stood then, Socialist Democracy, even under the most gifted leadership, would hardly have been capable of winning over the majority of the French people and of capturing political power within two months. It was necessary to prepare for a protracted fight, with Socialist Democracy in the role of the opposition. The meaning of the election results was perfectly clear to all French politicians. The National Assembly had a large and bellicose bourgeois majority, which was determined to defend private property. Consequently there was no room for any socialist ministers. The Socialist Democratic Party should have left the government immediately, enlightened the workers of Paris concerning the actual situation, and entered into opposition without hastiness or risky undertakings.

Yet when the National Assembly met in Paris early in May and a new government had to be formed, a peculiar situation resulted. Lamartine and his closer friends had gradually been frightened by the rabid Right wing of their own party comrades. They sensed the coming counter-revolution and turned towards the Left. They did not want to give up the coalition with the Socialist Democrats. The result was a compromise solution. The socialist ministers Louis Blanc and Albert were sacrificed to the new bourgeois majority of Parliament. In return the two of them were allowed to continue their activity in the commission of the Palais du Luxembourg. Ledru-Rollin, on the other hand, remained in the government. Until the National Assembly had decided upon the new French Constitution, an executive commission of five members was formed to supervise the individual administrative departments, approximately as in Germany after November 9, 1918 the six People's Commissars had the general political leadership and controlled the work of the departmental heads. Four men of the *National* group entered into the supreme government commission: Lamartine, Marie, Garnier-Pagès, and Arago. To these Ledru-Rollin was added as the fifth man. The five members of the supreme commission were freed from all departmental work. In this way Ledru-Rollin lost the Ministry of the Interior, which was now given to a reliable bourgeois republican. Marie gave up the Ministry of Labour and was succeeded by the rabid reactionary Trelat. General Cavaignac became Minister of War in place of

Arago. The bourgeois majority of the National Assembly were still uncertain during the first days of their parliamentary activity. They didn't know the exact relations of the various forces as yet, and so for the present they put up with the new government.

The fact that Ledru-Rollin's party remained in the government under such conditions had extraordinarily significant consequences. The most important of these was not that the so-called Socialist Democrats became more helpless from day to day, nor that the reactionary majority of the National Assembly became more and more conscious of its strength and began to disregard the government in its actions. For the French army and administrative apparatus obeyed the bourgeois counter-revolution and not the democrats who happened to be ministers. Much more important was the fact that Ledru-Rollin's party, and with it French democracy in general, had isolated itself completely from the workers since the early part of May 1848. It was clear that the majority of the National Assembly wanted to do away with the social achievements of the Revolution. By remaining in the government and lending themselves to the execution of the reactionary decrees of the National Assembly they alienated themselves from the workers. The feelings of friendship for the workers which Ledru-Rollin's party had asserted in its propaganda before the Revolution and during its beginning did not stand the test of the first serious trial of strength. When the class struggle actually broke out, it became evident that French democracy was not capable of defending the cause of the labouring masses openly and consistently. Since the French capitalist class likewise distrusted the democratic leaders, democracy after May 1848 found itself playing a ridiculous part between two hostile armies. There was nothing left of Robespierre's tradition.

If the official legal party of the Socialist Democrats had failed, then perhaps new leaders of the workers could have arisen from the ranks of the illegal democratic movement, of the secret societies, which had fought for the Republic during the reign of Louis Philippe. Among the revolutionary republicans whom the February Revolution had freed from prison, Blanqui and Barbès were the most important. Blanqui was by far the most significant figure among all the various groups of French democracy. He was the only realistic politician among those fighting for power, who did not allow himself to be misled by the slogans of the February Revolution and its parties. He demanded the complete disarmament of the capitalists and the militarists and at the same time the arming of the working people. He considered everything else unimportant as long as this condition was not fulfilled. Blanqui was neither a fomenter of abortive insurrections nor an adventurer. Instead he was the living conscience of French democracy and was therefore bitterly hated by the official politicians, by the ministers and their followers.

Blanqui's positive influence on the workers of Paris was slight. He founded a club, at whose meetings he expounded his ideas. There were many other democratic and socialist clubs besides his, however, and the heads of the other clubs, who lacked Blanqui's mental clarity, joined the agitation against him, which was carried on, in part, by despicable methods. Since Blanqui was reviled on all sides as the evil spirit of the French Revolution, as a terrorist and as a preacher of civil war, the bourgeoisie considered him its worst enemy. Blanqui became the terror of all philistines just as Karl Liebknecht and Rosa Luxemburg were to become in 1918 in Germany. The result was that Blanqui had to spend the greater part of his life in prison.

The historical significance of the agitation against Blanqui during March and April 1848 lies primarily in the fact that it prevented any recovery of the French democratic movement. When the official party collapsed, there remained nothing more than a confused mass of clubs and agitators. Blanqui's voice could not assert itself successfully in this chaos. As a result the Parisian proletariat, which had been deserted by the political parties, became the tool of adventurers and police spies. An armed uprising of the Parisian workers, for the purpose of carrying out a second revolution, was never quite so hopeless as in May 1848. Owing to the inept tactics of the democrats a profound estrangement had taken place between the workers of Paris and the peasantry. It is not true that Paris had regularly had the leadership of the French revolutions and that the provinces used to follow the slogans of the capital. On the contrary, actually the Parisian movements were victorious only if they were in accord with the wishes of the majority of the French people. The storming of the Bastille was only significant because at the same time the peasants throughout France were also about to storm their local Bastilles. In May and June of 1793 the party of the Mountain was victorious only because the great majority of the French people despised the Roland clique. The Revolution of 1830 had been fought by the Parisians in complete agreement with the provincials, and the movement against Louis Philippe during the winter of 1847–8 had actually started in the provinces and had later spread to Paris.

The counter-revolutionary current, which achieved a temporary predominance in the rural areas and in the provincial towns during April and May 1848, necessarily doomed every revolt in Paris to complete isolation. If the villages and the provincial towns opposed the revolt, and if the bourgeois middle class hated the " anarchists " and "terrorists," then it could be assumed that the regular army as well as the bourgeois section of the National Guard would fire fanatically upon the workers. In addition there was the fatal separation between the unemployed, who were strongly organized in the national workshops and who still supported the government, and the workers in the factories who were in favour of Socialist Democracy. The secret wire-pullers of the French administrative apparatus had seen to it that the workers of the national workshops had been received into the National Guard in very large numbers. These workers, who were loyal to the government, had received arms and they ruled the sections of the National Guard in the working-class districts. In addition to this the active democrats in the clubs were completely at variance with one another. Barbès hated Blanqui and was ready to unite with the government at any time if it were a question of destroying Blanqui. Finally the presence of Ledru-Rollin in the government necessarily confused certain classes of the population. The radical petty bourgeoisie, and also many workers, did not immediately understand the change of front of the Socialist Democrats, and a revolt against the government of Ledru-Rollin would have seemed a fratricidal adventure to them.

The result was that in May 1848 the political forces of French democracy and French socialism reached a low water-mark, and no leader who had even the slightest bit of common sense could seriously recommend a second revolution at that time. The workers of Paris had exhibited a maximum of discipline and restraint since Februray 24. To be sure, several peaceful mass demonstrations had taken place, but there had never been any violence nor spilling of blood. Nevertheless this pacific attitude of the Parisian workers was not desired by the Right wing of the bourgeois republicans. This group of rabid reactionaries from the provincial towns had long since decided that the governing five-man commission was much too weak. They did not want any compromises with the workers of Paris, but favoured the use of the mailed fist. The man whom the Right wing of the bourgeois republicans trusted most was the new Minister of War, General Cavaignac. It was desired to use the next opportunity to overthrow the Executive Commission, to shoot down the Parisian workers, and then to erect a military dictatorship under the leadership of Cavaignac.

Since the workers of Paris did not want to attempt a putsch, it became necessary to incite them to such action by suitable means. A large demonstration of all the democrats and socialists of Paris for Poland had been arranged for May 15. There was no objection to this, nor was it a political misfortune if the masses took this opportunity to march past the building where the National Assembly held its sessions and show their strength in a peaceful parade. Nevertheless the danger existed that certain shady characters might utilize the demonstration for their own purposes. Blanqui warned in vain. The enthusiasm of the Parisian workers for Poland, that old relic of the democratic tradition, was so great that no objection was of any avail. Blanqui, together with his club, participated in the demonstration in order not to exclude himself from the general democratic action.

The course of events on May 15, 1848 was extremely peculiar. The masses appeared before the building of the National Assembly according to schedule. The government had long since made all possible preparations to suppress any disturbances in Paris. The capital and its environs swarmed with troops. The regular army, the Mobile Guard, and the National Guard were at its disposal. The government had always considered the protection of the National Assembly from any disturbance as being especially important. Nevertheless, when the demonstrators arrived in front of the National Assembly on May 15, they found the entrances of the building undefended and open. Consequently a group of Parisian workers was able to enter the building and to appear on the floor of the house. They expressed their dissatisfaction to the deputies and created a great deal of noise. There was, however, no violence. For three hours the demonstrators controlled the floor of the house without any armed power rushing to protect the Parliament. So far all this had only been an unpleasant incident for Parliament, without any important political significance. Suddenly a dubious individual who was suspected of being a spy declared in the name of the people that the National Assembly was dissolved.

Now many of the demonstrators and even some of the democratic leaders convinced themselves that a second revolution had been victorious. The National Assembly had apparently collapsed and the armed power of the government had failed. A number of demonstrators marched to the Hôtel de Ville in order to proclaim a new revolutionary workers' government. Barbès and Albert were short-sighted enough to go along into the Hôtel de Ville. Once the fact of a political revolt against the legitimate government had been conclusively established, the troops suddenly appeared. The Hôtel de Ville was occupied without any resistance. Barbès, Albert, and several other well-known radicals, among them Blanqui, were arrested. The attempted revolt of the Parisian workers, which had been so fearfully awaited for months, was now past. It had terminated without any blood having been spilled, like a scene in an opera bouffe. Not only had Socialist Democracy been completely vanquished, but besides it had exhibited a ridiculous helplessness.

Anyone who has had any experience at all with the course of mass movements can hardly doubt that the action of May 15 was an unparalleled, preconcerted provocation arranged by police spies. The political purpose of the entire action is only too clear. The secret wire-pullers wanted to force the masses into the building of the National Assembly and to create a disturbance there. It had been intended to create the pretence of a socialist revolution in order to have an excuse for the overthrow of the government and the erection of a military dictatorship. Meanwhile everything had taken place too rapidly and too mildly. Since the reluctant revolutionaries had not offered any resistance, the soldiers had had no excuse to fire, and the generals together with their political backers had to create a new and better opportunity. The 15th of May showed French democracy in a fright-

ful state of disintegration. The official Socialist Democratic
Party was just as impotent in the government as among the
masses, and the leaders of the democratic clubs had neither
influence nor authority. As a result the Parisian workers became the prey of every adventurer. It was not by chance that
the Bonapartist agitation again became conspicuous in Paris
after the 15th of May. The workers, who had lost their faith
in all the republican groups, remembered the image of the
Emperor again and thought that, at the very least, conditions
could not become worse under a new Bonaparte.

The group of reactionary republicans who were hostile
to the workers and well disposed towards a dictatorship were
supported by the monarchist parties of the National Assembly and continued their activity. At first the government
commission for labour affairs in the Palais du Luxembourg
was dissolved. With that the workers lost their legal representation. War was declared upon the principles of the right
of association and of collective bargaining. Ledru-Rollin
continued to remain quietly in the government. The next
decisive blow was intended to strike the national workshops.
The provincial deputies did not know that the national
workshops had been a stronghold of the bourgeois group,
a guarantee of economic peace. They saw in the national
workshops only an institution for the purpose of wasting
taxes and promoting idleness. The capitalists detested the
principle of the right to work, to which the national workshops owed their existence. The manufacturers gradually
prepared again for a period of business prosperity, when
socialism in France had once been conquered. They again
wanted cheap and obedient workers for their plants, and
they saw in the national workshops a kind of state support
of strikes. The dissolution of the national workshops appeared to them a necessary condition for the recovery of
industry on a capitalistic basis.

The national workshops of Paris at that time, with their
wretched wages, their useless relief projects, their military

organization and political misguidance of the workers, certainly had nothing in common with any form of socialism. Louis Blanc was fully justified in denying any responsibility for the national workshops. No socialist would have had any interest in perpetuating them as they existed then. The return of the unemployed to productive labour would have been the only correct solution. But it was a matter of the conditions under which the relief workers should return to the factories; whether at reasonable wages or whether they should be abandoned unconditionally to the discretion of the employers. The majority of the National Assembly desired the latter course. The national workshops should suddenly be closed in a provocative manner, and the workers would have the choice of starving or of returning to the factories at the lowest wages. If a revolt should break out on this occasion, it would be ruthlessly suppressed by the army.

The question of the national workshops thus turned into a test of power between capital and labour, whereby particularly that part of the proletariat which was most moderate, anti-socialistic, and desirous of economic peace became the victim of capitalistic violence. Simultaneously a crisis developed among the liberal democrats as a result of the problem of the national workshops. Socialist Democracy in France had been dead politically since the 15th of May, despite the supernumerary roles which Ledru-Rollin and a group of his friends still played in the government and the Parliament. To all appearances, liberal democracy, personified by Lamartine, Marie, and others, was still in power. This group controlled the supreme ruling Executive Commission. It had been the liberal democrats who, guided by the idea of class conciliation, had created the national workshops and, with the aid of Thomas, had turned them into their own political machine. At the same time the brutal dissolution of the national workshops was also intended as a decisive blow at the liberal government. During the crisis which was expected to follow the closing of the national workshops, an opportunity would also be found to overthrow the government.

The governing commission, under the leadership of Lamartine, was likewise ready to dissolve the national workshops, but it wanted to do so gradually and considerately in order to avoid any provocation of the workers. Such provocation, however, was just what the majority of the National Assembly wanted, in order to be able to derive political benefits from it. The behaviour of the Executive Commission during this conflict was extremely deplorable. Garnier-Pagès had already come to an agreement with Cavaignac and his group and carried on intrigues behind the backs of his four colleagues. The other four saw no other way out and finally submitted to the threats of the National Assembly. The Minister of Labour, Trelat, did everything possible to drive the workers to despair. When Thomas, the director of the national workshops, warned the Minister about continuing his course of action and prophesied a revolt of the embittered relief workers, Trelat had him arrested and removed from Paris. This occurrence is the best proof of the ruthless and cunning manner in which the party which was then most powerful in France provoked the June uprising.

The government decrees regarding the dissolution of the national workshops appeared. The unemployed and the relief workers should immediately seek employment again in private industry. The young men who found no work were to report for military service, and the others were to be sent to the provinces to work on relief projects, though it was not at all clear what the authorities in the provinces would do with the relief workers. All this meant the complete subjection of the workers to the will of the employers. The workers of Paris had now been deserted by all parties and no one could advise them or show them a way out of their dilemma. The relief workers felt that they had been de-

ceived for four months; they had been used to fight socialism as long as they were needed and now, because they were
no longer needed, were being kicked out.

In this desperate situation the class consciousness of some
of these relief workers awoke again and they attempted to
get in touch with the revolutionary workers in the factories.
They reminded themselves of 1793, 1830, and February 24,
1848. As members of the National Guard they were armed,
and they had grown accustomed to a certain degree of military organization in the national workshops. They preferred
to die honourably rather than to starve to death slowly in
the name of the democratic Republic. On June 23 the revolt began in the working-class quarters of Paris. No political party and no prominent leader sided with the workers.
Since the Democratic Party no longer existed and since the
so-called successors of the party of the Mountain had deplorably renounced their task, the simple workers of Paris fought
alone for the tradition of Robespierre.

The first victim of the revolt was the liberal-democratic
government. On the morning of June 24 a group of excited
deputies forced their way into the offices of the Executive
Commission and demanded the immediate resignation of the
five members. The latter declared that they would yield
only to a formal decree of the National Assembly. They did
not have to wait very long for the decree. The National Assembly transferred complete executive power to General
Cavaignac, and with that the Executive Commission was deposed. If Socialist Democracy had collapsed in France on the
15th of May, then the 24th of June was the end of liberal
democracy. Opinions may vary as to which group disappeared more deplorably from the arena.

When the revolt of the workers began in Paris on June 23,
the spectacle of May 15 was repeated. The insurgents met
with no resistance at first and were able to take possession of
the working-class quarters and to erect barricades there.
Had the government also thrown its entire armed force into

the working-class districts of Paris on the same day on which
it published the decrees concerning the national workshops,
then a revolt of such dimensions would hardly have resulted.
However, the friends of a military dictatorship wanted a
real street struggle, so that they would be able to settle ac-
counts thoroughly with socialism and democracy. Now they
had attained their aim. The cunning provocation with
which Cavaignac's party prepared the revolt of June 1848
finds its closest analogy in the behaviour of the Tsarist government of Russia in January 1905, when it also allowed the
labour movement of the priest Gapon to develop in order to
have an opportunity for the blood-bath which it desired.

The revolt of the Parisian workers was completely hopeless from the beginning. But they fought with the courage
of despair. It was only after a three-day struggle, which resulted in the deaths of thousands of victims, that General
Cavaignac was victorious. The general remained at the head
of the government, gathered his Ministry from the Right
wing of the so-called moderate republicans, and suppressed
every oppositional impulse of the masses with brutal violence. In the meantime the majority of the National Assembly completed its labours with the composition of a
republican Constitution for France. General suffrage remained in existence, for the ruling class was not afraid of it,
as long as it was capable of suppressing any opposition with
the help of the police, the courts, and the army. If the ruling
capitalistic military dictatorship could suppress every party
and every club, every meeting and every newspaper whose
opinion displeased it, then general suffrage was an empty
formality.

This was the opinion of the French government party
when it introduced direct election of the president by the
people into the Constitution. Nevertheless general suffrage
played a mean trick on Cavaignac's party. The French people were supposed to elect the president of the Republic on
the 10th of December. The great majority of the wealthy

bourgeoisie, the owners of estates, and the bureaucracy supported the candidacy of General Cavaignac, the saviour of society and private property. After his elimination from the government Ledru-Rollin had continued his agitation with catchwords as if nothing had happened. His friends abused the name of the party of the Mountain by annexing it for themselves, and Ledru-Rollin presented himself to the French people as the presidential candidate of " Social Democracy." The candidate Lamartine personified peaceful democracy. A group of determined Socialists nominated their own candidate, Raspail.

No class-conscious French workers could vote for General Cavaignac or for Ledru-Rollin. Raspail's candidacy was completely hopeless. Consequently the majority of the French workers decided in favour of the other candidate who had been nominated alongside of the four party representatives, Louis Napoleon Bonaparte. The nephew of the great Emperor was a completely insignificant individual, and his election promises were non-committal. However, his name and its tradition worked for him. The French workers, who despaired of the Republic and democracy after the experiences of the past months, clung to the memory of the Empire. If the ballot for Napoleon did nothing else, it was at least the revenge for the June massacre, the answer of the proletariat to Cavaignac's provocations and his parliamentary majority. But the peasant masses also voted for Louis Napoleon Bonaparte. They distrusted royalty, and the Republic in all its phases had disappointed them. The provisional government had decreed the tax increase of forty-five per cent, and General Cavaignac collected it in the villages with the brutality which was characteristic of the man. The peasant, like the worker, answered with a vote for Louis Napoleon.

The result of the election exceeded all expectations or fears. Interest in the election had again been very great: 7,500,000 votes were cast. The 8,000 votes which Lamartine

received showed how much the French people cared for liberal democracy. Ledru-Rollin received 370,000 votes, Raspail 36,000, Cavaignac 1,500,000, and Louis Napoleon Bonaparte 5,500,000. The union of the French working masses,
which democracy had never achieved, was now consummated
in the name of Bonapartism. To be sure, the French workers
and peasants were to be bitterly disillusioned by their President. For Louis Napoleon hadn't the slightest idea of governing in the interest of the working people; on the contrary,
his government soon showed itself as the expression of reactionary capitalism and militarism. A group of French bourgeois politicians who turned towards the rising sun had
already supported Louis Napoleon's candidacy on December 10. No matter how much the sentiment of the French
masses was to change during the following years, for the
present Bonapartism sat firmly in the saddle. The road
from the presidency of Louis Bonaparte to the Empire of
Napoleon III was clearly marked after the 10th of December. The French Revolution of 1848 as a democratic popular movement had already been at an end since the June
battle. Nevertheless by choosing Bonapartism the masses
of the French people chose that form of bondage which appeared to them to be most convenient and most bearable.

3. The Defeat of the Revolution in Central Europe, 1848-9

The victory of the revolt in Paris on February 24 exerted
a powerful stimulatory effect on the democrats in the bour-
geois-parliamentary monarchies of Belgium and England.
As soon as they received the report of the proclamation of the
Republic in France, the democrats of Brussels, under the
leadership of Marx and Engels, immediately initiated an intense activity. The Democratic Union of Brussels congratulated the French upon their success, exhorted the Chartists
to obtain general suffrage in England as rapidly as possible

now, and prepared themselves for an attack upon the Belgian ruling class. The Belgian government, however, struck first. The foreign democrats in the country, among them Marx, were arrested and expelled, and the Belgian-French border was closed by soldiers. In March, Belgian democrats attempted to invade the country from France, but were beaten back. The Belgian government maintained itself. In London the Chartists organized a mass demonstration for April 10; all kinds of hopes and fears were attached to this meeting. Nevertheless, the day passed peacefully. The decline of the Revolution in France after the June struggle also exerted a paralysing influence on Belgian and English democracy.

In the meantime the Revolution had made great progress in the partially or totally absolutist countries of the European continent. Germany and Italy, Hungary and Poland had looked upon France as the leader for many years. As soon as the Revolution broke out in France, the other countries wanted to emulate it. So great had the influence of international revolutionary opinion already been on the minds of men! The bourgeoisie and likewise the broad masses of the people no longer wanted to endure the rule of a monarch and a nobility, of the police and of the bureaucrats. This feeling was augmented by the conviction that every people must conquer, once it has taken arms and mounted the barricades. The two French revolutions of 1830 and 1848 had produced an almost mystical belief in the invincibility of the barricade fighters. Actually the army of a modern major power is a match for any revolt as long as it maintains discipline and obeys its leaders. For reasons with which we are already acquainted the French army had no particular interest in the Bourbons and therefore fought only half-heartedly in 1830 as well as in 1848. However, the masses and European public opinion interpreted the events differently. In all the larger cities the masses of the people were imbued with an astounding feeling of victory, and the worries and the uncertainty of the governments were correspondingly great. The petty bourgeoisie and the workers of Berlin, who were otherwise so peaceful, attacked the Prussian Guards on March 18, without much deliberation. The impulsive action of the masses in Vienna, Milan, Budapest, and other cities was very similar.

In March 1848 the liberal revolution triumphed with surprising rapidity in Germany, Italy, and Hungary. The King of Prussia granted the demands of the liberal bourgeoisie. In Vienna, Metternich was overthrown and a liberal Constitution was granted. The Hungarians wrested an extensive concession of autonomy from the Habsburgs. The Italian people drove the Austrian troops out of Milan and Venice. The King of Sardinia placed his army at the disposal of the Italian national and liberal movement. The other Italian princes also granted the demands of the bourgeoisie. The King of Prussia not only appeared ready to fulfil the national demands of the Germans, but also to become the leader of the Polish movement. The Prussian Poles were granted self-government and began to prepare for a thrust against Russia.

Now everything depended on the manner in which the French Republic and the liberal movements in Germany and Italy, in Hungary and Poland would co-operate. If the democratic-liberal International held together now, the success of the European revolution would be certain. For Prussia, the German petty states, and also the Italian states had gone over to the side of the revolution. The Empire of the Habsburgs was in a state of complete dissolution, and if the revolutionary countries maintained their close association they could easily conquer the Russian Tsar. The French provisional government was ready to act in accordance with the idea of international democratic solidarity, for such an active French foreign policy was desired by the bourgeoisie as well as by the workers. The French workers wanted the extension of the democratic revolution to all the European

countries, and the bourgeoisie wanted to utilize this opportunity to enlarge the French economic and political sphere
of power. Consequently the provisional government offered
the Italians the aid of French land and sea forces against Austria. At the same time the French Republic entered into
negotiations with Prussia. In the event of a war with Russia arising out of the Prussian support of Polish national demands, France was ready to come to the aid of the German
and Polish revolutions against the Tsar.

Such a victorious revolutionary war, conducted conjointly
by the French Republic, Prussia-Germany, Sardinia-Italy,
Hungary, and the insurgent Poles, would have delivered the
death-blow to the Habsburg Empire. From a military point
of view, Tsarist Russia was not very capable of carrying on a
war with a major western-European power. Thus the conquest of the western parts of Russia by the allies and the
restoration of Poland would have been possible. During
1848 Marx and Engels, especially in the *Neue Rheinische
Zeitung,* repeatedly demanded and preached a revolutionary
war against Russia. It was by no means fantastic; on the
contrary, such a campaign was actually considered then by
influential people in Paris and Berlin. It would by no means
have meant a victory of international communism, but it
would have established the rule of bourgeois liberalism and
would thus have laid the basis for further development along
the path envisioned by the *Communist Manifesto.*

It soon became evident, however, that the revolutionary
European united front, which had been imagined so clearly
and frequently, didn't exist. The liberal bourgeoisie of Italy
desired greatly to drive the Austrians out of the country, but
their fear of a republic and the rule of the poor masses was
just as great. The Italian liberals had chosen King Charles
Albert of Sardinia as their leader so that the military monarchy might prevent any radical outgrowths of the nationalist movement. If French troops had marched into Italy in
March or April 1848, they would have been regarded as

propagandists for a republic, since the French army was sent by a government of which Louis Blanc was a member. Besides, the Italian liberals feared that the French would not be entirely unselfish, but might use this opportunity to obtain parts of Italy for themselves.

As a result the King of Sardinia refused the French offer. Italy wanted to carry on its struggle for liberation alone and it would also have been able to triumph over the disorganized Habsburg monarchy if the entire power of the people had actually been employed against the enemy. However, the liberals in power, together with King Charles Albert, were afraid of mobilizing the masses. The result was that the war was conducted in a weak and inadequate manner by the Italians, chiefly with the insignificant military forces of the Kingdom of Sardinia.

The liberal German bourgeoisie comprehended the need for a revolutionary united front just as little as the Italians. The German bourgeoisie saw in its revolution the road to national greatness and did not want to make any sacrifices. It was certainly not easy to find a boundary between Germany and a restored Polish state, but German liberalism and the Prussian government showed no serious desire to solve the Polish question. The project of a Prussian-French collaboration against Russia was dropped, and when the disappointed Poles in Posen turned against the Prussian authorities in April and May, they were violently suppressed. With that the decisive condition for a struggle of the central-European revolution against Russia was destroyed. It was these events in Posen that led to the great demonstration of the Parisian proletariat on May 15, in which it wanted to express its sympathy for Poland and from which such disastrous consequences were to result.

German liberalism also failed to solve the other great international problems of 1848 just as in the case of the Polish question. The German liberals, just like the Italians, wanted to attach themselves to one of the existing monarchies. Only Prussia or Austria could be the leader of the future Germany. Nevertheless in the revolutionary situation of 1848 an alliance of the liberal movement with the house of Habsburg was really objectively impossible, since the victorious revolution would have to deprive the Habsburgs of Italy, Hungary, and Galicia, the greatest part of their territory. Actually, then, nothing was left for German liberalism, if it rejected a republic and was satisfied with a parliamentary monarchy, but to reach an agreement with Prussia. Nevertheless precious time was lost before these simple facts were grasped by the leaders. The newly elected German National Assembly, which met in Frankfurt am Main, even went so far as to elect the Austrian Archduke Johann vice-regent — that is, provisional ruler — of the Empire. This was at least a moral support of the house of Habsburg. At the same time the German liberals in Austria refused to surrender any part of their Emperor's dominion. The German bourgeoisie approved when the Austrian government opposed the Italian Revolution with armed force. When the imperial troops suppressed an uprising of the Czech artisans and workers in Prague in June, the German bourgeoisie was also satisfied.

The new Hungarian government which had been formed in Budapest under the leadership of Kossuth also wanted to employ legal means. It was interested only in developing self-government in its own country and did not care if its King, in his character as Emperor of Austria, made war on Italy. Thus in the spring of 1848 the revolutionary united front in central Europe was already completely disrupted. The national egoism of the Italian, German, and Hungarian liberals prevented any common action. The first to derive any benefit from this situation was the house of Habsburg. Supported by leading circles in Vienna and Budapest, the Austrian generals had suppressed the revolution in Bohemia and prevented it in Galicia. In addition, Radetzky won decisive victories over the King of Sardinia during the summer. The Austrians reconquered Milan. In August the King of Sardinia concluded a deplorable armistice which first of all doomed the Revolution in Italy to defeat.

The Italian democrats, under the leadership of Mazzini, observed with profound exasperation how the liberal bourgeoisie, together with the King of Sardinia, his bureaucrats and officers, ruined the Revolution. For the moment, however, the Italian democrats had no possibility of intervening. In Hungary the movement was completely in the hands of the patriotic nobility and the wealthy bourgeoisie, so that no possibility existed here for the democrats to take any separate action. In Poland the revolutionary movement had already been suppressed at the very beginning, so that here, too, the democrats had no opportunity of differentiating themselves by their deeds from the patriotic party of the aristocrats. In Germany democracy was somewhat stronger. Nevertheless it was not capable of changing the fateful course of events.

According to its social development, Germany was divided into three parts. In the agrarian regions east of the Elbe a suppressed mass of rural labourers and small peasants opposed the great landowners of the nobility. In these old Prussian provinces a serious democratic movement would primarily have had to mobilize the poor rural population and to demand the expropriation of the large estates. Secondly there were in Germany regions with large cities and modern industry, such as Berlin, Vienna, Saxony, the Rhineland, Westphalia, and the industrial districts of Silesia. In all these districts the bourgeoisie and the workers made common cause against the ruling feudal bureaucracy. In addition, however, the conflict between the capitalistic employers and the workers was evident from the very beginning. A serious democratic movement in these parts of Germany would have had to organize the struggle of the working class against feudalism and the employers into a joint movement.

Thirdly there were those parts of Germany, primarily in

the south, where the class struggle was not so acute. There were but few noble landowners in southern Germany and they had little influence socially. Almost the entire countryside belonged to independent peasant proprietors. There were but few factories. Neither the capitalists nor the workers exerted a decisive influence. The petty bourgeoisie was influential throughout all of southern Germany. The opinions of the independent peasants, the business people, the artisans, and the intellectuals, who were united with them, were to a large extent uniform. There was, it is true, a confessional difference in southern Germany, but apart from religion the Catholic peasant and artisan of southern Germany thought exactly like his Protestant class comrade on all practical and political questions. Since the religious question was not very real in 1848, it did not disturb the unified sentiment of the south-German people.

Because of these conditions two types of democracy developed in Germany in 1848. There was first of all a social democracy of the western-European type, which wanted primarily to organize the struggle for the liberation of the urban and rural proletariat. Marx and Engels became the most brilliant representatives of this group. After the outbreak of the Revolution they returned to Germany, renewed their old connexions in the Rhineland, and founded the *Neue Rheinische Zeitung* in Cologne. Marx and Engels called their paper " The Organ of Democracy." The *Neue Rheinische Zeitung* elucidated the events of the German and the international revolution with remarkable clarity and authority and pointed out the paths along which the bourgeois revolution could be achieved. For the bourgeois revolution must first have triumphed before the class aims of the proletariat could be realized by means of the democratic republic.

Outside of Cologne, however, there were very few men in Germany who were ready to work consistently for the ideas expressed by the *Neue Rheinische Zeitung*. The workers in

Berlin, in Vienna, and in the industrial districts were willing to fight for a democratic republic as soon as they were called. Among the students there were many honest friends of the poor people who would gladly give their lives for democracy. The rural proletariat east of the Elbe waited only for a signal from the democrats to expel the large landowners. The wealthy bourgeoisie of northern Germany, however, shrank from all radical measures because they feared that if the masses were unleashed, capitalist property might also be threatened. All the conditions were lacking, then, for the creation of a north-German mass party as proposed by the *Neue Rheinische Zeitung*. The so-called Left wing of the Prussian Parliament sometimes flirted with the name and the slogans of democracy, but the policies which they proposed did not differ fundamentally from those of bourgeois liberalism.

Democracy had a much broader basis in southern Germany, but it was by no means the democracy of the *Neue Rheinische Zeitung* that had taken hold of the masses in Baden, in the Palatinate, and other places. The population of southern Germany had eagerly adopted the ideas of liberal reformism because they hated the bureaucrats and the actions of the police. Wherever the neighbouring French and Swiss states had exerted their influence, the people were also sympathetic towards the idea of a republic. Thus in southern Germany a general opposition movement existed, which first demanded liberal reforms and a parliamentary government. The class struggle hardly played a role. The teacher and the apothecary, the farmer, the merchant, and the master artisan were socially equal. The few workers and manufacturers who were also present were submerged in the general whirl of democratic fraternity. Understandably enough south-German democracy favoured general suffrage. Any discrimination against an honest German citizen was incomprehensible.

Such a uniform popular feeling, which united city and

country firmly and which found its chief expression within the boundaries of the individual historic states, would have been able to produce an extraordinary revolutionary force. At first glance one is reminded of the thirteen American colonies. However, a tradition of political liberty and independence was lacking in southern Germany. For centuries the population had been accustomed to obey their superiors. The single states had not been founded by independent farmers and citizens, like the British colonies in North America, but were rather the result of dynastic accidents. The harmless and uninfluential Diets of the south-German states, which had been instituted since 1815, were likewise incapable of producing a desire for political struggle. Thus the masses of the south-German people did indeed participate enthusiastically in the liberal movement of 1848. They were delighted with the accomplishments of March, with the liberal ministers and the citizens' militia. The leaders and their followers considered themselves good German democrats. The great majority of these so-called democrats were useless, however, for any serious revolutionary action, at least beyond the boundaries of their beloved individual states.

Sentiments similar to these present in southern Germany also existed in north-German states with a corresponding social composition of the population. The peasant and petty-bourgeois democracy of Schleswig-Holstein and Hanover corresponded approximately to the movements in Baden or Württemberg. This was the normal form of German democracy in 1848, a political type which differed essentially from the social democracy of western Europe. It was actually only a popular version of upper middle-class liberalism, which had been translated into petty-bourgeois terms. Among the German émigrés prior to 1848 Arnold Ruge was the best-known representative of such petty-bourgeois democracy. Ruge had originally been a friend and collaborator of Marx. Because of his different conception of the social question he had then separated from Marx and Engels. After the outbreak of the Revolution, Ruge worked for the cause of bourgeois democracy in Germany. Democrats of the south-German type controlled the Diets of southern Germany and formed the nucleus of the Left wing in the Frankfurt National Assembly. The bourgeois Left wing in the new Prussian Parliament in Berlin pursued approximately the same political course.

There was, however, a small group of men among the petty-bourgeois south-German democrats who were not satisfied with the general slogans of liberty and who wanted to act in a revolutionary manner. The most outstanding of these men was Hecker, a deputy in the Diet of Baden. He rejected all compromises with the monarchy, such as the German democrats were making everywhere. His goal was a democratic German republic, which the armed people were to establish by force of arms. The historical tradition with which Hecker was imbued derived from the great German Peasant War of 1525. He was much further removed from the modern working-class movement, since he was chiefly influenced by the petty-bourgeois conditions of his native country. Hecker was the only one of the German politicians of 1848 who actually made an impression on the broad masses of the people and enjoyed personal authority. In April Hecker decided to rise in revolt with the aim of expelling the German princes and of erecting a republic. Thus Hecker challenged not only the German princes and the nobility but also the entire official liberal movement.

In April 1848 Hecker began his revolt in Konstanz in Baden. His undertaking was by no means a putsch, but was well founded upon an objective appraisal of the existent political conditions. As a result of the impression left by the recent events of March the German governments were still morally paralysed. The army, and the police were confused and incapable of any action. If the German people were really in earnest about the slogans of liberty and nation,

then they would have to act now. Hecker drew the consequences of the events of March 18. If the German people
did not follow him, then the German Revolution was actually lost. When Hecker proclaimed the Republic, he had
some friends with him, among them the Badenese deputy
Struve and the former Prussian officer Willich. Despite
Hecker's great popularity, only a few thousand volunteers
followed him in southern Baden. They were generally sons
of peasants and small business men. Proletarian elements
played no part. The government troops easily dispersed the
insurgents. The leaders of the undertaking fled to Switzerland or to France. It had been demonstrated that all of the
many so-called democratic and " Left " organizations in Germany were useless for a revolution, even at such a favourable
moment. When, towards the end of June, Hecker also wit-
nessed the collapse of the Parisian proletariat during the
June days, he abandoned the cause of the European revolution. This fact again emphasizes the correctness of his political judgment. Hecker went to America. In September
Struve once again proclaimed a republic in Baden, but he
had no success and was arrested.

Meanwhile the Austrian military power, which had triumphed in Italy and Bohemia, was also preparing to strike
at Hungary. If it should succeed in removing the autono-
mous Hungarian government too, then the Austrian Empire would be restored to its old form and the constitutional
charter which the house of Habsburg had been compelled
to recognize after March could be torn to pieces. The Viennese workers and students recognized the danger and arose
in October in order to prevent the departure of the troops
from Vienna towards Hungary. The democratic masses took
possession of the city. This is the most glorious example of
international democratic solidarity to be found in the entire
history of 1848 and 1849. The situation of the Hungarians
was more favourable than that of the other European revolutionaries. The Hungarian nobility had maintained its

Constitution for many centuries. In Hungary at least the upper classes had a tradition of parliamentary self-government, which was reminiscent of England. Besides, the Hungarian government had taken advantage of the transitory weakness of the Habsburgs in March 1848 to develop an army, in which the troops of the house of Habsburg who had been recruited in Hungary were under the control of the Hungarian authorities.

Vienna had revolted in favour of the Hungarian cause. Kossuth's Hungarian government should therefore have had every interest in coming to the aid of the Viennese as rapidly as possible and with united forces. A common victory of the Hungarians and the Viennese over the imperial army would have smashed the Habsburg Empire, would have reawakened the Revolution in Italy and allowed events in Germany to take a new turn. Unfortunately Hungarian aid was inadequate and came too late. The Viennese democrats were forced to conduct the struggle against the overwhelming imperial power alone. In Germany the democratic Left wing contented itself with expressions of sympathy. The Left wing of the Frankfurt National Assembly sent several deputies to Vienna. One of them, Robert Blum, who was personally courageous, participated in the defence of the city and was shot in accordance with martial law after the conquest of Vienna by the Austrian army. In 1848, just as later in 1934, the Viennese workers had to suffer because they were superior to the other democrats and socialists of central Europe in courage and understanding. When the imperial army had reconquered Vienna the Revolution in Austria was ended. Now the imperial troops also marched into Hungary. When the King of Sardinia ventured to attempt a new passage at arms in March 1849, he was again beaten by Radetzky. After this Sardinia finally withdrew from the revolutionary struggle.

Nevertheless in the spring of 1849 events took an unexpected turn in various European countries and appeared to usher in a revival of the revolution. First the Hungarians won a series of victories over the Austrian troops in April and May and again forced them out of the country. In central Italy the republicans had started to act independently. The Pope was driven out of Rome and a republic was proclaimed in Rome with Mazzini at its head. Garibaldi assumed the military leadership of the Roman democrats. Besides the Austrians and Naples, the Roman Republic found itself faced by still another opponent, whose intervention on the side of the counter-revolution would not have been expected by anyone several months earlier. This was France. The new President, Napoleon Bonaparte, wanted to win over the French Catholics to his side by carrying out an action for the benefit of the Pope. French troops landed in Italy and attacked Rome, but in April they were driven back by Garibaldi. The brilliant military achievements of the Roman Republic offer a characteristic contrast to the inadequacy of the royal Sardinian army.

Meanwhile in France the National Assembly had concluded its activity and in May 1849 the regular Parliament, the legislative body, was elected on the basis of the new republican Constitution. Under the stormy tide of Bonapartism, republicanism gradually lost its significance in France, but for the present republican forms were still observed. The elections of May 1849 were very peculiar. President Napoleon was indeed backed by the great majority of the French people, but the development of Bonapartism had proceeded in such a stormy manner that the President did not yet have any organized party of personal adherents. As a result he was forced to depend on one of the old parties temporarily. Napoleon chose the old monarchist party, from which he selected his ministers. During the election campaign the monarchists presented themselves as the friends of President Napoleon and thus obtained a majority in Parliament. On the other hand many voters who had voted for Napoleon during the presidential elections did not want to vote for the compromised adherents of the Bourbons. The result was that in May 1849 Ledru-Rollin's party obtained a surprising success in a number of electoral districts. The Socialist Democrats occupied one quarter of all the seats in Parliament. Ledru-Rollin and his friends convinced themselves that May and June 1848 had only been an evil dream, that now everything was in order again, and that the French workers and peasants would follow the tested banners of revolutionary democracy. Ledru-Rollin's party began a lively propaganda campaign against the President and the reactionary government and launched an impassioned indictment at those in power because of the attack on the Roman Republic. The commotion which the party of the Mountain created was so great that many people expected a new working-class revolution in Paris. If it should succeed, then the June days would be erased and France would again march at the head of the democratic European revolution.

Following the victories of the Hungarians, the new revolutionary wave in France, and the successes of the Roman Republic, a new crisis also developed in Germany. The German National Assembly at Frankfurt am Main had finally finished the Constitution for Germany. However, the National Assembly, together with its government, was suspended in the air, since the individual German states continued to exist despite the speeches in St. Paul's Church in Frankfurt. The police, the army, and the administrative apparatus belonged to the governments of the individual states, and the Parliament of the German Reich exercised no real political power. Nevertheless the Frankfurt Parliament was considered the legal representative body of the German people and enjoyed considerable moral authority. The majority of the German liberal bourgeoisie had finally decided to create a united Germany under the leadership of Prussia. It was intended to found a constitutional German Empire and it was desired to present the German imperial crown to the King of Prussia, Friedrich Wilhelm IV.

The bourgeois-liberal party in the National Assembly, so far as it favoured the Prussian solution of the national question, agreed upon a compromise with the democrats of the Left wing in order to obtain a majority for their constitutional plan. This compromise favoured the south-German Left-wing democrats considerably. If the Constitution of 1848 had actually been put into effect, then the King of Prussia would indeed have had the formal title of Emperor, but little real power. A German imperial parliament, elected by means of general suffrage, would have exercised the supreme power. According to the letter of the Constitution, the south-German petty bourgeoisie would have had supreme power, a completely unnatural condition. The clearest-thinking leaders of north-German capitalism rejected the compromise which their party friends in Frankfurt am Main had concluded with the democrats. They didn't want to have anything to do with a constitution which made the fate of Prussian capitalism and the Prussian army dependent upon general suffrage. King Friedrich Wilhelm IV was even more reluctant to accept the imperial crown under such conditions. In April he refused the Frankfurt offer.

The destruction of the German Constitution by the princes excited the masses profoundly. The workers were just as embittered as the south-German democrats. Early in May the Saxon workers rose in revolt in Dresden and were suppressed by the Prussian army. Disturbances also occurred in other parts of Germany. Most important were the events in Baden. Hecker's ideas had taken root among the Badenese soldiers, with the result that a revolutionary mood, such as existed in no other part of Germany, prevailed among the troops. From the 9th to the 12th of May the soldiers revolted in the most important garrisons of Baden. The Grand Duke, together with his loyal officers and officials, were forced to flee, and consequently the executive committee of the popular democratic societies of Baden, led by Brentano and Goegg, suddenly and unexpectedly found itself with the entire political power in its hands. The Revolution also triumphed in the neighbouring Rhenish Palatinate. The first days of the Badenese military revolt remind one of the rebellion of the German sailors at the end of October and the beginning of November 1918. It was of the utmost importance to extend the military revolt beyond the boundaries of Baden as rapidly as possible and at the same time to legalize the movement by having the Frankfurt National Assembly adopt it. After the failure of the Constitution almost all the moderate deputies had left Frankfurt am Main. Consequently the Left wing controlled the National Assembly and was still qualified to speak in the name of the German people. It could confer the character of a legal struggle for a legal constitution upon the mutiny of the soldiers in Baden. Once again the possibility of saving the German Revolution was present.

One after another, however, all the hopes of the revolutionaries in Europe were disappointed. When Ledru-Rollin's party attempted to organize a revolutionary street demonstration in Paris on June 13, the demonstrators were dispersed by Napoleon's soldiers without any trouble. With that the soap-bubble of the rejuvenated party of the Mountain burst. Ledru-Rollin went into exile in England, following the example of Louis Blanc. The defeat of the French Mountain party likewise destroyed the chances of the republicans in Italy. After a courageous resistance the Roman Republic succumbed in July to the superior reactionary forces. The Russian Tsar placed his army at the disposal of the house of Habsburg for the purpose of vanquishing the Hungarian Revolution. In the summer of 1849 Hungary was conquered by the combined Russian and Austrian troops. One sees how all four major powers of the European continent, Russia, Austria, Prussia, and Bonaparte's France, put aside their differences and first subdued the revolution together.

The Prussian army, together with the troops of the German petty states, got under way against Baden and the Palatinate. The Revolution in Baden, which had begun with so much élan, soon assumed the character of a farce. At first the boundaries of the petty state of Baden were scrupulously respected by the revolutionaries. Three irretrievable weeks were lost before they decided to permit the revolutionary troops of Baden to cross the frontier. At the same time the Left wing of the Frankfurt National Assembly did not have the courage to join their cause to the fate of the revolt in Baden. One of the Frankfurt Left-wing leaders, Raveaux, appeared in Baden, but only as a private individual, and did nothing more than to increase the confusion there. On May 30 when the Badenese troops were finally ordered to cross the Hessian frontier in the north, they were already completely demoralized. The soldiers refused to cross the border. The leader of the revolutionary army of Baden, the fomer Badenese lieutenant Sigel, sought to encourage his troops. At the border he himself captured a Hessian, whereupon the nearest Badenese army corps actually advanced into " enemy territory." When the first shots fell, however, the Red troops turned back again and fled into Baden.

To such a degree had the leadership of the Badenese democratic politicians, Brentano and Goegg, ruined the mood of the revolutionary soldiers in the course of three weeks. It is understandable that the revolutionary soldiers lost their courage, as soon as they saw that the movement made no progress, that Baden remained isolated, and that the worst confusion prevailed in the leading democratic party. Upon the report of the failure of May 30, Brentano and Raveaux wanted to capitulate immediately, to recall the Grand Duke and indict Sigel because of his "attack upon Hesse." Soon thereafter Brentano reversed his decision and wanted to continue the struggle. The situation had certainly become hopeless, because the revolutionary troops of Baden were not equal to the superior power of

Prussia. Only small reinforcements came from the neighbouring Palatinate. Among them was also a volunteer corps
led by Willich. Willich's adjutant was Friedrich Engels, who
had left Cologne and gone to the Palatinate after the suppression of the *Neue Rheinische Zeitung* by the Prussian
government.

When Hecker, who was in America, heard of the revolt
in Baden, he embarked for Europe in order to take part in
the struggle. He came too late, however, for any decisive
action. Since Hecker was missing, the resolute democrats
in Baden had no really popular leader. Struve had been
freed by the Revolution. He started an opposition movement against the Brentano government. Brentano and
Goegg remained at the head of the revolutionary government of Baden. A Constituent Assembly for Baden was
elected. It is characteristic that Struve received no mandate
in the election. Towards the end of the revolt he entered
the Constituent Assembly as an alternate for someone else.
The revolutionary Parliament of Baden was entirely in the
hands of the official moderate democrats. In his reminis-
cences Sigel remarks concerning the deputies: " They were
in fact an élite of capable, well-meaning men — well-situated
business men, manufacturers, lawyers and writers, clergy-
men, professors and other teachers, doctors, state and municipal officials, and so on." Proletarian elements played no part
in the entire revolt. It was a typical undertaking of the
south-German provincial democrats. The popular clubs of
Baden would never have opened the attack if the revolutionary soldiers had not shown them the way.

Meanwhile the rest of the German National Assembly at
Frankfurt am Main no longer felt secure. The Left-wing
deputies did not go to the insurgents in Baden, but to Stutt-
gart. On June 18 the National Assembly was dispersed there
by soldiers of Württemberg. Shortly prior to this the Assembly had appointed an imperial regency consisting of
five members. They were the aforementioned Raveaux,

who had returned to the German Parliament, together with Karl Vogt, Heinrich Simon, Schüler, and Hecker. These five men were actually the democratic revolutionary government of Germany. Their activity was a worthy conclusion to the democratic labours of the Revolution of 1848-9. Sigel, who absolutely belonged to the moderate group himself and who did not want to deride anyone, wrote concerning them:

" The unhappy regents moved into Baden, inspected the beautiful region and the old castle of Baden-Baden under the guidance of Raveaux, and waited very anxiously there for news of the encounters of Waghäusel and Rastatt. They were soon freed from the tragicomical situation by the refugees who fled to Baden-Baden from Gernsbach and Freiburg and went into exile from there." The remaining revolutionary troops were driven across the Swiss border by the Prussians and were then disarmed in Switzerland. Most of the leaders of the movement went into exile in England. The farce was followed by serious consequences in the form of executions under martial law, which were ordered by courts martial in Baden, and of long sentences of penal servitude, which were inflicted upon well-meaning patriots. The well-known democratic writer Kinkel was among those condemned to penal servitude. Towards the end of 1850, however, he succeeded in escaping from prison and likewise went to England.

By the summer of 1849 the democratic as well as the liberal and the national revolutions had been completely defeated. In some countries which were subject to foreign domination the national movements soon recovered of course, and the defeat of the capitalistic liberal bourgeoisie in the revolution of 1848-49 was likewise only an episode. On the other hand, revolutionary democracy, of the type which had been created by the Great French Revolution, was now finally finished. Ledru-Rollin, speaking with great pathos and without misgivings between the classes, and Raveaux, anxiously visiting the Black Forest, buried the movement that Robespierre and Saint-Just had founded.

4. *Why did Democracy Fail in 1848–9?*

After February 24, 1848 an English woman painter named Goldsmith, who was filled with enthusiasm for liberty, sketched an allegorical picture of the French Republic and of general suffrage. It portrays a stern, solemn landscape with fields and factory chimneys in the background. In the foreground France is represented as the well-known symbolic female figure. The goddess France holds the rights of man in her hand, and beside her is the mighty ballot-box of general suffrage. Workers and peasants approach in long columns, in order to place their ballots in the box. In the background stands a liberty tree, such as was planted everywhere at that time, decorated with flags, and against which Ledru-Rollin leans pensively.

The proclamation in which the provisional government of Lamartine and Ledru-Rollin called upon the French people to elect a National Assembly exhibits the same spirit. In it they say: " The provisional electoral law which we have decreed is the most far-reaching law which has ever summoned the population of any nation of the earth to exercise the greatest of the rights of man: namely, its own sovereignty. Everyone without exception has the right to vote. Since this law has been announced, there are no longer any proletarians in France. Every adult Frenchman is a political citizen, every citizen is a voter. Every citizen is sovereign. This right is absolutely equal for all. There is no citizen who can say to any other: ' You are more sovereign than I.' Consider your power, prepare yourselves to exercise it, and be worthy to take possession of your empire. The Republic is the people's empire."

The picture of the private artist, as well as the official proclamation of the French government, both reflect the illusions which inspired the various democratic tendencies in France. A fetish-like cult of the Republic and of general suffrage was fostered. They actually persuaded themselves that the people had already achieved all that was essential, once the monarch had been expelled and every adult inhabitant had an equal right to vote. The bold assertion of the provisional government that the proletariat had been abolished in France with the introduction of general suffrage is perhaps defensible, if the word " proletarian " is interpreted according to its meaning in antiquity. If a proletarian is nothing more than a poor citizen without political rights, then the existence of a proletariat would actually be incompatible with general suffrage. However, if one thinks of the modern industrial proletariat in the factories of Paris or Lyons, or even of the unemployed, who found a meagre employment in the national workshops, then the assertion of Lamartine and Ledru-Rollin seems to be either childish nonsense or mockery.

Since the great French Revolution social democracy in a historical, traditional sense was a coalition of workers, peasants, and petty bourgeoisie, collectively called the " people," against the aristocracy, under which both the nobility of birth and that of money were comprehended. It was completely false to think that social democracy was already realized with the abolition of the old monarchist power and the introduction of general suffrage, and that now nothing further was necessary but to allow the machine to function. Social democracy is not a miracle which comes to life at a particular moment and then continues to function automatically, but it is rather a political task upon which it is necessary to work continuously. In France after February 24 social democracy demanded a careful compromise between the interests of the peasants and those of the workers, since the " people " can only function politically if one understands its individual parts, serves their special interests, and thus secures their co-operation for a greater unity. It is useless to do nothing but tell the masses about liberty and equality and to wave the republican banner. It has been described above how the absurd tax policy of the republican government drove the French peasants out of the popular front and created differences between city and country which contributed essentially to the decline of the Second French Republic. However, the history of the spring of 1848 teaches still another thing. Just as a union of workers and peasants is not self-evident but must first be created by laborious political activity, similarly harmony among urban workers is by no means a natural and given quantity. During every greater period of unemployment a difference of interests and sentiment exists between those workers who are inside the factories and those who are outside. Thanks to the activity of Louis Blanc, the French Socialist Democratic Party was in close touch with the workers in the factories, but it allowed the organization of the unemployed to be taken out of its hands without any resistance, and the official Socialist Democrats could certainly claim no credit for the fact that the workers of the national workshops later fought the June battle against capitalism.

In addition early in May Socialist Democracy made the serious mistake of remaining in the coalition government together with the majority of the National Assembly, which was anti-socialistic and hostile to the workers. Since then Ledru-Rollin's party was completely isolated socially. It had the support neither of the peasants nor of the unemployed nor of the workers in the factories, and it was only the expression of certain radically clamorous petty-bourgeois groups. The catastrophe of Social Democracy in France during 1848 was not that it succumbed in battle. Democracy should have had the task of warning the workers against isolated and hopeless struggles. If a battle was fought and the democratic party was honourably defeated, then at least the movement would remain alive. Actually, however, the Socialist Democratic Party in France had no longer anything to do with the real class struggle after May 1848. The capitalists and the generals, supported by the misguided peasants and soldiers and by mercenaries who had been recruited from among the unemployed, struck at the proletariat. The workers defended themselves heroically during the June uprising. The Democratic Party stood aside and bewailed the terrible times; they took no part in the struggle. With that the historical democratic movement had become completely isolated from the revolutionary worker's movement. In June 1849 when Ledru-Rollin's party called upon the masses to fight the despotism of Bonaparte, the workers of Paris did not stir.

The personalities of the leaders of great mass movements are certainly very important. Robespierre or Saint-Just cannot very well be imagined in the situation of Ledru-Rollin and Louis Blanc. From the very beginning Robespierre paid the greatest attention to the French peasantry. He sided with the poor peasants in all practical questions and no one could have been convinced that any action of the Paris party of the Mountain, led by Robespierre, could be harmful to the interests of the peasants. Employing ruthless methods, Robespierre safeguarded and guaranteed the existence of the unemployed. He was more likely, however, to have come into conflict with the factory workers as a result of his policy of maximum wages and prices. But even in this case every understanding worker knew that the government of the Mountain party defended the collective interests of the working people. Robespierre and his friends carried out a realistic plan of action in order to obtain power; first they acquired control of Paris and upon this foundation they were able to develop their plans. Ledru-Rollin and Louis Blanc, on the other hand, relinquished their positions of power without any resistance, just as small children are deprived of their toys. The slogan of a republic and general suffrage would never have misled Robespierre to enter into the Girondist government and thus to confuse and paralyse the Parisian revolutionaries. On the 9th of Thermidor, when Robespierre succumbed to the superior forces of capitalism and reaction, he fell together with democracy and the proletariat. The memory of Robespierre's deeds kept the tradition of revolutionary democracy alive in Europe until 1848 and still influenced the French workers decisively in 1871. When Ledru-Rollin was defeated, however, only ridicule accompanied the exile.

Although it would be very convenient to be able to throw the blame for the collapse of 1848 on the leaders of French Socialist Democracy, and even though the figure of Ledru-Rollin, the sentimental popular orator, provokes criticism especially easily, still historical research cannot remain satisfied with such an answer. For the decline of Socialist Democracy in France is paralleled by a corresponding development in other European countries; besides, every mass movement is responsible for its own leaders. If Ledru-Rollin and his friends remained the uncontested heads of the Socialist Democratic Party, it proves that, despite any inadequacies, they personified the ideology of the movement. European Social Democracy did not perish only because of its inadequate leaders in 1848–9, but primarily rather as a result of the internal contradictions of the movement itself.

At the time of the great French Revolution an urban proletariat already existed in France, but it was far less important than in 1848. The peasants had no landed property as yet. In 1789 the task of democracy was to combine the struggle of the dependent peasants against the landed nobility with the struggle of the urban poor against capitalism. It had been much easier then than a corresponding course of action was in 1848. In the meantime the industrial proletariat had become so important, even though most of the workers were still employed in small factories, that every serious political debate came to a head in the question: proletariat or capitalists. Every detail in the course of the French Revolution of 1848 and 1849 shows this. On the other hand, the French peasants were now free and the landed nobility had been eliminated. To be sure, in France around 1848 the independent proprietors were still only a minority of the rural population. The majority of the rural inhabitants were small tenants, farm labourers, and so on. Nevertheless the wealthy peasant was most influential in the village. In 1848 the wealthy peasant, as well as the urban worker, had a class consciousness, which was very differently developed from that in 1789, and great tactical ability on the part of the democratic party was already required in order to combine the movement of the peasants and the workers. However, if it was to approach the mass of the small tenants and the farm labourers while excluding the peasant proprietors, then there was an even greater need for a tactical policy that was thoroughly realistic, even though it would be difficult to execute in detail.

In this manner the task of social democracy had become more difficult during the fifty years after Robespierre, while at the same time the intellectual capacity of the democrats to cope with these problems had continually decreased. At the time of Robespierre social democracy had already hardly comprehended the actually decisive economic forces of its own period. During the course of the next fifty years its insight into economic problems by no means improved. While Louis Blanc broadened the program of French Socialist Democracy by his petty-bourgeois co-operative projects, he did not thereby increase its fighting ability. Louis Blanc's practical work as Minister in 1848 was much better than his co-operative theory. However, Louis Blanc erected his social policy in a vacuum, so to speak, without any connexion with the real conditions of power, and when democracy in France collapsed, the social achievements also vanished with it. As the leaders of French Social Democracy grew less and less capable of coping with facts, their attachment for the traditional slogans and illusions increased. The empty and idle talk concerning the Republic and general suffrage, with which such a great show was made in 1848 in France, would have been impossible at the time of Robespierre.

In Germany Social Democracy began where it stopped in France: namely, with the pseudo-radical petty bourgeoisie. The decisive social forces of Germany were to be found in the north, chiefly in Prussia. On the one hand there were the landed nobility, the industrial and financial capitalists, and on the other the urban and rural proletariat. Owing to certain external causes, however, democracy as a social movement did not gain a footing in northern Germany, with its sharp class contrasts, but rather in the south, with its pleasant, petty-bourgeois uniformity. In the course of the German Revolution south-German democracy was faced with problems which it could not solve, and as a result it collapsed completely. In France during 1848 and 1849 the crisis of democracy had led to a separation of the working class from the petty-bourgeois political leaders. In Germany, on the other hand, petty-bourgeois democracy had never really approached the workers. The problem of social democracy and the working class would first have become acute in Germany if the Constitution of 1849 had been realized, or if the revolt in Baden had spread and triumphed throughout the Reich.

Thus in Germany as well as in France the class coalition of workers, peasants, and petty bourgeois, which represented the actual essence of the older democracy, had been destroyed by the course of the Revolution of 1848–9. In France as well as in Germany the defeat of democracy had resulted in the moral bankruptcy of its leadership. Events in Italy took a different course. There the Revolution had increased Mazzini's personal authority tremendously. The glorious history of the Roman Republic emphasized only too well the pitiable failure of liberalism and of the Sardinian monarchy, which was allied with it. Nevertheless, although Mazzini opposed a popular republic to the monarchy of the upper classes with the greatest determination, he was incapable of dealing successfully with Italy's economic questions. An industrial proletariat was just arising in Italy. The important social question of the country did not yet concern the workers, but rather the oppressed rural masses, the small tenants of central and southern Italy, who were repressed in a mediæval manner by the feudal landlords. Several advanced Italian republicans criticized Mazzini for not taking a clear stand on the agrarian question, because he did not want to attack private property. Mazzini's personal authority, however, was strong enough not to permit any such opposition to arise. Despite that, after the defeat of 1849 the Italian question was more than ever chiefly the problem of national liberation, before which the individual social issues receded into practical politics. The same was true of Hungary and Poland.

The second tendency of European democracy, which in France was called moderate, honourable, or orderly democracy, in contrast to social democracy, and which, seen historically, might best be designated as liberal democracy, suffered no better fate in the Revolution. Its spokesmen were enlightened and broad-minded representatives of the liberal bourgeoisie, who considered every connexion with any feudal or monarchist traditions as harmful. They hoped that the rule of the wealthy and educated classes could also be maintained in a republic with general suffrage, if the masses were only approached with trust and reason. This tendency, which was personified by Lamartine and his closer friends, had first come to power in France after the 24th of February. However, it soon showed itself incapable of bridging the gap between the classes. The majority of the capitalists and of the wealthy classes in general feared the socialist workers so much that they did not want to approach the poor masses with concessions and trust, but rather to proceed against them with blood and terror. It is characteristic that at the decisive moment the greatest part of the party of the *National* abandoned the benevolent slogans of orderly democracy and deserted to General Cavaignac.

Another lesson of the movement of 1848 and 1849 concerned general suffrage. If humane, liberal democracy turned into its opposite, into a White Terror and military rule, then general suffrage could also withstand this change. By misguiding unenlightened masses and by a cunning exploitation of transient moods among the people, even a capitalistic or military group could obtain a majority under general suffrage. The ruling class would then have the army, the police, and the courts at its disposal, and besides that, they could cite the judgment of "democracy" in the elections. The opposition, which took the part of the workers and of the poor masses in general and which advocated freedom of expression for the people, would be ruthlessly suppressed and silenced by the authorities. If the opposition was not permitted to appear, and if the administrative authorities took care that the elections were carried out in the right way, then a terroristic counter-revolution could also accommodate itself to general suffrage. For instance the French republican Constitution which was produced under Cavaignac's military terror allowed general suffrage to exist, and Louis Napoleon used general suffrage as his trump card from the very beginning. Thus the Revolution of 1848–9 taught the real democrats and socialists the lesson that general suffrage is indeed a necessary and preliminary condition for popular self-government, but that at the same time it is compatible even with the most brutal oppression of the masses.

5. Struggles among the Émigrés, 1848–59

The destruction of historical European social democracy was a well-established fact after 1849. A certain period was still necessary, however, before this fact could be completely recognized and appreciated by politically active individuals and organizations in Europe. The process of clarification within the political movements of the European continent was rendered more difficult by the fact that during the decade from 1849 to 1859 police persecution everywhere prevented any discussion. As a result the controversies which were necessary for this process took place in exile, chiefly in England but also in the United States. Comprehensibly enough, the quarrels among the émigrés in London at that time were often no more than petty and personal squabbles. Nevertheless they have an extraordinary historical importance, because during that period the political parties began to develop along certain lines which were to become decisive for the history of Europe, and which to a certain extent have remained so until the present.

The type of person who was forced to emigrate from the European continent to England and America was purely a matter of chance. Anyone who had come into conflict with the police at home was forced to go into exile. In Poland, Hungary, and Italy all patriots were included, no matter what their rank or class, and among them were aristocratic descendants of ancient families. The French exiles were chiefly compromised bourgeois opponents of Bonapartism. The Germans were mainly men who had played prominent parts in the various uprisings or during the final days of the Frankfurt Parliament. It is understandable that Ledru-Rollin's French friends and the Germans who gathered around Ruge and Kinkel looked for support from the Hungarian and Italian exiles, since the German and French bourgeois democrats had not covered themselves with glory during the revolution. On the other hand, not only was Mazzini's personality generally recognized, but the military and political accomplishments of the Hungarians in 1849 had made an international figure of Kossuth.

The various émigré groups combined in London to form a European Central Committee, at the head of which were Kossuth, Mazzini, Ledru-Rollin, and Ruge. The Central Committee was also in touch with the Polish exiles. It was an attempt to continue the revolutionary International of

1848 just as if nothing had happened in the meantime and as if matters could be resumed in 1851 where they had been dropped in 1847. The only difference was that in 1847 the democratic International had been a powerful force, while in 1851 it had become a joke. In 1847 it could have been expected that the next revolution in France would carry the Socialist Democratic Party into power, and that this would automatically be followed by a bourgeois revolution in Germany and by national revolutions in Italy, Hungary, and Poland. Even after the defeat of 1849, nationalist movements continued to exist in Italy, Hungary, and Poland. Nor was the liberal bourgeoisie in Germany destroyed, and at the next opportunity it would be forced to resume its struggle against the feudal bureaucracy. In France there was also a considerable bourgeois group, which rejected Bonapartism and wanted to replace it by a more liberal form of political organization.

It is evident, then, that the joke was not that someone believed in a continuation of the national struggle in Italy, Hungary, and Poland and of the liberal struggle in Germany, but it was rather the assumption that between these real patriotic and liberal movements on the one hand and the labour movement on the other a third movement— namely, so-called European democracy— still had a right to exist. The difference between the bourgeois politicians of the opposition who had remained in France and Germany and those who were in exile was purely accidental and was based upon police persecution and the existence of warrants for their arrest. In 1851 there was no social class or political movement in either France or Germany which would have supported Ledru-Rollin and Kinkel. Nevertheless the groups around Ledru-Rollin and Kinkel and Ruge attempted to continue their political existence in exile. They maintained that they were the representatives of uncompromising democracy in contrast to the vacillating liberalism of the other bourgeois groups. In order to retain any significance on an international scale, however, Ledru-Rollin and Ruge were compelled to join forces with Kossuth and Mazzini.

As a result of this situation, a remarkable reversal of position had taken place, particularly when compared with conditions in 1847. As long as European social democracy was still a real and powerful movement, the French and English parties, which were predominantly proletarian, had been the leaders. Now the socially backward countries where no modern proletariat existed as yet and where the nobility still fought for national independence were supposed to take the lead. As the national leader of the Hungarian nobility and bourgeoisie, Kossuth was certainly a distinguished personality, but the labouring masses of central and western Europe could permit neither him nor Mazzini nor some patriotic Polish general to determine the tempo of their development. Hungarian-Italian leadership of a so-called European democratic movement meant nothing more than the bankruptcy of the German and French parties, the elimination of every important social question, and the depression of the movement to the level of those countries which were socially most backward.

The co-operation of this renewed continental European democratic movement with the English labour movement was just as impossible. The English Chartist Party had been declining since 1848, but it still existed and during the fifties it was still the political representative of the British proletariat. The English workers still sympathized whole-heartedly with Poland and Italy and with the liberal forces of the European continent in general, but they could not accept the slogans of an international association which had no interest at all in the struggle of the workers with the capitalists, or which evaded the issue with innocuous catchwords. The Revolution of 1848-9 had failed chiefly because of the differences between the bourgeoisie and the labour movement. The entire course of events in France from the 24th of February to the triumph of Louis Napoleon Bonaparte shows this. In Germany, too, the leading bourgeois groups had likewise avoided all decisive measures against the monarchy and feudalism because they wanted to remain within the bounds of legality and had no desire to pave the way for the " anarchist " and " communist " masses. Even in Italy the national Revolution had been wrecked on the opposition of monarchist-liberal upper classes to the broad masses. How could anyone expect the democratic International to triumph in 1851, when it was much more backward and confused in all social questions than the democratic movement of 1847 had been?

The new attitude of Marx and Engels with regard to the official democratic movement in Europe after 1850 corresponds to its completely changed objective significance. Marx had supported the party of Ledru-Rollin and Louis Blanc not because he had any special faith in its leaders, but because millions of revolutionary workers and peasants followed its banners. Marx and Engels had participated in the official European democratic movement as long as even the faintest hope existed that this movement could influence the masses. Although Marx immediately grasped the full significance of the June days of 1848 in Paris, he still shared some of the hopes which were placed on the apparent rise of the French party of the Mountain in 1849. At the beginning of June 1849 Engels was with the insurgent democrats in the Palatinate, and Marx was in Paris, as a kind of liaison officer between the German democrats who were fighting in Baden and in the Palatinate and the French party of the Mountain. At the same time Marx and Engels praised the deeds of the Hungarian army.

After 1850, however, it was completely clear that the official democratic leaders, who had organized their committees and released their proclamation in exile, had nothing to do either with the German and French workers or with the bourgeoisie of those countries. They were nothing more than the remnants of a period which had been got over. Therefore after 1850 Marx and Engels emphasized the differences which separated them from the official European democrats, in a sharply defined manner, and warned the workers against the slogans of Kossuth, Ledru-Rollin, Ruge, and others. As an individual Ledru-Rollin was no better and no worse in 1851 than he had been in 1847, but during the latter year he had been the representative of a great progressive mass movement, while in 1851 he was only an individual. The change in the tactics of Marx and Engels does not mean that they had abandoned the basic idea of democratic revolution; on the contrary, as long as they lived they remained democrats in the best sense of the word and in the spirit of 1848. They never advised the workers to adopt a narrow-minded class policy and to separate themselves from the other groups of working people. Particularly after 1848, Marx and Engels devoted a large part of their labours to the study of the agrarian question in all countries. Wherever the liberal bourgeoisie fought against feudalism Marx and Engels absolutely demanded that the workers support the struggle of the bourgeoisie, in order to be able to carry the movement beyond its bourgeois-liberal limits after the common victory.

According to the doctrine of Marx and Engels, the proletariat would "organize itself as a nation" at the head of the victorious working people and thus make possible the transition from the capitalistic individual economy to a socialistic collective economy. Nevertheless this statement of faith in democracy and a democratic revolution by no means signifies any agreement with the actions of an impotent and, in view of the objective situation, counter-revolutionary group of leaders. After 1850 Marx and Engels hoped that new parties would arise in the decisive countries with the advent of a new revolutionary wave; these parties would complete the work of 1848. They hoped that these new movements of the future would have a much clearer character and would be based to a much greater degree upon the class-conscious proletariat. However, these future movements should not burden themselves with individuals and ideas that had demonstrated their inadequacy in 1848–9.

The separation of the labour movement from the remnants of official bourgeois democracy had been in full swing everywhere since 1849. Nevertheless it appeared at first as if the leadership of an independent European labour movement would not devolve upon Marx and Engels but rather upon other individuals and groups. The Communist League, which was led by Marx and Engels, had but few adherents left in Germany after the defeat of the Revolution, and their activity was soon paralysed by the police. Consequently the German Communist Workers' Society in London remained the most important organization. After 1850, however, intense opposition to Marx and Engels arose within this society. They were not always very successful in the actual leadership of workers' societies. Marx and Engels presented the proletariat with tasks of such a far-reaching political character that the simple workers could not follow them easily. According to the doctrine of Marx, the proletariat must place itself at the head of the democratic revolution, must conclude or avoid alliances with other classes as it finds necessary, and must always keep the national as well as the international necessities of the movement in mind. After the victory of the democratic revolution a new human society would have to be erected. But the simple worker understood only the direct needs with which he was faced in his daily life. The minds of the workers were not yet equal to the enormously complicated tasks of an international revolution.

In the opinion of Marx and Engels the proletariat must first undergo a lengthy period of development before it would be capable of solving independently the tasks with which history confronted it. In the meantime the workers must submit to the leaders, who, equipped with the achievements of bourgeois science, are able to point out the correct course of action. Marx and Engels always decided alone and in a completely autocratic manner just what the proletariat should or should not do in a definite situation. They never tolerated or even took notice of any opposition from "narrow-minded" workers. It is therefore understandable that the Geman workers in London, particularly when faced by the depressing experiences of a lost revolution and a troubled life in exile, did not understand or endure the leadership of Marx and Engels. The immediate cause of the open break, which appeared in 1850, was a difference of opinion concerning a future revolution. Marx and Engels recognized the full import of the defeat which international democracy had suffered, and did not believe that the struggle could simply proceed as if nothing had happened. On the other hand the simple and impatient workers did not want to believe that for the present the revolution was ended. The result was that the greater part of the German workers in London left Marx and Engels. When Engels had gone into exile in England after the defeat of the uprising in Baden, he brought his former military leader Willich with him. Willich joined the Communist League. He was a capable soldier, but had no political experience. The result was that he soon became an opponent of Marx and Engels and during the quarrel of 1850 he sided with the simple members. Willich and an older functionary of the Communist League, Schapper, became the leaders of the German workers who had separated from Marx and Engels. This occurrence had considerable significance because at that time it was still generally assumed that the movements among the exiles gave a true picture of the tendencies in the homeland, where they were forced to be silent under police pressure.

Willich and Schapper reached an understanding with the proletarian wing of the French émigrés in England. The socialistic French workers no longer wanted to have anything to do with Ledru-Rollin and his friends. On the other hand the imprisoned Blanqui exercised a great moral authority over the French workers. They had subsequently recognized that in 1848 he had been the only one who had opposed the prevailing illusions and who had warned the workers. At that time there was indeed no actually flourishing Blanquist organization either in France or in England, but the great name of Blanqui had its effect and was a symbol for the fighting French proletariat. Consequently the French socialist exiles who wanted to differentiate themselves from the bourgeois democrats usually called themselves Blanquists. Louis Blanc had failed as a politician, but as an individual he still enjoyed a certain esteem. When the French socialist émigrés combined with the German group of Willich, Louis Blanc followed them and was also admitted into the organization.

The English Chartists wanted to maintain their connexions with the politically active workers on the Continent. They were more concerned, however, with the political attitude of the French and German workers in general and less with any individuals. Thus the Chartists were ready to enter into an official union with the Willich-Schapper group and their French friends. The radical wing of the Polish exiles and even several democratically inclined Hungarians joined the organization. In November 1850 the United Socialist Democrats of Germany and France, together with the Polish and Hungarian democrats, published a common proclamation, in which they exhorted the democrats of all nations to continue the revolutionary struggle and announced a democratic and social world republic as their goal.

Thus around 1850 and 1851 there were two competing democratic Internationals. One was essentially bourgeois, while the other was predominantly proletarian in character. The bourgeois International had the great names of the political past on its side, yet the other International defended the class interests of the workers in central and western Europe and of the poor peasants in the east. The great moral success of the socialist International was its recognition by the Chartist Party, which together with Willich and Louis Blanc continued the tradition of the Fraternal Democrats of 1847. The personal situation of Marx and Engels was extremely unfavourable, since they were now eliminated from both Internationals and all real democratic and socialist movements. On February 24, 1851, the anniversary of the French Revolution of 1848, a large international mass meeting was held in London. Willich presided and among the speakers were Louis Blanc, influential Chartist leaders, as well as Hungarian and Polish émigrés. When two friends of Marx appeared at the meeting, they were driven out by the outraged audience as alleged spies.

This situation of 1851 represents the lowest point in the political career of Marx and Engels and in their relation to the working class. Marx was personally very embittered that the former Prussian lieutenant Willich had so easily deprived him of the leadership of the international labour movement. Nevertheless, as far as their cause was concerned, Marx and Engels remained completely unshaken. They did not make the slightest concession, either in their theory or in their personal relations. Engels lived in Manchester as a business man, and Marx as a writer in London. Remaining in constant and close communication with Engels, Marx continued his scientific and literary activity; he was firmly convinced that the future would be his and that the two democratic Internationals were only transitory phenomena without any serious significance.

It was soon evident that the bourgeois-democratic International had no future, in so far as it wanted to represent any tendency apart from the national and liberal movements of individual countries. Nor could the socialist-democratic International of Willich and his friends maintain itself under the conditions of the period. It was based on the illusion of a section of the German and French exiles that the

revolution could simply be continued from that point where
the armed struggles of 1849 had ceased. Marx knew, however, that at that time no real revolutionary movement existed among the workers in France or in Germany. If the
revolution still did not appear after a certain interval, then
the organization of Willich and his French friends would
disintegrate of its own accord. Willich and his collaborators
lacked any scientific and political knowledge. They were
incapable of leading the workers through a long period of
decline. Consequently Marx and Engels could wait patiently
until the destiny of both Internationals had been fulfilled.

No new revolution developed in Europe during the next
decade. On the other hand, the legal bourgeois-liberal opposition gradually regained its strength in Germany as well
as in France. By taking advantage of amnesties some of the
exiles returned to their homes. Others abandoned politics
and sought new vocations abroad. The remaining bourgeois-democratic émigrés from Germany and France who
wanted to remain politically active were only an unimportant
branch of the liberal opposition at home. Ruge sided with
Prussia, since the Prussian government appeared to have
turned liberal. Kinkel and the other London émigrés of
the same group became members of the local branch of the
German National Union in London. The history of the
German democratic émigrés in England, which had begun
so significantly in 1849, ended during the sixties in petty
squabbles in the London branch of the National Union. At
the same time no one bothered any longer with Ledru-Rollin. He was only important as a foreign echo of the legal
bourgeois-republican opposition in France.

The nationalist movements, which had played such an
important part in the revolutionary International during
1848 and thereafter, degraded themselves to the status of vas-
sals of Bonapartism. Louis Napoleon, since 1852 Emperor
Napoleon III, played with the idea of a revision of the
treaties of 1815 and claimed to be supporter of all harassed

and oppressed nations. The Hungarian National Party, led by Kossuth, as well as the aristocratic section of the Polish exiles and the liberal-monarchist group of the Italian patriots, entered into negotiations with Napoleon and hoped that he would fulfil their desires. Mazzini, however, remained true to his principles and rejected any association with corrupt Bonapartism, which could only ruin the Italian movements.

While the bourgeois-democratic International disintegrated into its component parts, the proletarian-democratic International of Willich had no better fate. When it was realized that the movement could not achieve any positive successes, new quarrels developed in the Communist Workers' Club in London, which soon brought about its complete disintegration. Willich temporarily approached the bourgeois democrats of the Ruge-Kinkel group and then emigrated to America. Schapper and the rest of the politically interested German workers in England returned to Marx. At the same time the organization of the French socialist exiles lost all significance, and thus the anti-Marxist labour International was only an episode, despite the tumult which it had created in 1850 and 1851.

While all the various groups of European democratic exiles were disintegrating and their leaders were sinking into insignificance, Marx continued to work indefatigably in London. His unparalleled scientific work attracted thinking representatives of the labour movement like an irresistible magnet. The leaders of the English workers resumed their relations with Marx and Engels. This is equally true of the Chartist Party during the last years of its existence, and of the English trade unions as soon as they too began to interest themselves in the political tasks of the proletariat. In a like manner the few people in Germany around 1860 who were concerned with the class politics of the workers also considered Marx as their scientific guide. The political struggle among the European émigrés ended about 1860, although its echoes, in the form of unimportant personal feuds, continued to resound for some time. The historical democratic movement no longer existed. There remained only bourgeois liberalism in its various national forms on the one hand, and Marx and the labour movement on the other.

6. The Beginnings of Social Democracy

The paralysis of the political and social movements, which had followed in the wake of the unsuccessful Revolution of 1849 had again been overcome by 1859. New beginnings became evident in all the important countries. In Europe and America events had progressed so far by 1863 and 1864 that a new world-revolutionary situation like that of 1847 could be recognized. In England, to be sure, the Chartist Party had gradually and gently passed away, but the trade unions had succeeded it and represented not only the economic interests of the English proletariat but likewise its political demands. The trade unions in England resumed their agitation for general suffrage, and in 1863–4 it already appeared as if the resistance of the ruling bourgeoisie was weakening. Influenced by events in America, the radical Left wing of English liberalism also supported the workers' demands for the franchise. If the English workers finally succeeded now in obtaining general suffrage, incalculable consequences would necessarily ensue.

In France, Bonapartism had lost all its charms. In the meantime the French workers had realized the mistake that they had made by voting for Louis Napoleon on December 10, 1848. Napoleon III was not the Emperor of the masses; on the contrary, he sought the favour of the wealthy upper classes. The workers had again been deprived of all the social achievements of the Revolution of 1848. The French workers no longer had the right of association, and any strike attempt was cruelly persecuted by the imperial police and the courts. The working day was again increased to twelve hours. Wages and working conditions were dictated by the manufacturers. Under Napoleon III the French peasants were not mistreated quite so badly as the workers, but for them, too, the Empire was a great disappointment.

Napoleon I had introduced a just and honest administrative apparatus in France. He had no need to repress the masses by force, because they trusted him voluntarily. Under Napoleon I the possibility for any capable individual to rise in the imperial army had been a kind of substitute for the loss of political democracy. All this was completely different under Napoleon III. The army and the administrative apparatus were controlled by the old upper class, except where the personal adherents of the Emperor had established themselves. This latter group was a clique of adventurers, fortune-hunters, and stock-exchange speculators which was despised by all of France. An enormous police apparatus, which was as brutal as it was corrupt, oppressed the urban and rural population. The French peasant obtained no positive advantage from the government of Napoleon III. He saw in the imperial splendour only the arbitrary power of the police, and stock-exchange swindles.

After 1849 the wealthy bourgeoisie had gradually grown accustomed to the Empire. Nevertheless it demanded of Napoleon III a strong foreign policy, which would open up new fields of activity for the French bourgeoisie. As a matter of fact Napoleon III created enough noise with his foreign policy. He conducted two victorious wars in Europe, the Crimean War against Russia, and the war against Austria in 1859. In addition there were wars in eastern Asia, in Mexico, and in Africa. Nevertheless the positive result of all these actions was extremely small. In 1864 Napoleon had been the leader of France for fifteen years. During this period he had obtained Savoy and Nice in Europe and had begun the colonization of Indo-China in Asia. It was a meagre result. The political balance of power had by no means changed in favour of France; on the contrary, the very opposite was true. The four old major European powers, with whom France dealt, had not been weakened. In addition Napoleon's inept policy in Italy had permitted a new major power to arise. The new Italian kingdom was naturally opposed to France, since Napoleon had not permitted the Italians to occupy Rome, where French bayonets defended the secular rule of the Pope.

In 1863 the French army had become enmeshed in a dubious adventure in Mexico, and Napoleon III attempted in vain to protect the insurgent Poles against the Russian Tsar. The question of German union under the leadership of Prussia had again become acute. Owing to the creation of an Italian kingdom for which Napoleon was responsible, Prussia had obtained an active ally to support her in any controversy with Austria. Critical observers of French foreign policy already saw that the mistakes of Napoleon III would also result in a centralized unification of Germany under Prussian leadership, in addition to the unification of Italy. As soon as this happened, the European balance of power would shift to the great disadvantage of France.

The French bourgeoisie discerned the personal incapacity of Napoleon, who was nothing more than a miserable adventurer, having surreptitiously obtained power over a great civilized people by exploiting his name and social crises, and who now maintained it by means of the most unworthy methods. Napoleon's worst political characteristic was his boundless personal untrustworthiness. He was capable of thrusting France into a dangerous war at any time because of some sudden fancy, and a stable internal policy, such as the bourgeoisie desired, could not be expected of him. During the first decade of his government he had indeed zealously advocated the interests of the capitalists, of the bureaucracy, of the Church and the officers' families. French economy as a whole had progressed and the government aided business by means of public works and similar enterprises. As soon as Napoleon began to fear the loss of his throne, however, he was also capable of sudden changes in his internal policies.

The conclusion of the Anglo-French trade treaty in 1860 was a typical occurrence. The Emperor noticed how his popularity with the masses was disappearing. Desiring to oblige the poorer population by making necessary commodities cheaper, he concluded a trade treaty with England in 1860, to the great astonishment of the French public. The treaty lowered the French tariff rates considerably and produced an intense agitation among the French manufacturers. Since that time, certain individuals, whom the Emperor employed for his personal political machinations, showed a striking interest for the distressed condition of the French workers. Nevertheless Napoleon III did not regain the favour of the French proletariat with such manœuvres, but he did increase the feeling of distrust and insecurity among the bourgeoisie. What good did it do the French bourgeoisie to endure the imperial despotism with its repulsive concomitant excrescences if Napoleon III as a result of his foreign policy dragged France into uncertain adventures and if he were ready to attempt all kinds of experiments in his internal policies?

All honest and independent people in France, irrespective of class, despised Napoleon III and his entourage. After 1860 this feeling was intensified by growing doubts among the bourgeoisie as to whether a continuation of the dictatorial Empire would be at all useful. Napoleon III and his satellites were seized by a feeling of insecurity. The repressive machinery could no longer be employed as in the past, at least not in the large cities. The various groups of the opposition cautiously resumed their political activity. Until then the parliamentary elections had been a wretched comedy under the terrorism of the police. In 1863, however, the elections assumed a serious character. To be sure, the rural districts again elected the prescribed government candidates, but all the larger cities voted against the Empire. In Paris primarily, only candidates of the liberal and republican opposition were elected.

As a whole the election of 1863 was a serious blow for the Empire. It was the beginning of the end. Not only the labouring masses but also the wealthy bourgeoisie rebelled against Napoleon III. A new bourgeois revolution was to be expected in France during the following years. It had become very doubtful whether the army would fight for the despicable heir to a great name and against the nation. Thus, as far as England and France were concerned, it appeared as if the situation of 1847 had reappeared. Apparently in England the workers would soon obtain general suffrage, and France was on the verge of a republican revolution. However, if the revolution triumphed anew in Paris, then the workers would again be found in the centre of the political stage.

The other European countries likewise exhibited a strange return to the conditions which existed prior to the Revolution of 1848. Since 1859 the liberal bourgeoisie in Germany had again awakened from the slumber into which it had fallen after the lost Revolution. Liberalism regained the leadership of the south-German states. The Emperor of Austria was forced to grant a progressive Constitution and in Prussia a decisive struggle developed between the ruling feudal nobility and the bourgeoisie. In Prussia the Revolution had left behind it a Constitution and a Diet, which had no real power, to be sure, but which could become an instrument for the expression of public opinion in periods of unrest. Now a constitutional conflict had developed between the King and the nobility on the one hand, and the liberal bourgeoisie on the other. In this struggle the workers, the artisans, as well as the majority of the peasants, sided with the liberal opposition. Almost all the electoral districts, even those in the darkest corners of East Elbia, the backward agrarian country east of the river Elbe, elected opponents of the government to the Diet. King Wilhelm I and his Prime

Minister, Bismarck, had overstepped the bounds of the Constitution. They ruled in a dictatorial manner, in opposition to Parliament and nine tenths of the people. Apparently a revolutionary situation was developing in Prussia, and in his weaker moments the King himself expected the fate of Louis XVI.

At the beginning of the sixties the nationalist movements had also reawakened. In 1863 a revolt broke out in the Russian part of Poland, which met with intense sympathy in central and western Europe. Hungary was in a state of increasing turbulence, since the Hungarians rejected Viennese centralization in any form, no matter whether it appeared under the cloak of absolutism as after 1849 or of German liberalism after 1860. Owing to the war against Austria, which Napoleon III had conducted together with Sardinia in 1859, the nationalist movement in Italy was again in full swing. At first Napoleon had obtained only the cession of Lombardy by Austria, a meagre result for the Italian patriots. Then, however, the movement of the Italian people went ahead alone. It overflowed into central Italy and in 1860 Garibaldi undertook his famous expedition to Sicily. In the course of a brilliant triumphal march Garibaldi, at the head of his republican and patriotic volunteers, destroyed the corrupt feudal Kingdom of Naples.

The impression which Garibaldi's victories made upon all of Europe was enormous. It was the first time in many years that the democratic revolution had conquered by force of arms. The radical elements of all countries conceived new hopes. The moral authority of the Italian republicans and of their leaders, Garibaldi and Mazzini, who had already stood the test of 1849 so brilliantly, was greater than ever before. However, it was soon evident that the Italian republicans could indeed triumph, but that the liberal monarchists gathered the fruits of their victories. With all their courage and all their love of the broad masses, the Italian republicans had no social program with which they would have been able to oppose the liberal monarchists. The military conquest of southern Italy was not so very difficult, but it was not enough unless the social conditions of the country were radically changed at the same time. As long as millions of wretched and ignorant tenants remained the slaves of the landlords in southern Italy, then Sicily and Naples were a doubtful gain for the progressive northern part of Italy. Garibaldi and Mazzini, however, had no intention of unleashing an agrarian revolution in Italy. Practically, then, they served only the cause of national union, and the fruits of their victories were gathered by Cavour, the great liberal statesman of Sardinia. Little Sardinia was transformed into the great Kingdom of Italy. It included all the Italian states with the exception of Venice, Trentino, and Trieste, where Austria maintained itself, and Rome, where French bayonets protected the secular rule of the Pope.

Consequently the Italian national question was still not completely solved as long as Rome and Venice remained outside of the national union. At first the monarchy and the ruling liberal party submitted to the command of Napoleon III and attempted no new attack upon Rome. Nevertheless Garibaldi considered his mission unfinished as long as any foreigners still remained upon Italian soil. He and his volunteers were in a certain sense a revolutionary opposition army, which could be mobilized at any moment independently of the army of the state. In the event of any new attempts against Rome, Garibaldi would not only be opposed by the French army, but also by the royal Italian government. Consequently the national crisis continued to exist in Italy and the disappointment over Rome again widened the gap between the King and the ruling liberal group on the one side, and the republican-democratic movement on the other. In Italy, too, the revolution was not yet at an end.

Thus in 1863-4 critical observers in Europe saw the agitation for the franchise in England, the crisis of the Empire in France, the constitutional conflict in Germany, the revolt in Poland, Garibaldi's movement in Italy, and the unrest in Hungary. This was approximately the same group of countries within which the movements between 1847 and 1849 had taken place. This time, however, two more great countries were involved in struggles, of which the end was not yet in sight. In the United States the Civil War between the North and the South had brought about a mighty renewal of fighting democracy. The American Civil War had resulted in a new connexion between the European and the American movements, in that all class-conscious workers and democrats in Europe sympathized with the North, while the capitalist governments, on the other hand, supported the slave-holding South. There were already suggestions of French and English interference in the American struggle, and European democracy had the task of preventing any such intervention. Should the Civil War in the United States end with the collapse of the slave-holders, then apparently America would again be the centre of a powerful democratic movement, based upon the support of the masses.

During the same period the Tsar of Russia had been compelled to abolish serfdom. Nevertheless the distribution of the land among the peasants in Russia remained extremely unsatisfactory. It appeared very probable therefore that a fighting political movement of the Russian peasants would begin to develop now and would furnish the necessary mass basis for the opposition of the bourgeoisie and the intellectuals to tsarism. Now Russia was no longer the reactionary block of 1848 upon which the waves of the central-European Revolution had been broken. It now had its own revolution within itself.

Consequently in 1863 and 1864 all the conditions for a renewal of the international revolutionary movement were present. This renewal was dependent, however, on the answer to the question who was to lead the movement now since the democratic parties of 1848 no longer existed in the important European countries? Apparently the working class itself would now have to fill the gap consciously. The proletariat as a class would have to take up the arms which the older democratic movement had cast aside. In theory this was clear and simple, but its practical political execution was all the more difficult. The strength and the weakness of the older democratic movement had been the fact that it had been a mobilization of the " people." On the one hand this explains the phraseological vagueness of most of the older democrats on the social question, but on the other also the impassioned energy with which workers and peasants, artisans and students had united under the democratic banner. In 1848 the democratic idea had actually moved the masses and had carried them to the barricades. Only recently Garibaldi, with his democratic and patriotic slogans, had mobilized all the people in southern Italy to fight against a small ruling group.

The democratic movement had then been wrecked every time on its social contradictions. It had made a glorious beginning, however, by stirring up the people, by arousing the will of the masses to sacrifice their lives for freedom and a better future. If the labour movement now appeared as the successor to the older democratic movement, would it be capable of making the same glorious beginning? Any labour organization was capable of seeing the real problems of social life much more clearly than the older democratic movement had seen them. Would the organized working class, however, be capable of finding the connexion between the minor specialized questions of its daily activities and the great problems of the revolution? Would the workers be capable of organizing the masses of peasants and artisans and others as a part of the working class and then of leading them in an attack upon the ruling system?

In 1848 the political idea had pushed all other considerations into the background. The workers in all countries were convinced that the people must first obtain political power. Everything else would then follow. The movement was so strong that in many cases it even carried the unpolitical socialists with it. It is typical that in 1848 in France even Proudhon allowed himself to be elected to the National Assembly, not, to be sure, as a member of any party, but as an independent socialist. The defeat of the political revolution necessarily shook the faith of the workers in the power of purely political action and with that also their faith in the older revolutionary democratic movement. During the decade between 1860 and 1870 four tendencies or forms may be recognized according to which the workers sought to shape their class movement in contrast to that of the older democratic tradition. These were the political labour party, the political trade unions, unpolitical anarchism employing peaceful methods, and finally unpolitical anarchism advocating revolutionary methods. Lassalle's party in Germany represented the first form; the second was typified by the English trade unions. The two anarchist groups consisted of the adherents of Proudhon and Bakunin.

During the sixties the Left wing of the bourgeoisie in Germany formed several parties. These were movements of uncompromising liberals, who attempted to win over masses of the petty bourgeoisie and of the working class. The specific German form of the democratic movement of 1848, which had never been anything else but a Left wing of liberalism with petty-bourgeois tendencies, merged with the new parties. In Prussia there was the German Progressive Party and in southern Germany the German People's Party. Men who had been considered democrats in 1848 worked in both parties — for example, Schulze-Delitzsch in the Progressive Party, and Karl Mayer in the People's Party. It is remarkable, however, that in their official names both parties avoided any designation as democrats. It was felt that the word " democrat " was not very suitable for a peaceful and legal bourgeois party, or, as Lassalle bluntly expressed it: " The old, honourable, and intelligible word ' democracy ' was obscured by the furtive, mendacious name of the ' Progressive Party.' "

At the beginning of the sixties the Communist League had long since ceased to exist. Only a few people had any direct connexions with Marx and Engels in England. The workers who had any interest at all in a radical political movement joined the Left wing of the bourgeoisie, the Progressive Party, and the People's Party. Later the two independent Social Democratic parties were formed by the separation of the workers' clubs from the two bourgeois parties. The popular goal of the social-reformist movement among the workers, just as among the distressed petty bourgeoisie, was still the co-operative in the spirit of Louis Blanc. If matters were considered in the right light, the liberal bourgeoisie had no occasion to fear the co-operatives. Thus Schulze-Delitzsch himself founded co-operatives in the name of the Progressive Party, and as a result the workers in Prussia could be really satisfied with their party. The party also led the struggle for political freedom. Particularly in 1863 the Progressive Party opposed the King and Bismarck, and at the same time the workers received their co-operatives. However, Schulze-Delitzsch differed with Louis Blanc by demanding that the co-operatives should not be organized with the help of the state, but that they should be maintained with funds contributed by the members themselves.

It was nevertheless an unnatural condition for the German proletariat, which was constantly growing in number and self-confidence, to remain permanently attached to the leading-strings of the wealthy bourgeoisie. For the workers in 1848 democracy had not meant a policy of class conciliation with the manufacturers and the bankers. After the collapse of revolutionary democracy in 1849 the democratic remnants had hidden themselves beneath the wings of bourgeois liberalism. The fact that the workers had accompanied this retreat for a certain period was only an expression of the defeat of all the popular forces in Germany. Yet the moment had to come when the German working class, after the decline of the older revolutionary democratic movement, would found its own democratic party.

When the German workers began to become politically independent, they found a great leader in Lassalle. He was by far the most important thinker among the younger politicians and sociologists in Germany who had accepted the teachings of Marx. Lassalle used the differences of opinion within the progressive workers' clubs in order to enter into a struggle with Schulze-Delitzsch and the bourgeoisie. He explained the facts of the class struggle very trenchantly to the workers. He demanded general suffrage for the German workers, a right which they possessed neither in Prussia nor in southern Germany nor in Austria at that time. He demanded that the state should aid the productive cooperatives of the workers. Only in this way would it be possible to obtain any positive results, while the co-operatives of Schulze-Delitzsch would expire owing to a lack of funds.

In 1863 Lassalle founded the General German Workers' Society. It was the first independent and vital working-class party on German soil. The Communist League had been but a small group without any independent following among the masses. Lassalle's Workers' Society was a democratic party, for he demanded general suffrage and the assumption of political power by the working class. Marx and Engels greeted the founding of Lassalle's party with mixed emotions. They were disturbed first of all by the co-operative theory, which Lassalle had not borrowed from Marx, but rather from Louis Blanc. Marx did not believe that the controversy over the correct form of co-operatives was a particularly suitable starting-point for a new labour party. Marx feared that the propaganda for co-operatives would lead to nothing but confusion and reverses. The worst of it was that a few producers' co-operatives might very easily be founded with some help from the state, even under capitalism. Thus a few co-operative experiments were started in France right after the massacre of the workers in June 1848. Schulze-Delitzsch proved that the liberal bourgeoisie could likewise create co-operatives. Even the King of Prussia might finance several workers' co-operatives if he felt like doing so. In this way the vanguard of the proletariat would be changed into pensioners of the Prussian police state.

Nevertheless the fundamental objection which Marx and Engels made to Lassalle and his followers did not deal with the subject of co-operatives, but rather with general political tactics. Precisely in 1863 when Lassalle started his agitation, the liberal bourgeoisie in Prussia was in the midst of an intense fight with the monarchy and the government. In order to establish his labour party, Lassalle was forced to direct his attack upon bourgeois liberalism at this moment, with the result that, willingly or unwillingly, he became a tactical ally of Bismarck — that is, of the government of the Prussian nobility. Lassalle, as an independent and uncommonly sagacious thinker, realized the consequences and did not fear them. Lassalle did not believe that any of the groups of the liberal German bourgeoisie was capable of a revolutionary struggle. At the decisive moment the bourgeoisie would yield to the monarchy and the nobility just as they had done in 1848–9. It would not serve any purpose to check the agitation of the labour party against liberalism because any expectations of revolutionary deeds from the liberals would never materialize.

In Germany the national democratic movement of the future could only be founded by the working class, and only by a working class which had inexorably broken with liberal capitalism. The tactical appearance of an alliance between the labour party and the Prussian government was unpleasant, but there was no need to abandon the main goal on that account. Furthermore, Lassalle recognized that a solution of the German question was imminent, and that this solution would only be possible under the leadership of Prussia. It would therefore be necessary for the working class to adapt itself to the new unified Germany led by Prussia. It would be of the utmost importance to obtain general suffrage in this new Germany. Under the influence of increasing difficulties and the growing pressure of the masses, it was not at all impossible that Bismarck would finally grant general suffrage. At first such a German parliament, elected by general suffrage, would not have any too much power alongside of the Prussian militaristic monarchy. It would furnish a basis, however, upon which the democratic German labour party could develop. For the moment it would appear perhaps as if the democratic labour movement were a tool of Bismarck, but the ultimate result would reveal the true dupe.

These were approximately Lassalle's basic ideas from the founding of his party to his early death in 1864. It must be admitted that he saw the future of Germany with a remarkable clarity of vision, such as but few political prophets possess. Everything happened more or less as Lassalle had predicted. A few years after his death Germany was united under Prussian leadership, with the elimination of Austria. The opposition of the liberals to the Prussian militaristic nobility collapsed deplorably, but Bismarck granted general suffrage anyway. The labour party grew constantly and in 1918 the political offspring of Bismarck and Wilhelm I had to retreat before the followers of Lassalle. It would therefore appear to be very simple for a historian to establish that Lassalle had been completely right and that Marx and Engels would have been completely wrong. In the special German case, Lassalle certainly employed the correct tactics for the creation of an independent labour party. Yet Marx and Engels, with their more general criticism, located the weak point of the entire socialist labour movement from 1863 to the present.

In his criticism of Lassalle, Marx was chiefly concerned with the political situation in Prussia at that time and with the struggle of the bourgeoisie against the monarchy and the nobility. Marx was far removed from any exaggeration of the fighting ability of the Berlin Progressive Party, but a great fundamental conflict did exist between liberalism and the military aristocracy, and in a struggle of this kind the labour party should never side either directly or indirectly with the feudal nobility. The General German Workers' Society did indeed fight the capitalists, but in the opinion of Marx it neglected agrarian conditions. Lassalle's party did nothing about the oppressed rural workers of East Elbia. It suppressed all agitation against the nobility and the monarchy.

After Lassalle's death Schweitzer assumed the leadership of the movement. He was likewise a clever and skilful politician, who continued to lead the General German Workers' Society according to the ideas of its founder. Towards the end of 1864 Schweitzer, who wanted to found a party newspaper, requested Marx and Engels to contribute to the paper. They had not yet published their criticism of Lassalle and at first they promised their co-operation in the hope that they would be able to influence the German labour movement. However, when the tendency of Schweitzer and his party did not change, a split developed. In February 1865 Engels wrote to Marx with regard to the agitation of the followers of Lassalle: "In a predominantly agricultural country such as Prussia is, it is a dirty trick to attack the bourgeoisie alone, in the name of the proletariat, while at the same time not a word is uttered about the patriarchal exploitation of the rural proletariat by the great feudal nobility." A few days later in a letter to Schweitzer, Marx informed him of his break with Lassalle's party and stopped contributing to the paper of the General German Workers' Society.

Marx's letter is a biased but imposing document. Marx states that he has never demanded that the Lassalleans conjure up a conflict with the police and the courts through unrestricted agitation. "A form of agitation against the government, which would be possible even in Berlin, is certainly very different from any flirtation or even any pseudo-compromise with the government. . . . There is no longer any doubt that Lassalle's unfortunate illusion of a socialistic intervention by a Prussian government will be followed by disappointment. The logic of facts will speak. However, the honour of the labour party demands that it reject all such illusions, even before their emptiness has been demonstrated by experience. The working class is revolutionary or it is nothing."

Marx did Schweitzer a great wrong, when he considered him in any way an agent of the Prussian government. Schweitzer, and Lassalle before him, never betrayed the working class and democracy, even for one moment, in the interest of Bismarck. Schweitzer's tactics are explained rather by the practical needs of his party and by the desires and sentiments of the German workers themselves. The small party of the Lassalleans was in an enormously difficult situation at that time. In order to attain any significance, the party first had to separate a considerable number of workers from bourgeois liberalism. This was possible only by carrying on an intense polemical agitation against the liberal catchwords. If the party had simultaneously begun such a propaganda campaign among the rural population, it would have dissipated its forces and would probably have achieved nothing in either field. On the other hand it was just the class-conscious part of the German proletariat that desired a genuine labour party, a party which clearly and definitely represented the workers and would not mingle the cause of the workers with the causes of other groups.

Marx and Engels, on the other hand, were not concerned with the problem of founding some kind of socialist party in Germany as rapidly as possible, but only with advancing the revolution in Germany. But a revolution in Prussia was impossible if the urban workers isolated themselves. The workers must unite with the poor rural population and defeat the military monarchy together, thus completing the actual bourgeois revolution in Germany without waiting for the bourgeoisie. Marx and Engels demanded of Lassalle's party that it behave like a party of revolutionary democrats. It should continue the work of 1848, but it must get rid of all petty-bourgeois admixtures and phrases. At that time, however, it was difficult to interest just that part of the European proletariat which was most class-conscious in a policy of this kind. The more clearly the vanguard of the proletariat realized its own position within bourgeois society, the greater became its tendency to isolate itself and to emphasize those qualities which were specifically proletarian and which differentiated it from all the groups and tendencies of the wealthy classes. At this stage the radical proletarian movement tended particularly to see the nobility and the peasants, the manufacturers and the intellectuals as " a uniform reactionary mass." However, in this manner the working class isolated itself and made it impossible for itself to carry on a revolutionary policy.

It has already been emphasized that Lassalle reproached the liberal bourgeoisie and particularly the bourgeois radicals with the fact that they renounced the name of democrats. The result was that the rising independent labour movement claimed the democratic name for itself. The political German labour movement began to call itself " social-democratic," in accord with the tradition of 1848. Linguistically this name was unobjectionable, since it was intended to designate a movement which demanded self-government by the people based upon general suffrage and at the same time the social transformation of society in the interest of the labouring masses. Historically, however, the designation was less correct, for, by their policy of class isolation, the new labour parties abandoned the essential idea of the historical democratic movement.

Marx and Engels were not at all satisfied with the characterization of their labour movement as " social-democratic."

In 1864 Schweitzer had informed them in England that the new paper of the General German Workers' Society would be called *The Social Democrat*. Consequently Engels wrote to Marx: " What a disgusting title — *The Social Democrat*! Why don't those fellows frankly call the thing: *The Proletarian?* " Marx replied diplomatically: " *Social Democrat* is a bad title. Yet one shouldn't immediately use the best title for something which may turn out to be a failure." In 1848 Marx and Engels had by no means been ashamed to be called democrats. In 1864, however, the name " Social Democrats " seemed to them to be a revival of the bankrupt party of Ledru-Rollin and Louis Blanc. They finally put up with the name, being convinced that such a poor name was good enough for the Lassalleans. In this strange manner did the designation of Social Democrats for the Marxist labour parties come into being.

Nevertheless the name of social democracy remained popular among the politically active German workers. When a second labour party in addition to the General German Workers' Society arose after 1866 in Germany, it called itself simply the Social Democratic Labour Party. Lassalle had founded his party by separating the Prussian workers from the Progressive Party; now Wilhelm Liebknecht and Bebel did the same for southern Germany and Saxony. In these regions the workers had to be separated from the People's Party. The two parties differed chiefly in their different attitudes towards the German question. Lassalle and his successors had put up with the Prussian solution of the German question. On the other hand, in central and southern Germany the People's Party represented the uncompromising anti-Prussian wing of liberalism.

After 1849 the south-German provincials had completely lost any inclination for revolutionary deeds. However, they still rejected unification and centralization by Prussia and defended the easy-going independence of their small states. This was the practical form in which the "democratic" movement in central and southern Germany still carried on a vegetating existence after 1866. The modern progressive section of the bourgeoisie favoured Bismarck and German unity. This group was now represented by the National Liberal Party. In southern Germany it was opposed by the petty bourgeoisie of the People's Party, as well as by the Catholic friends of Austria. In Baden and in the Palatinate the democratic movement had been ruined so completely after 1849 that the National Liberals were in control there. In Bavaria the Catholic peasants and artisans had their own particularistic party. This left the People's Party with a restricted sphere of action comprising Württemberg, Frankfurt am Main, and several parts of Saxony. The workers' societies which had originally been associated with the People's Party became independent and formed the Social Democratic Labour Party.

The new party was led by Wilhelm Liebknecht. As a young man he had taken part in the revolt in Baden during 1849 and had belonged to Struve's group. He had then been an exile in London, where he had joined Marx. He always wanted to be a loyal follower of Marx and to shape his policies according to the latter's views. Nevertheless it was impossible for him to carry on his practical political activities in agreement with Marx and Engels. After his return to Germany, Wilhelm Liebknecht, in his capacity as party leader, proved to be an outstanding speaker and organizer. He knew how to gain the confidence of the workers and how to keep the movement together under difficult conditions; but he lacked any comprehension of profounder scientific problems and of the broader relations of politics. For thirty years Liebknecht's methods drove Marx and Engels to despair.

Liebknecht's party differed from the Lassalleans chiefly in its intense anti-Prussian agitation. The result was that the party's propaganda took on an apparently revolutionary character. After 1866 one of the tasks of a democratic Ger-

man labour party could have been to unite all the opponents
of Bismarck's system. However, Liebknecht and his friends
were not capable of steering an independent course in the
great political questions of the day. To be sure, they represented the trade interests of the German workers courageously, but at the same time they were completely under
the influence of the People's Party's anti-Prussian particular-
ism. Just for the sake of annoying Bismarck the leaders of
the Social Democratic Labour Party waxed enthusiastic over
Austria, over the rulers of the petty German states who had
been deposed by Prussia, and over the narrow-mindedness
of the petty states. The anger with which Marx and Engels
observed Wilhelm Liebknecht and his tactics is entirely
comprehensible. This example again illustrates how difficult it was at that time for an independent labour party in
Europe to steer its own political course. As soon as the
workers and their leaders abandoned the well-known road
of revolutionary democracy, they were confronted by tangled
forests of unexplored political territory. Every advance was
dangerous and as a rule it was easy to go astray.

The founding of an independent labour party was not
due to Lassalle's ambitions, but developed out of the conditions of the period. The corresponding events in France
prove this. Ever since Napoleon III had begun to feel in-
secure and had observed the growth of the opposition, he
had begun to toy with the labour movement. In 1862 the
imperial government had permitted the French workers to
elect a kind of industrial representative body. These workers' delegates were to represent the French proletariat at
the London World Exposition, which was then being held.
This contact between the French and English workers, which
had been encouraged by Napoleon III, was later to become
important for the origin of the First International. In a positive sense Napoleon did nothing for the French workers.
However, at least a few working-class organizations, with
moderate aims, were now legalized in France. In Paris these

labour groups determined to play an independent part in the parliamentary elections of 1863. The labour candidates appealed to the electorate with declarations in which they emphasized the class differences between the workers and the capitalists, as well as the necessity for an independent labour party, with extraordinary clarity. This occurred in the same year during which Lassalle started his great agitational campaign in Germany.

The two movements were completely independent of each other. The leaders of the political labour movement in Paris were exceedingly honest men, who had nothing to do with Napoleon's manœuvres. However, they had a perfectly good right to utilize as advantageously as possible the increased freedom which the working class had obtained. Nevertheless the nomination of independent labour candidates in Paris at such a time meant a split in the ranks of those who opposed Bonaparte. Just as the German liberals had considered Lassalle's agitation as an aid to Bismarck, the French bourgeois republicans also regarded the nomination of labour candidates as one of Bonaparte's manœuvres. It is characteristic that in 1863 the labour candidates in Paris were decisively defeated, and received but a few hundred votes. During the early period the electoral successes of the two socialist parties in Germany were just as moderate. From 1867 to 1877 five general elections, based upon general suffrage, were held in northern Germany, but the first Social Democratic deputies were not elected in Berlin until 1877. The idea of an independent labour party, separated from the bourgeois-democratic or bourgeois-republican opposition, gained adherents among the proletariat very slowly.

The second form of proletarian dissociation from the policies of the older democratic parties developed in England. Together with all possible kinds of personal, local, and more accidental factors, two main causes were important for the decline of the Chartist Party. First of all the complete collapse of the revolutionary democratic movement on the European continent after 1849 also tended to paralyse the related movement in England. Furthermore the one-sided concentration of Chartist propaganda on the political franchise no longer satisfied the English working class. To be sure, the politically thinking English workers still demanded electoral reform, but they gradually felt themselves repelled by a party which continued to speak only of parliamentary reform and disregarded the practical daily needs of the proletariat. In the long run, the promise of the Chartists that everything would change after the electoral reform did not satisfy the English workers. As a result, during the sixties they turned to their trade societies, the unions, and also found a political haven in them.

This does not mean that the English workers had now become fundamental opponents of political activity. On the contrary, the English trade unions fought with increased zeal for general suffrage at that time and were very influential particularly in international political questions. Yet the English workers no longer believed that only a democratic political party of the proletariat could advance their interests. Perhaps pressure exerted by the workers who were organized in unions on the existing bourgeois parties could accomplish the same, if not more. In England, too, the masses were evidently drifting away from the older ideal of a democratic party of the working people.

In Germany and France the friends of independent labour parties agreed with the politically active English trade-unionists by attributing great significance to political activity within the bounds of the existing states and their constitutions. The Germans and the French wanted to have their labour deputies in Parliament; the English wanted to exert pressure on the bourgeois parliamentary parties from outside. All of them believed in the importance of political activity in Parliament and in the state. Alongside of these groups, however, a completely different movement developed among the European workers. This tendency also opposed the traditional democratic ideas. It went beyond this, however, and completely rejected all political activity within the framework of the existing political order. It has already been pointed out that the older utopian socialism had rejected the use of political methods for the transformation of the state. The complete collapse of the European revolution in 1849 and the failure of all the political movements of the masses, which had been started with so much enthusiasm and devotion, appeared to bear out the views of these sceptics.

From the beginning many utopian socialists had exhibited anarchist tendencies; that is, they demanded the dissolution of all centralized political organizations based upon compulsion, and their replacement by smaller, loosely connected, self-governing communities. This older criticism of centralization and of political states based upon compulsion was developed by Proudhon. Not only did he absolutely reject the existing capitalistic and feudal states, but he also distrusted intensely any attempt to realize socialism by means of a large centralized organization based upon force. People who think like Proudhon do not consider it a great advance for the working class to be commanded by an organization of government officials, even though it takes place in the name of "socialism." At the present time the followers of Proudhon's ideas generally refer to Soviet Russia as proof of the correctness of their fears. Proudhon and his school did not consider any revolution progressive as long as it was directed by a centralized party machine, since such revolutions only led the masses from one form of dependency to another.

The rejection of the political party is closely connected with the criticism of the centralized state. A party is, in a certain sense, a state in miniature and tends ultimately to become the state itself. A party embodies authority just as a state does. Even though a party may make extremely radical demands and promise its followers republicanism, democracy, or socialism, still in a practical sense these promises and demands have no great value; for if a party once obtains political power, it rules the people, with the aid of its machine, just like the former government. A parliament is the soil in which political parties develop. The party politicians prevail upon the masses to vote for them and promise them all sorts of possible achievements which are to be obtained in parliament. Actually, however, the party leaders utilize the parliament for the aggrandizement of their personal power. Therefore the anarchists teach the people to shun political parties and not to participate in elections.

Peaceful anarchism, which utilized certain ideas of Proudhon, increased its influence among the French workers during the sixties. Distrust of the political parties and movements of the bourgeoisie, emphasis on the special class interest of the workers, and rejection of any strongly centralized labour organization were characteristic of these workers. At that period the majority of the Parisian workers were still revolutionary democrats, for whom the name of Blanqui was the symbol of their goal. This group, however, which only waited for the next opportunity to revolt, was unable to build up an organization, owing to the pressure of the Bonapartist police. The possibility of organization existed only for a moderate, peaceful minority, among whom a popular form of Proudhonism was combined with projects for the formation of a new labour party.

Actually a peaceful character corresponds best of all with the nature of anarchism, since every violent revolution or movement presupposes a certain organization of the masses. Such an organization requires leaders and discipline, and consequently authority. The sceptical anarchist, however, has no respect at all for any authority, particularly for a new form which calls itself revolutionary. It is therefore apparent that consistent anarchism must lead its adherents to avoid any premature action. Instead they want to advance the education and enlightenment of the masses until the people will become mature enough to introduce a better social order of its own free will.

Besides the moderate anarchists, who considered themselves disciples of Proudhon, there was still another group. These were impassioned revolutionaries who hated existing conditions just as bitterly as did the radical democrats — for example, the Blanquists. They, too, wanted a revolt. However, the revolt was not to be the work of an organized party, but rather an outburst of the masses themselves. The masses would break their yoke, without having been commanded to do so, and would then replace the old centralized state of the capitalists and the kings by small free co-operatives. This type of revolutionary anarchism, which preaches a philosophy of action, necessarily contains serious internal contradictions. If the movement should have any success, this very circumstance would soon compel it to create an organization which contradicted its own ideas.

During the sixties this second form of anarchism was advocated chiefly by the Russian revolutionary Bakunin. He was most active in western Europe and in 1849 participated in the revolt at Dresden. Bakunin wanted a revolution, but without the consequent erection of a new political authority. It later became evident that his peculiar form of the movement could find a considerable number of adherents only among especially backward, embittered and disillusioned masses of people. The rural proletariat of Spain and Italy was the chief representative of this category. Since the beginning of the nineteenth century one revolution had followed another in Spain. The monarchists fought the republicans, the feudal nobility opposed the bourgeoisie, and the free-thinkers attacked the Church. Various groups of officers and civil politicians struggled to attain influence within the state. Every party made extravagant promises to the masses, but the social condition of the people remained unchanged. The poor rural population continued to obey the great landowners. In Italy the course of events had been similar.

There the traditional feudal clericals opposed the modern liberals, who were reinforced by Mazzini's republicans. Mazzini's party had also founded a few workers' societies, but nothing was done for the masses of the rural proletariat in the south. These oppressed rural labourers of southern Europe, who could neither read nor write, were ready to revolt against their masters, but they distrusted all politicians and parties and preferred to act individually and without any "leaders" — each village for itself. The revolutionary anarchist propaganda appeared to have been created for just such groups.

During the sixties the European labour movement exhibited a colourful and varied picture. There was an intermingling of the most diverse tendencies. Nevertheless an inclination to turn away from the democratic movement of 1848 and a struggle to create new forms for the proletarian movement are recognizable in all countries. It was felt everywhere that the class-conscious workers of all countries belong together and have certain common tasks.

7. *The Founding of the First International*

The acute political situation in Europe around 1863-4 mobilized the workers. At their head were the English workers. They not only fought for electoral reform, but also demonstrated for Poland and Italy. When Garibaldi visited England the workers prepared an official reception for him.

The American Civil War occasioned serious distress among large numbers of English workers. The Northern fleet blockaded the Southern ports and prevented the export of cotton to Europe. Consequently the English textile industry lacked the necessary raw materials, and hundreds of thousands of workers lost their jobs. Simple trade egoism should have led the English workers to demand the end of the blockade and the free importation of cotton and to favour the South against the North. In an imposing demonstration of international democratic solidarity, however, the English trade unions and their members supported the North. They demanded the defeat of the slave-owners, even though they themselves might suffer need. During the American Civil War, European sympathies coincided in an exceedingly characteristic manner with the existing class divisions. In England the majority of the ruling class supported the South, while almost the entire proletariat sympathized with the North. The demonstrations of the English workers for Lincoln and against slavery played an important part in preventing the European major powers from intervening in the war.

As the long struggle in America gradually turned in favour of the North, this fact increased the feeling of self-reliance of the English workers extraordinarily. The unions increased their agitation for general suffrage and wanted to develop their international relations. In doing so the English workers made use of the friendship which had again united them with the French proletariat since 1862. In the autumn of 1864 the English trade unions invited the French workers' societies to participate in a common demonstration for Poland. The leading men of the English group were Odger, the chairman of the London Trades Council, and Cremer, secretary of the Society of Carpenters and Joiners. Odger was also the chairman of the trade-union society which agitated for general suffrage. Odger and Cremer had also organized demonstrations for America and for Garibaldi.

The French workers' societies, with which the English were in touch, were the legal organizations, which had been able to develop during the past few years and which were tolerated by Napoleon. They were friendly to the idea of a labour party and were also influenced by certain Proudhonistic ideas. These two currents of thought could be reconciled by striving for a labour party which should not be a political party, like those of the bourgeoisie, but rather a class organization without any authority in the hands of any leaders and with complete self-government by the members. Tolain, one of the labour candidates in the recent elections, came to London as the representative of the Paris workers. On September 24, 1864 a large international labour meeting was held in London. Besides the English and the French representatives, several delegates of the Italian workers' societies which supported Mazzini participated in the meeting. Marx was invited to take part as the representative of the German workers. Marx recognized that he was dealing with a serious movement and accepted the invitation.

At the meeting in London it was decided to organize an international workers' association, which for the present would include the English, French, Italian, and German labour organizations. The workers of other countries were invited to join. A general council with its seat in London took over the direction of the International. Marx soon obtained a decisive influence in the General Council. He drew up the program of the International and directed its policies.

It is worth noting that Marx and Engels did not found the "first" International, but that the idea came from the workers themselves, chiefly from the English unions, and Marx then accepted the plan of the English workers. Furthermore it was not the narrower trade interests of the workers that led to the founding of the International, but rather broad, general questions of international policy. The immediate occasion for the founding of the International was not a strike, but a demonstration of sympathy for Poland, a matter which had no direct connexion with the workers' jobs. The formation of the International would have been inconceivable without the older tradition of collaboration of the European democratic movement. The foreign policy of the Chartists furnished the most important precedent for the International. The London meeting of 1864 was the direct continuation of the London assemblies of the Fraternal Democrats before and after 1848. The First International was an imposing attempt on the part of the European

In France the police did not allow the formation of a revolutionary workers' party, nor was there anyone among the émigrés who would actually have been able to speak in the name of this section of the Parisian workers. In September 1867 Marx wrote in a letter: "The worst of it is that we haven't even a single person in Paris who could get in touch with the working-class sections (and they form the majority) that are hostile to the Proudhonists." Marx sympathized sincerely with old Blanqui. He was actually the only one among the leaders of the democratic movement of 1848 whom Marx valued highly as an individual. Blanqui reciprocated this feeling of sympathy. However, opportunities to get in touch with Blanqui, inside or outside of prison, were rare, and the practical significance of such attempts was small, since Blanqui had no party and was actually only a great, half-mythical name for the workers of Paris. Since the French revolutionary workers had no organization, Marx was forced to allow the theorizing and captious Proudhonists within the International to speak in the name of France.

Despite these enormous internal difficulties, Marx was able to maintain a unified International until great and tragic events in European politics made its further existence purposeless. At first Marx was satisfied with the results despite any momentary unpleasantness. In September 1867 he wrote to Engels in the jargon which he had acquired in exile and which he employed for such communications: "Meanwhile our society makes great progress. . . . Les choses marchent, and in the next revolution, which is closer perhaps than we suspect, we, i.e. you and I, will have this mighty engine in our hands. Compare with this the results of Mazzini's etc. operations since 30 years! And all this without funds, despite the intrigues of the Proudhonists in Paris, of Mazzini in Italy, of the jealousies of Odger, Cremer, Potter in London, and despite Schulze-Delitzsch and the Lassalleans in Germany!" (Potter was an English trade-union leader.) In speaking of the coming revolution Marx apparently thought of an uprising in Paris, which was expected momentarily then.

8. *Napoleon's Collapse*

At first the International actually achieved political successes. One of these was the acquisition of general suffrage in 1867 by the urban workers in England. This result had become possible only because it was supported both by the radical wing of the liberals and also by the revived Conservative Party of Disraeli. With this step England had completed its transformation into a bourgeois democratic state, wherein the organized workers played an important part. In addition in America the Northern states had obtained a decisive victory during 1864-5 and had completely destroyed the slave-holding aristocracy. The International congratulated President Lincoln formally upon his success. The address was composed by Marx, and Lincoln replied with an exceedingly friendly answer. Simultaneously in France, Napoleon's decline grew more evident. The French strike movement, which was supported by the International, helped to render any contradictions more acute. The violence of the imperial police on such occasions embittered even the most peaceful Proudhonists and proved to them that even the most modest social progress would be possible in France only after the expulsion of Napoleon. Napoleon's apparent friendliness for the workers had disappeared long ago.

In Germany at the same time the authority of the ruling class had been greatly strengthened by Bismarck's successes. Since 1866 the liberal bourgeoisie had become completely reconciled to Bismarck. Bismarck was now at the head of a solid bloc composed of the King of Prussia and the minor German princes, the militaristic Prussian nobility, and the liberal bourgeoisie. As Lassalle had predicted, Bismarck had

actually granted general suffrage for the North German
Reichstag. Since 1867 the government had received overwhelming majorities in the elections. The Catholic Pan-
Germans, the anti-Prussian People's Party, and the two Social Democratic groups were completely impotent politically.
A formal and final solution of the German question, through
the entrance of the south-German states into the confederation led by Prussia, was apparently only a question of a
short time.

From a democratic and socialist point of view, this entire
development in Germany was not very gratifying. Nevertheless, in a certain sense it advanced the aims of the International. In the first place the unification of Germany was
followed by a powerful development of industry and consequently strengthened the proletariat. The solution of the
German question removed the differences which had separated the friends and the opponents of a greater Germany
and thus paved the way for the unification of the German
labour movement. Even more important at this moment
was the fact that anything which strengthened Germany likewise weakened Napoleon and so helped to bring on a French
revolution. French public opinion considered the result of
the war of 1866 as a serious defeat for France. By his political
mistakes Napoleon III had brought about the unification of
Italy and then the centralization of Germany under Prussian
leadership. The result was that France's international position had become exceedingly serious and unfavourable.

The collapse of Napoleon's American policy followed
upon the heels of his diplomatic defeat in Germany. Napoleon had taken advantage of the weakening of the United
States during the Civil War to erect a kind of French pro-
tectorate in Mexico. In Mexico the party of the great landowners and the Church was opposed by a popular peasant
movement. The republican party led by President Juárez
represented the interests of the poor rural population. The
large landowners, on the other hand, sought aid abroad.

Napoleon III intervened in Mexico, certain shady financial deals of the imperial court also playing a part. A French army occupied Mexico. Nevertheless the republicans continued to resist and carried on guerrilla warfare. In Mexico Napoleon produced a parody of his own Empire. He installed the brother of the Emperor of Austria, Maximilian, as "Emperor" of Mexico. A fake plebiscite confirmed Maximilian in his office. The new Emperor behaved like a legitimate ruler and executed captured republicans according to martial law.

The erection of a Mexican Empire was a serious violation of American political principles as they had been promulgated by President Monroe. During the Civil War in the United States, however, President Lincoln avoided any decisive action. He even gave Napoleon the impression that the Northern states would tolerate the Mexican Empire. The result was that Napoleon was prevented from siding openly with the Southern states at a critical period. When the North finally triumphed, however, the American politicians dropped all pretences and demanded the withdrawal of the French from Mexico. Napoleon yielded to the American threat. The sham Emperor Maximilian was left to his own resources. Since practically the entire nation opposed him, his Empire collapsed. Maximilian was taken prisoner by Juárez. The Mexican republicans regarded Maximilian as a foreign robber who had attacked their country without any justification and had murdered patriotic Mexican citizens. Juárez executed the Emperor Maximilian according to martial law — an American counterpart to the execution of Louis XVI. Nevertheless it was not yet possible at that time to establish a permanent democratic republic in Mexico, because the Indian peasant masses were still too ignorant and backward.

By 1867, then, Napoleon's foreign policy had collapsed both in Europe and in America, and one can only regard with astonishment the fact that France still endured such a ruler until Sedan. The chief reason for the preservation of Napoleon's throne was the same which had previously maintained Louis Philippe's kingship — namely, the fear which the French bourgeoisie felt for any subsequent developments. The French bourgeoisie had long since broken with Napoleon III. If they had been certain that Napoleon would immediately be succeeded by a bourgeois kingdom of the Orléans line or by a conservative republic like that of Cavaignac, they would have expelled the Emperor immediately. Nor would the French officers and soldiers have sacrificed their lives for Napoleon. But the course of a revolution could never be determined very precisely in advance. If such a movement had to develop in a metropolis like Paris, with its proletariat, it could only too easily end in a Red republic. Compared with a Red dictatorship, even the Emperor with all his repulsive characteristics, with his police tyranny, his despicable entourage, and his political adventures, appeared the lesser evil to many French citizens.

Nevertheless after 1867 all the parties and political groups in France were compelled to occupy themselves very earnestly with the question of what would follow the fall of the imperial despotism. Actually Bonaparte could rely only upon the police, the administrative apparatus, the shady adventurers who were personally interested in the existence of the Empire, and a few stock-exchange speculators. By employing the necessary combination of fraud and violence the imperial machine was still capable of manipulating the elections in the rural districts and provincial towns. Since everyone knew how such election results were obtained, however, they had no great practical significance.

The old French monarchists were divided into two groups, the adherents of the older line of the Bourbons and the friends of the house of Orléans. This was not only a dynastic but also a fundamental social division. The friends of the older legitimate line wanted a restoration of France as it had been before 1789, or at least before 1830; that is, they de-

sired the predominance of the historical nobility and of the
Church. It was evident that this legitimist party could never
regain power in France if they relied upon their own forces.
The Catholic clergy had come to an understanding with
Bonapartism after 1849 since Napoleon did everything to
satisfy the Church and zealously supported the secular rule
of the Pope. While the Second Empire was at its height the
legitimate royalist party had been weakened by the defection
of the clergy. However, as soon as Napoleon's throne became untenable, the old alignment was restored; the older
line of the Bourbons, the aristocracy, and the bishops united.
But since the overwhelming majority of the French people
had outgrown feudal forms of life long ago, the party of
the orthodox monarchists could regain political significance
only in alliance with other groups.

The adherents of the Orléans party were not concerned
with French feudal traditions. They did not want the monarchy because of any romantic memories, but because they
were convinced that a hereditary king was the best guarantee
for the maintenance of order and property. During the sixties Thiers, who had been elected to the imperial Parliament
and who criticized Napoleon's amateurish foreign policy
with particular vehemence, emerged as the most important
leader of this group. There was no fundamental difference
between Thiers's group and the conservative republicans.
Both groups wanted a strong government to protect the interests of the wealthy classes and to curb the poor masses
energetically. They were divided only by a question of expediency: whether it would be tactically better to place a
king at the head of the state or to establish a republic.

The party of the moderate republicans maintained the
traditions of General Cavaignac and of the *National*. This
party was burdened with the blood-guilt of the June massacre of 1848, a fact with which the Bonapartists readily reproached them. For the wealthy bourgeoisie this episode out
of the past of the moderate republicans was only a recom-

mendation. Towards the end of the sixties there was still a group of men among the leaders of the conservative republicans who had already been prominent in 1848. Among them were Garnier-Pagès as well as Jules Favre, who had been Under-Secretary for Foreign Affairs under the five-man government of 1848. Among the younger leaders of the conservative republicans Ferry was especially prominent.

In 1848 the party of the bourgeois democrats, represented by Lamartine, had existed alongside of the conservative republicans. They had been men who wanted to maintain capitalistic property, but who also had faith in the people, being convinced that a popular republic, based upon general suffrage, was the best guarantee for an orderly and reasonable government. A corresponding party developed in France towards the end of the sixties. Its leader was the young lawyer and deputy Gambetta. With great fearlessness he carried on a fight against the Empire; he prophesied the revolutionary downfall of Napoleon and the establishment of a democratic republic. He wanted a government based upon general suffrage, with all its consequences, and the ruthless destruction of the monarchist administrative machine which had ruled France since the beginning of the century. On the social question, however, Gambetta's opinions were very indefinite and reserved. Gambetta opposed the conservative republicans, who steered clear of the people and sought feeble compromises. As a result he attained great popularity among the masses in Paris. Whether his own group represented any real social force, apart from the wealthy bourgeoisie or the class-conscious proletariat, remained doubtful. Only the future could show this.

So far the reorganization of political life in France during the sixties had proceeded along the lines of the historical parties. The Bonapartists, the two royalist parties, and the conservative republicans represented a direct tradition which had never been interrupted. In substance at least, Gambetta revived the policies which Lamartine and the progressive

National group had followed after February 24, 1848. After that, however, the formation of parties in France ceased during 1869–70. There was nothing else to the left of Gambetta. Here is the great difference between the situation of the political parties in 1847 and in 1869. At that time the large mass movement of the Socialist Democratic Party existed to the left of Lamartine. Now the organized party formations stopped with Gambetta's group. It was known that the masses of the French workers approved of Gambetta's political slogans, but that they went far beyond him in their social demands. However, no leader and no party existed which would have been justified to speak in the name of these masses.

To be sure, a small group of Proudhonists and social reformers formed the official French section of the Workingmen's International, but no one thought of these peaceful theoreticians as the future leaders of the Red army and as the successors of Robespierre. At that time the French public looked for a representative of the extreme proletarian Left wing and found none. Marx and Engels likewise looked, but they too found no one. In this strange situation an unpolitical Parisian journalist and editor of a popular magazine fell under suspicion of being Robespierre's successor.

Rochefort's historical significance lies in the fact that he manifests the lack of an organized revolutionary democratic movement in France very clearly. The courage and the wit with which Rochefort attacked the Emperor, the Empress, and the entire Bonaparte family caused a great sensation. His conflicts with the imperial police and the courts only increased his popularity. When a prince of the house of Bonaparte shot one of his collaborators, Rochefort dared to print a statement in Paris during the reign of Napoleon that every Bonaparte was a murderer. Rochefort was jailed, but when the murdered journalist was buried, Paris was on the verge of revolution and Napoleon already thought that he would have to flee. This exaggerated opinion of Rochefort, which can only be explained on the basis of the odd political situation in France at that time, was held even by the most experienced observers. Thus Engels wrote on August 15, 1870: "The worst of it is — who should be the leader in case a revolutionary movement actually appears in Paris? Rochefort is the most popular and the only useful one — Blanqui appears to be forgotten."

The French elections of 1869 were an improved edition of the 1863 elections. To be sure, the manufactured imperial majority was returned again, but all the large cities, headed by Paris, had definitely voted against Napoleon. The frightened Emperor sought to compromise with the bourgeoisie. He changed the military despotism into a parliamentary monarchy, and he even found a very conservative republican, Ollivier, who was ready to usher in Napoleon's new era as Prime Minister. Napoleon then held a plebiscite to confirm or repudiate the establishment of the new "liberal" Empire. Once again the plebiscite brought victory for the tried and trustworthy imperial electoral swindlers. Paris, however, again repudiated the Empire. The liberal comedy of Ollivier's Ministry was only the beginning of the end, or, as Gambetta expressed it, the bridge between the Republic of 1848 and the republic of the future.

In July 1870 war broke out between Napoleon and Prussia and brought the swindle of the Empire to a bloody conclusion. After the first defeats of the French army in August 1870, everyone prepared for Napoleon's fall. Even the generals speculated on the political future, in which the Red republicans at home appeared much more dangerous than the Prussians. The plan of action which the leader of the main French army, Marshal Bazaine, initiated during the middle of August was dictated entirely by internal political considerations. He wanted to maintain his army, supported by the fortress of Metz, as strong as possible in order to be able to employ it against the revolution in Paris after the conclusion of peace. Consequently Bazaine delayed his departure from

Metz and gave the German troops an opportunity to trap him in Metz. In order to save Bazaine from his own trap, the second French army, led by MacMahon, had to undertake its useless march, which ended with the catastrophe of Sedan. MacMahon's behaviour during the war of 1870, both in a military and in a personal sense, was above reproach. Bazaine's actions, on the other hand, were definitely treasonable; to be sure, they were not carried out in the interest of Germany, but rather in the interest of the internal counter-revolution. After 1871 the French conservative government court-martialled Bazaine, but it did not hesitate to use the instruments of power which Bazaine had preserved for it. The officers and soldiers of Bazaine's army suppressed the Paris Commune after their return from captivity.

When Paris learned that Napoleon had also been taken prisoner at Sedan, the filthy and shame-bedecked edifice of the Empire automatically collapsed. On September 4 a Republic was proclaimed in Paris. For the moment the provisional government of 1870 was composed of the leaders of the various republican groups. Together with Favre, Garnier-Pagès, and Ferry, Gambetta also entered the government. In addition there was General Trochu, who had attained prominence as a critic of the imperial military system. He acted as liaison officer between the republican government and the monarchists. Thiers placed himself at the disposal of the new government for diplomatic missions. It was also felt that a representative of the extreme Left would be desirable in the " government of national defence." Actually there was no other course but to release Rochefort from prison and make him Minister. How the actual relation of the forces within this variegated coalition government would develop depended on the future course of events. Above all, however, the unfortunate fact of war and the invasion of France by the German army necessarily endowed all political questions with a special character.

9. The Paris Commune and the End of the First International

In September 1870 one part of the regular French army had been captured, while the other part was trapped in Metz. Only recruits and militia formations were left in the rest of the country. France appeared defenceless. A German army began to surround Paris. Nevertheless the republican government attempted to continue the war in order to exact more favourable peace terms. It had soon become evident, within the provisional government, that Rochefort was unable to exert any influence. Instead Gambetta opposed the conservative majority. The fact that Paris was besieged necessitated a division of the government. Gambetta, equipped with extraordinary plenary power, left Paris in a balloon and undertook the organization of national defence. Trochu, Favre, and the others remained in Paris. As a result France had two opposed centres of power. In the provinces Gambetta ruled in the name of radical bourgeois democracy, supported by the peasants, workers, and artisans and hindered by the distrust of the wealthy upper classes. On the other hand, the conservative republicans, together with their monarchist friends, ruled in Paris. They were supported by the rich bourgeoisie and the bureaucracy and were opposed by the growing distrust of the workers.

Within a few weeks Gambetta became a figure of national importance. With the same energy with which he had fought Bonapartism in the courts and in Parliament, he now opposed the hostile invasion. Almost out of nothing, Gambetta created a new French army, which still resisted the German advance five months after Sedan. Gambetta hoped that the French Republic would revive the spirit of 1793 and that the foreign invasion, too, would be defeated again. The willingness of the French people to make sacrifices was not smaller in 1870 than it had been in 1793. Nor were their leaders any worse. As an organizer Gambetta was the equal of Carnot, and the new leaders of the French army did their best under desperate conditions.

If the French Republic of 1870-1 was nevertheless denied the success of 1793, it was due to the fact that this time it faced a very different opponent. At the time of Robespierre the French popular army fought against the antiquated armies of European feudalism, which were numerically weak and difficult to manœuvre. On the other hand, owing to a remarkable development the Prussian army of 1870 was simultaneously both the most progressive and the most backward institution in Germany. Its backwardness lay in the fact that the Prussian army recruited its corps of officers chiefly from the feudal nobility of East Elbia, and that the Prussian military machine was the instrument with whose help the militaristic nobility repressed the masses. At the same time, however, since the Wars of Liberation of 1813-15, the Prussian General Staff had appropriated all the methods of modern bourgeois warfare which the French Revolution and Napoleon I had developed. The Prussian General Staff had an army recruited by universal conscription at its disposal, and under the highly gifted leadership of Moltke the German army employed a strategy of extermination, which had nothing in common with the methodical slowness of the eighteenth century.

On the German side the war of 1870 was a struggle for national unification. The German liberal bourgeoisie was united in its support of Bismarck and carried the great mass of the people with it. In 1793 the armies of the European monarchs were so weak that the French popular militia was able to fight all of Europe simultaneously. Furthermore the monarchist troops were so slow and difficult to manœuvre that the French army was able to gain time in order to learn the art of war gradually. In contrast to this, in 1870-1 the Germans had an army of millions, based upon universal conscription, and the German command was so energetic that the French had no time to organize a new army. The Ger-

man soldiers who fought in the battles of the winter of
1870–1 had a background of military training with an average duration of three years, while that of the French soldiers
was only three months. The German army had trained professional officers, while the French army had improvised,
newly appointed officers.

When two armies of such an unequal nature confronted
each other, the outcome was a foregone conclusion. The
French recruits, whom Gambetta sent into the field in the
name of the Republic, certainly had the best of intentions
and were filled with honest patriotic enthusiasm. During
the winter battles the young French soldiers attacked with
great determination on the first day, but on the following
days they simply had no power in their loose-knit formations
to withstand cold and fatigue. In all military history there
is actually no analogy to the winter campaign of 1870–1.
Even the World War of 1914–18 furnishes none. At the beginning of the last war every country sent only its trained soldiers into the field, and the deterioration of the armies
which resulted from the enlistment of poorly trained soldiers was fairly even in all the warring countries. Gambetta's defeat therefore does not prove at all that a militaristic
monarchy would be superior to a democratic republic in the
event of a war. The result of the war of 1870–1 was simply
the consequence of special conditions which existed for both
armies at that time.

In 1870 the French masses were certainly not capable of
judging the real situation soberly. The Parisian workers
joined the National Guard with great enthusiasm and hoped
that the Republic would repeat the wonder of 1793. As the
iron ring of the German siege forces closed around Paris and
the sorties of the besieged remained in vain, many workers
began to believe that the capitalistic government was inten-
tionally sabotaging the defence because it did not want the
Red Republic to be victorious. Actually, even if the greatest military genius had led the people of Paris then, he would

not have been able to avert disaster. However, the provisional government in Paris saw to it that the dissatisfaction of large groups of the population with the new rulers increased.

The development of the revolution once again made the question of municipal autonomy for Paris a matter of major importance. In 1848 the moderate republicans had immediately seized power in Paris in order to prevent a repetition of the Commune of 1792. In 1870 the members of the government acted in a similar manner. Actually it was not very wise for the new democratic Republic to deny the capital of the country its right to democratic self-government, particularly since the existence of the government depended on the armed Parisian workers, who manned the fortifications and resisted the Prussians. However, just because the power of the provisional government was restricted to the city of Paris for the present, it wanted to retain control and refused to tolerate any other authority. The conservative element predominated among the ministers who had remained in Paris. Either the Germans or Gambetta were in control outside. During the winter of 1870-1 the Paris government was the legal nucleus for a conservative capitalistic reconstruction of France.

If a democratic municipal government had been formed in Paris on the basis of free elections, it would have been composed of revolutionary workers or at least of Gambetta's followers. In case of conflicts the National Guard would have obeyed the municipal government and not the ministers. For all practical purposes Paris would have been a branch of Gambetta's government, and the ministers of Favre's group would have been isolated. This eventuality had to be prevented at all costs. The government appointed Ferry Mayor of Paris and prevented the establishment of a democratic commune. The radical Parisian workers and National Guards, who were again led by Blanqui, began to agitate for a commune. This was by no means an adventure or a slogan symbolic of socialism or anarchism; the Parisians simply demanded their democratic rights. Riots and demonstrations occurred within besieged Paris. The government helped itself by means of a cunning manœuvre. It held a plebiscite in Paris for the people to express their confidence or lack of confidence in the " government of national defence." In the interest of national defence the majority of the Parisians felt obliged to vote for the government. The result was that Favre and his friends obtained a vote of confidence from the people of Paris. Supported by the plebiscite, they continued to delay the formation of a democratic communal government and were able to proceed against the radical agitators. Blanqui was forced to leave Paris secretly.

In the course of January 1871 the military situation grew more and more hopeless for France. The armies in the field had been defeated and supplies in Paris were rapidly approaching their end. Nevertheless the question of war or peace had been removed from the sphere of objective judgment and had become a party and class question. Gambetta demanded the continuation of the war to the very last, and in this he was supported by the masses of the large cities. On the other hand the wealthy upper class demanded peace, for, once the war was ended, Gambetta's dictatorship and the arming of the working class could also be eliminated. At the end of January the rump government in Paris ceased fighting and concluded an armistice with Bismarck as the first step towards the negotiation of peace. In a strict sense the Favre government was not qualified to undertake such negotiations, for if Paris once capitulated, the members of the government who were present there would be prisoners and would have just as little right to speak for the rest of France as Napoleon had had at the surrender of Sedan, or Bazaine at the capitulation of Metz. The advantages which the wealthy classes in France derived from the non-existence of a democratically elected municipal government in Paris now became evident. Only because no independent municipal government existed alongside of Favre at the end of January 1871 could the Minister dare to declare in the name of France that the war was at an end.

Bismarck was clever enough to treat the ministers in Paris as apparently free men and not as prisoners of war. He formulated the conditions of the armistice in such a manner that the German army remained outside of Paris and did not enter the Parisian witches' cauldron. The armed National Guard of Paris was left to its own resources for the present. Gambetta, who was then in Bordeaux, did not recognize the armistice at first and attempted for a short time to carry on the war with the support of the revolutionary democratic movement and without any regard for the scrap of paper which Favre had signed. He was soon forced to recognize, however, that the mass of French peasants were tired of war and sacrifices and did not want to continue the hopeless struggle. Gambetta resigned, with the result that the conservative ministers in Paris were free to act as they pleased.

In February a National Assembly based upon general suffrage was elected in France. It was to convene in Bordeaux and decide upon peace or war. The German army of occupation did not interfere with the elections. The monarchist parties and the conservative republicans campaigned for peace. The bourgeois democrats led by Gambetta and the revolutionary workers wanted to continue the war. The result was that the elections gave a completely distorted picture of actual popular sentiment. The rural population and the provincial cities voted for the monarchists because they wanted peace. The result was that of 650 deputies about 400 were adherents of the Bourbons, partly friends of the older line and partly followers of the Orléans party. In addition there were 30 adherents of the Empire. The remainder consisted of republicans, some belonging to Favre's group and others following Gambetta. In Paris, almost without exception, only opponents of peace had been elected. The deputies from Paris presented a variegated group of radical republicans and socialists. Together with Gambetta and Rochefort, Paris had also elected Tolain, the co-founder of the International, as well as old Louis Blanc. Among the Paris deputies who belonged to Gambetta's faction was the young physician and district mayor Clemenceau.

The National Assembly in Bordeaux elected Thiers as Provisional President. Thiers formed a new government composed of monarchists and conservative republicans. Gambetta's party was entirely eliminated. The National Assembly declared itself in favour of an armistice and peace. Bismarck's conditions, which included the cession of Alsace-Lorraine besides the payment of an enormous indemnity, had been accepted. Until this sum had been completely paid, German troops would continue to occupy northern France. Thiers's government and the National Assembly moved to Versailles.

Thiers's next task was to disarm the workers of Paris, who as members of the National Guard were armed. The National Guard of Paris, which had developed in the course of the war, was actually a workers' militia consisting of more than a hundred thousand men and was liberally supplied with guns, cannon, and other war materials. The individual battalions of the National Guard had their councils, and these soldiers' deputies had formed a central body. Until now the conservative French government had prevented the rise of a democratically elected municipal government in Paris; now in its place a new institution, which completely made up for the lacking commune and which was even more dangerous for the ruling class, had developed in Paris. This was the Central Committee of the National Guard, the head of the Red army of Paris.

The siege had brought the entire economic life of Paris to a complete standstill. The unemployed had enlisted in the National Guard. The daily wage of the soldiers of the National Guard was a military form of unemployment relief. In certain respects, therefore, the Paris National Guard of 1871 corresponded socially to the national workshops of 1848. Both institutions were equally hated by the wealthy bourgeoisie. From the point of view of a conservative bourgeois like Thiers it is entirely comprehensible that he did not want to perpetuate the Red army of Paris. If all the military formations which the war had produced were demobilized in France, the conservative government saw no occasion to make an exception of the Paris National Guard. In March the decision had to be made whether the Parisian workers would surrender their weapons and return to the factories, which the return of peace would reopen, or whether they would utilize the accident of war and employ the existing Red army for a decisive battle with capitalism.

As soon as the Franco-German War broke out, the attitude of Marx and the International which he directed was very clear. If the details of diplomatic manœuvres were disregarded, there could be no doubt that as a whole this war was a product of Bonapartist adventurousness. The war would free the European working class and the democratic movement from the nightmare which had oppressed it for twenty-two years — from Napoleon Bonaparte and his system. Marx had not the slightest sympathy with Bismarck and his policy. Nevertheless, because of general considerations, he desired the victory of Germany and the downfall of Napoleon III. Accordingly he advised the German workers to support the national war and recommended that the French workers assist in overthrowing Napoleon.

Sedan and the proclamation of a Republic in Paris changed the situation. It was clear that the peace treaty would force the French people to pay for Napoleon's guilt, so that the chief consideration now was to make the peace terms as bearable as possible for France. Marx absolutely opposed the annexation of Alsace-Lorraine by Germany, for, in the first place, Germany would never be able to assimilate the two provinces, and, secondly, this blow would drive France into the arms of Russia. An alliance between France and

Russian tsarism, however, was an equally great misfortune, both for Germany and for the international working-class movement.

Therefore after Sedan, Marx advised the French workers to support the new republican government in its defensive struggle against the German invasion, while at the same time the German workers were to carry on propaganda favouring a moderate peace and opposing the annexation of Alsace-Lorraine. The English workers also expressed their sympathy for the French Republic, and Garibaldi, at the head of a group of Italian volunteers, came to the help of the French. In this way the last democratic party which remained from the period of 1848, the party of the Italian republicans, demonstrated its international solidarity. To be sure, all this had no great practical significance. Garibaldi too was unable to stop the triumphal march of the German armies. The propaganda of the German Social Democrats was suppressed by Bismarck's police, and the ruling English bourgeoisie saw no occasion for any active intervention in the liquidation of the Napoleonic bankruptcy. During the entire war Bismarck's foreign policy had been so clever that neither Russia nor England had any excuse for intervention.

The completely negative result of all efforts in the interest of the French Republic was certainly regrettable from the point of view of Marx and the International. Practically, however, there was no other course for the German and French workers than to declare mutually that they did not recognize the annexation of Alsace-Lorraine. A better solution of the Franco-German controversy would have to wait for a future and freer settlement by both nations. For the present the main thing was to end the war as soon as possible and to see to it that the German as well as the French workers strengthened and organized themselves under the new conditions. After Sedan, Marx and Engels knew very well that French military resistance was hopeless, and they deplored the illusions which were current among the French workers concerning the possibility of a revolutionary war of liberation. Early in September a French confidant of Marx went to Paris; his report was rather dismal. He wrote that anyone who told the truth would almost certainly " be torn apart," and even " the élite still live among the memories of 1792."

In view of the confusion and the illusions which were rampant among the workers in Paris, Marx and Engels were greatly worried that the proletariat of Paris would permit itself to be misused for adventures with incalculable consequences. As early as September 12, 1870 Engels wrote to Marx: " If anything at all could be done in Paris, it would have to be the prevention of any undertaking by the workers before the conclusion of peace. . . . Whatever the terms may be, peace must be concluded before the workers can do anything. If they should triumph now — in the service of national defence — they would have to accept Bonaparte's legacy; they would be suppressed in a useless struggle with the German armies and would be retarded by twenty years. They can lose nothing by waiting. Any possible boundary changes are only provisional and will again be reversed. It would be madness to fight for the bourgeoisie against the Prussians. . . . After peace is concluded all conditions will be more favourable for the workers than they were previously. But won't they allow themselves to be forced by the pressure of the foreign attack into proclaiming a social republic on the eve of the storming of Paris? It would be hideous if the last act of war were to be the struggle of the German armies against the French workers upon the barricades. It would throw us back about fifty years."

Marx absolutely shared Engels's fears. For many years these two men had shaped all their policies with an eye to this event, the downfall of Napoleon, and the new revolution in France which would follow was to be the first step in the upsurge of a new revolutionary wave in Europe. Now Bonaparte had been expelled, the Republic had triumphed in Paris, the existing social order in France, and all its institutions, were shaken most seriously, and the outlook for the social democratic movement was better than ever. It was also necessary, however, that the workers of Paris should follow judicious and intelligent leaders and not permit themselves to be misled into undertaking any premature actions. The French workers were completely justified in regarding the Thiers government as the beginning of a monarchist and capitalist counter-revolution. They felt that they would be exposed and defenceless before their worst enemies if they now surrendered their cannons and guns. Nevertheless sober consideration of the facts did not favour the idea of a workers' revolt in March.

At the moment the military forces at the disposal of Thiers were weak. They were the tired and demoralized remnants of the popular army in the provinces. If the Red army of Paris carried out an energetic surprise attack, it could quickly capture Versailles and disperse the monarchist National Assembly. It is very improbable that the provincial troops would have fired upon the Parisians in such a case. At this moment, however, the decisive factor was not Thiers, but Bismarck; not the remnants of the French militia, but the victorious German army corps. How would Bismarck react to a revolution of the French workers? The slightest incident would be sufficient excuse for the German army to drown the uprising of the French workers in their own blood; or Bismarck could permit the French conservative government to form a White guard, consisting of imperial officers and soldiers who were prisoners of war in Germany, for the purpose of suppressing the proletariat. At any rate the French workers should have delayed any action until the German troops had withdrawn from the country.

Besides that, however, the danger existed that the French workers would isolate themselves in March 1871 just as they had done in June 1848. In 1871 the question of class rule and the political constitution of the state mingled most unhappily with the problem of war or peace. The rural and provincial masses — that is, the great majority of Frenchmen — absolutely wanted peace. If the Parisian workers struck a blow now, the majority of the people might easily regard their action as a manœuvre to prolong the war. In addition the insurgents in Paris would carry the responsibility for having conjured up a civil war in war-torn France while the enemy was still within its borders. After all, how was the rural and provincial population to arrive at an objective opinion regarding the Parisian workers and their policies? Consequently a serious danger existed that the Parisian workers would isolate themselves just as in 1848, and that the masses of peasants and provincials would be forced to sympathize with the capitalists. With the French people in such a frame of mind, a victory for the Parisian workers was almost impossible.

The cause of proletarian democracy in France could only gain by waiting, for the National Assembly did not really represent the actual sentiment of the nation. The peasants had absolutely no interest in a return of the Bourbons. As soon as the German troops should have left France, the conflict between Parliament and the urban and rural masses would necessarily break out again, with the result that the Parisian workers would not have been isolated in a struggle for a democratic republic. As a political party they would have been able to combine with Gambetta's group. The history of the Commune proves that the Parisian workers did not even think of establishing socialism at that time. They were satisfied for the present with the foundation of a democratic republic of a bourgeois type, with a development of local self-government and complete self-expression for the masses. On this basis they would have been able to join forces with Gambetta's party without any more ado. At the moment Gambetta, as the advocate of war to the very end, was eliminated from the government. As soon as the peace controversy should be settled, however, Gambetta and his party would necessarily reappear in the foreground. Unlike 1848, this time bourgeois democracy was no castle in the air; thanks to the activity of Gambetta, it had become the typical patriotic party of France. At least Gambetta's party was the only existing organization through which the French peasants could express their faith in a democratic republic. If the later MacMahon crisis of the seventies is imagined, but coincident with the existence of an unconquered Parisian proletariat, then one can conceive of the political possibilities which then existed.

More than anything else the Parisian workers needed a capable and intelligently directed political party, to a certain extent a renewal of the Socialist Democratic Party of 1848, but without the mistakes which the latter had made. It has already been emphasized repeatedly that such a party did not exist in March 1871. The French section of the International contained a number of honest and intelligent men, but almost all of them were influenced by Proudhonist ideas. They had no desire for political power and were completely incapable of directing the proletariat of Paris. Through an unfortunate accident Blanqui had again been arrested outside of Paris. Thus his advice and his authority were lacking at a time when they would have been most necessary for the workers. An actual Blanquist party — that is, a systematically recruited mass organization — did not exist. The Red soldiers' deputies, who actually had power in Paris then, frequently called themselves Blanquists. This did not mean, however, that a definite party and its organization had obtained power, but only that the armed revolutionary workers called themselves " Blanquists " in order to have a political name of some kind. Actually it was just the revolutionary section of the Parisian proletariat, which had no political leadership of any kind. The old democratic movement had disappeared. A new one had not yet been formed. It now became evident that the attempt of Marx and the International to create a new democratic movement which

would be capable of fighting had not succeeded. This was
due first of all to the purely external, technical circumstance
that the International had not even come into contact with
the most important section of the French workers. In addition there was yet a second and more profound reason. In
Europe after 1848 the entire course of development had isolated particularly the politically active workers from the rest
of the masses. Consequently when the proletarian vanguard
needed contact with the slow peasant and petty-bourgeois
masses more than ever, this contact was missing. The result
was that the urban workers once again fought alone and
rushed to their destruction.

On March 18, 1871 the Thiers government ordered the
regular troops to remove the artillery of the National Guard.
The Central Committee was not prepared for this moment,
just as in general it had no definite policy during those decisive days. Nevertheless the people of Paris spontaneously
opposed the removal of their cannon. A revolt developed.
The government troops refused to fire on their brothers.
Now the National Guard had not only retained its cannon,
but was suddenly in possession of the capital. The government together with its officials and the remainder of its
troops evacuated Paris. The workers of Paris had been impelled to revolt by their feelings and their fighting will, since
no one whom they trusted had been capable of showing them
a political path. By virtue of this situation the Central Committee of the National Guard had become a revolutionary,
republican government in opposition to the disguised or
open monarchists of Versailles.

The misfortune had now occurred and one can imagine
with what feelings Marx in London received the news from
Paris. Now the least that could be done was to attempt to
enhance the success of the revolt as rapidly as possible. The
Central Committee would have to install a strong dictatorial
government in Paris immediately. Then all the forces of
the National Guard would have to be collected and dis-

patched against Versailles to disperse the monarchist National Assembly and to win over or disarm the vacillating government troops. Furthermore, the republican government in Paris should have definitely declared for peace, given pledges to Germany of its intention to fulfil the terms of the peace treaty, and quieted the French peasants by means of a moderate program. As his letters of that period prove, Marx would have considered a policy of this kind correct.

Nevertheless none of these necessary steps were taken. Above all, the government in Paris undertook no military offensive, although in the National Guard it had an organized, reliable, and well-armed Red army at its disposal, a fortunate circumstance such as but few popular revolutions enjoy. The military direction of the Paris revolt was wretched. No active steps were taken and the confusion in the military administration was so great that within the next few weeks most of the National Guard had become useless for any action. A small minority of armed workers fought heroically, but they could not avert disaster. In the midst of a desperate civil war the Central Committee of the National Guard had no other worries than to give the Parisians their fervently desired democratic municipal government. Instead of marching upon Versailles, the republican soldiers' government of Paris first announced elections for a municipal government!

The newly elected Paris Commune was composed of a majority who were advocates of armed revolt and were called Blanquists or Jacobins, and a minority consisting of representatives of the International. Those municipal deputies who were in sympathy with the bourgeois parties did not participate in the work of the Commune. The election of the Commune did not strengthen the political leadership; on the contrary, the coexistence of the civil Commune and the military Central Committee only served to increase the prevailing confusion. Without any leadership and without any plan the Paris revolt drifted towards its end. The most significant achievement of the Commune lies neither in its political not in its social acts; for the Commune did not take any measures which could be called socialistic. Their present task was actually only the defence of the bourgeois-democratic Republic and proletarian self-government. The greatness of the Commune resides rather in certain attempts, which were partly accidental and partly experimental, to find a new form of popular self-government on the European continent.

The government and its officials had left Paris. Consequently the insurgent workers had to help themselves. The army and the police of the state, as organizations existing apart from the people, had vanished. Their place was taken by an armed workers' militia. Until now the officials and judges of the state had been representatives of a centralized apparatus based upon force. They were now replaced by simple commissaries of the working people. The normal bourgeois-liberal state is characterized by a separation of powers; the legislative, the executive, and the judicial departments are separated strictly from each other. The purpose of this arrangement is to impose restrictions on parliament, since it is the chief representative of popular sentiment. The administrative and judicial apparatus must be as independent of parliament as possible so that the radical advances which arise among the electorate can be defeated by the resistance of the bureaucracy and the judges.

These relations were particularly evident in those countries of the European continent where the centralized apparatus was headed by a monarch. For example in France under Louis Philippe and Napoleon III the Parliament played a secondary role to the extremely powerful administrative machine. The Prussian Parliament was still weaker when compared with the royal government, and the same was true of the Austrian Parliament in its relation to the imperial government. In Italy a large centralized government machine had also developed since 1860, even though under somewhat different conditions. The reproach which has been and is still being hurled at parliaments, that they " palaver " but do not act, is only a popular, critical formulation of this division of powers. The Commune of Paris, on the other hand, by overcoming the centralized governmental machine, was both the legislative and the executive body. The communal representative body of Paris was divided into several commissions which took the place of the historical ministries.

In Paris all this had arisen more or less spontaneously or as the result of a natural development. At the same time, however, it corresponded to the ideals of the Proudhonists. The Proudhonist minority of the Commune made a virtue of necessity and induced the majority to pass decrees which were to contribute to the reduction of the traditional political order. The decrees of the Paris Commune represent a sketch of a future France in which every community enjoys complete self-government and where the army, police, bureaucracy, and judiciary are replaced by simple executive organs representing the working people. The old centralized national government was to be replaced by a federation of the self-governing urban and rural communities. Thus during the stormy weeks of the Commune the first, as yet unclear beginnings of a new type of democracy became evident. It was based upon the idea that a centralized state, maintained by force, is incompatible with self-government by the labouring masses. A social democracy cannot remain satisfied with simply taking possession of the existing governmental machine, but must destroy it. The new form of communal democracy which was attempted in Paris in 1871 exhibits astonishing analogies to the self-government of the mediæval free cities and of the small republics of antiquity.

All these new thoughts certainly did not help the Paris Commune in its desperate struggle against its foes. Paris remained isolated. Several attempts by workers in other cities to bring help to the Parisians and to extend the movement failed completely. An alliance directed against the Parisian workers was actually formed by the conservative French government and the new German Empire. In the district which they occupied, the Germans suppressed every movement which was in any way sympathetic to the Commune. The German troops helped to surround Paris and, at the request of Thiers, Bismarck even permitted the return of many French prisoners of war who had formerly belonged to the old imperial army.

Since the Commune was completely helpless in military matters and without initiative, the government army constantly grew larger. Marshal MacMahon, one of the few remaining imperial generals, who still retained a great deal of authority, became the commander-in-chief of the government forces. It is apparent that the so-called republican government of France employed the imperial military machine in order to render the workers of Paris and the real republicans innocuous. A true slaughter was organized among the insurgents and even among the non-combatant population. The number of dead in Paris amounted to at least twenty thousand. In addition thousands of Parisian workers were thrown into prisons and concentration camps or were forced to flee. The defeat of the Commune was accompanied by the physical destruction of the proletarian and republican vanguard of France. To find another example of such a horrible defeat of the working classes one must go back to the Peasant War of 1525.

For Marx the defeat of the Paris Commune meant the end of the revolutionary plans to which he had devoted his entire life. The initiative of the French workers was destroyed for at least a generation, just as Marx and Engels had predicted since September 1870. It meant that the outlook for proletarian democracy in the other European countries was hopeless for a long time to come. Marx was confronted by a serious decision. Personally he was not at all responsible

for the Paris Commune. From the very beginning he had
considered such a revolt as hopeless, and when the uprising
of the Parisian workers had become a fact, Marx, in his letters, had criticized their mistakes ruthlessly. The great majority of the members of the Commune had not even been
connected with the International, and the minority, because
of its Proudhonist opposition, had always made the work of
Marx more difficult.

Furthermore the Proudhonist position on the question of
the state, which the Commune had accepted, differed completely from that of Marx. To be sure, Marx also regarded
the state as the repressive apparatus of the ruling class, and
he also hoped that at some future time, while evolving
towards communism, the repressive state would "wither
away" and would be transformed into a free association of
producers. However, in the event of a revolution the working class should not dissolve the centralized political apparatus of the state, but should rather employ it ruthlessly
for its own purpose. According to Marx, the first task of
the victorious proletariat was to form a strong, fighting, centralized government like that of Robespierre. Marx did not
consider such a "dictatorship of the proletariat" as a contrast to democracy, but rather as its armed consummation.
During the revolution the proletariat acts in the name of the
labouring masses — that is, the overwhelming majority
of the nation. Through discipline and the employment of
armed force democracy must first conquer its foes. The
"withering away" of the state can only occur during a much
later period.

In accordance with these ideas Marx would have wanted
the Central Committee of the National Guard to seize dictatorial power in Paris after the Revolution of March 18 and
to open an offensive against Versailles; for Marx at this moment the peaceful election in the midst of civil war and all
the experiments with decentralized self-government were
nothing more than Proudhonistic childishness. It would

therefore have been very easy for Marx to criticize the mistakes of the Commune publicly and to refuse any responsibility for the unfortunate events in Paris. But Marx was not so much concerned with maintaining the correctness of his ideas in public as with safeguarding the future of the movement. Despite their mistakes, in a more profound sense the revolutionary workers of Paris were Marx's party comrades; for by his " party " Marx did not mean any accidental society, but the great association of all the revolutionary fighters of all countries. To be sure, the heroic struggle of the Parisian workers irrevocably ended a very long period of democratic development in Europe, but now the main thing was to retain and to utilize the tradition of the Commune for future times.

Thus with the vivid impression of the White Terror of Paris still in mind, Marx, in the name of the International, wrote his famous pamphlet *The Civil War in France*. In it he suppresses completely every theoretical or tactical difference of opinion which he himself had had with the Communards. From beginning to end he approves the Commune, even with its experiments for the immediate dissolution of the centralized state, and presents it as a glowing example to the workers and revolutionaries of all countries. Theoretically this was a partial retreat of Marxism in the face of Proudhonism. For Marx, however, theoretical dogmatism was always unimportant in comparison with the great tasks of movement.

The work of Marx on the Civil War of 1871 has an extraordinary historical significance; for by this bold step Marx annexed the memory of the Commune. It is only since then that Marxism has possessed a revolutionary tradition in the eyes of mankind. By 1870 Marx had already acquired a reputation as an outstanding theoretician of the labour movement, but the general public knew nothing of the political and revolutionary activity of the Marxists. It is only since Marx's resolute public defence of the Commune in 1871, with which he drew upon himself the entire indignation of bourgeois society, that he achieved his aim of identifying his International and the Commune in the public mind. It is only since 1871 that Marxism has been clearly associated with the labour revolution. The Paris Commune as interpreted by Marx exerted an extraordinary influence on the development of Russia.

In this manner Marx provided an important tradition for the future movements of the working class, and he placed his own doctrines in the centre of these movements. At the same time, however, he saw clearly that the Workingmen's International, which had been founded in 1864, no longer had any right to exist. The basic political idea of Marx and Engels had been to establish, with the aid of the International, co-operation between the French and the English workers in accordance with the tradition of revolutionary democracy. Since the collapse of the Commune the French movement was destroyed. In the meantime the English workers had obtained the franchise. For the present, however, they were satisfied with this political victory and sought to carry it to its logical conclusion by making the position of the trade unions legally secure. On the other hand, the English workers showed no inclination to found an independent proletarian political party. After 1871 the relation of the English workers to the International became untenable. In the long run it was impossible for the same English trade-union leaders to defend the revolutionary Commune in their capacity as members of the International and at the same time to support the Liberal Party in England. During the same period the majority of the trade-union members even voted for the Conservatives!

Even though a split between the English unions and the International had become unavoidable, and at the same time the opposition of Bakunin and his anarchists was becoming unpleasantly conspicuous, nevertheless Marx and Engels would have been able to maintain the existence of the International. Even after separating from the English and the Bakuninists, Marx could still count upon all the German Social Democrats. Since the Commune he had also become the leader of the French émigrés. In addition, Marx also had followers in Austria, in Italy, and in the smaller European countries. He also had connexions in the United States and among the Russian émigrés. Marx was never afraid of a struggle within the International, and he never shrank from a split. Even during the seventies he would have been able to maintain an International which would have united the most important sections of the proletarian vanguard. But what would such an International have been able to accomplish? It would have held congresses, issued proclamations, distributed positions, and discussed the international trade interests of the workers. However, Marx did not want to work for an International of this kind. Owing to the changed situation in the world after 1871, the International could no longer be the driving force towards a new revolution. Therefore, as far as Marx was concerned, it was unnecessary.

All that Marx wanted now was to prevent the anarchists from obtaining the name and the authority of the International. Consequently, at the congress of the International in 1872, at The Hague, he inspired the strange resolution that the seat of the General Council be moved from London to New York. Even in the age of the steamship and the telegraph, it was impossible for the European labour movement to be directed from America. Besides, the American section of the International was very insignificant at that time. Marx believed, however, that in New York the General Council would be removed from the grasp of the anarchists. It was the interment of the International, and after 1872 it slowly expired.

The Paris Commune marks the end of the attempt of the working class to solve the tasks of the older revolutionary democratic movement independently. If Switzerland is disregarded, the democratic movement had been completely defeated in all of continental Europe by 1871. In France the monarchist National Assembly ruled in conjunction with the generals. Thiers was ousted from his post in 1873 and Marshal MacMahon became acting head of the state. He was generally considered as the man who would clear the way for a return of the Bourbons. In Germany it was apparent that Bismarck's Empire was not to be shaken in the near future. Within the Habsburg Empire the Hungarians had again obtained autonomy in 1867. Since then the Kingdom of Hungary had been ruled by an oligarchy of the nobility and the wealthy bourgeoisie. In this manner the Hungarian national movement had been completely diverted into the camp of reaction. After the pacification of the ruling class of Hungary, the power of the Habsburgs had also been reinforced in the Austrian half of the Empire. Through the acquisition of Venice and Rome, the national unification of Italy was now essentially completed. Political power was divided among the capitalists of the north, the feudal landlords of the south, the professional politicians, the bureaucrats, and the military. The broad masses were eliminated. Mazzini did not capitulate before the new order in Italy. He criticized the maladministration of the new Kingdom unrelentingly and carried on propaganda for a democratic republic. However, as a genuine representative of the democratic movement of 1848, he did not understand the new movement of the urban and rural Italian proletarians, who had no intention of keeping their hands off private property. Sincere and courageous, but at variance with all classes and isolated, Mazzini died in 1872. A whole period in the history of European democracy was buried with him. Since the defeat of the revolt of 1863–4 the Polish revolutionary movement was also at an end.

Thus since 1871 democracy, proletarian as well as bourgeois, had been eliminated as a vital political force on the European continent, with the exception of Switzerland. In the meantime, however, bourgeois democracy in the Anglo-Saxon countries had developed new forms.

10. *Bourgeois Democracy in America, England, and Switzerland*

In the United States approximately since 1815, Jefferson's Republican-Democratic Party had completely halted its struggle against financial capitalism. Since then this party had become the expression of the great national community (at least of all the white citizens) which existed in the United States. Amicable relations existed between the large landed slave-owners and the small farmers, as well as between the capitalists and the factory workers. To such a degree had American democracy lost all characteristics of a movement based upon social struggle. Nevertheless the American commonwealth retained its peculiar character, which differentiated it sharply from the European states.

In his *Capital*, in the chapter on the modern colonial system, Marx clearly presented the difference between American and European economy, at least as it existed until the sixties of the nineteenth century. Under " colonies " Marx comprehended a " virgin territory which is colonized by free emigrants." The underlying principle of such colonization is free land. Every healthy and energetic emigrant, even though he may have but little capital and few implements, can acquire a piece of uncultivated land in order to become an independent farmer through his own labour. The existence of free land simultaneously deprives the manufacturer of a so-called industrial reserve army. The masses of supernumerary wage workers who are always offering themselves to the employer, and who consequently depress the wages and the standard of living of the proletariat, are lacking here. In colonies with free land the manufacturer is forced to pay such high wages that he eliminates any inducement which would tend to make his workers exchange their work in a factory for the existence of the small independent farmer. As long as land is still available for the mass of the people, the industrial proletariat is automatically guaranteed a liberal and high standard of living.

It was this peculiar colonial economy that justified the existence of American democracy, even after 1815. The political franchise which the poor whites — that is, chiefly the workers — obtained in almost all the states of the Union after 1815 was no empty formality, for the colonial economy, based upon the principle of free land, conditioned the nature of American democracy. The existence of free land united capitalists and proletarians, large landowners and small farmers in a community of labour.

In the course of the nineteenth century this idyll of American democracy was first disturbed by the enormous growth of a slave-holding aristocracy in the Southern states. If the slave-barons had succeeded in seizing power in the Union, both the principle of free land and the democratic state would have been destroyed. This collapse of colonial democracy had to be prevented. In the mighty Civil War of the sixties the revived Republican Party, under the leadership of Lincoln, destroyed the slave-holding aristocracy and restored the principle of free land, with all its consequences, to its original importance.

Marx followed Lincoln's political work with the greatest sympathy. Nevertheless he saw clearly that this episode of colonial democracy in the United States was untenable in the long run. In *Capital* Marx emphasizes the fact that the American Civil War brought in its train a colossal national debt, accompanied by increased taxation, the rise of a financial aristocracy, the squandering of a huge part of the public domain on speculative companies for the exploitation of railroads and mines; in brief, the most rapid concentration of capital. " The great Republic has therefore ceased to be the promised land for the emigrating labourer! "

In the Introduction to the 1882 edition of the *Communist*

Manifesto, Marx and Engels likewise call attention to the economic and social changes which had taken place in America during the past decades. " The small independent farmers who are the backbone of the American political order succumb in ever increasing numbers to the competition of giant agricultural combines, while at the same time in the industrial regions a numerous proletariat is arising for the first time, coincident with a fabulous concentration of capital."

Marx and Engels predicted that the class compromise upon which colonial democracy rested would disappear in the United States and would be replaced by new and mighty class struggles of the workers and farmers against the capitalists. In fact free land disappeared in the United States around 1890. The resulting destruction of the economic and social basis of the older American democratic tradition led to the development of a new mass movement for social democracy after 1890. Under various guises this struggle for political and economic power between the labouring masses and monopoly capitalism has continued until the present.

Originally the conditions for colonial democracy had also existed in the great dominions, the self-governing transoceanic possessions of the British Empire, where virgin territories had likewise been opened up by white settlers. In Australia, however, unfavourable agrarian legislation, to which Marx had already called attention in his *Capital,* had made possible the early development of enormous estates, particularly in New South Wales and Queensland. Consequently around 1890 the working people were also forced to organize an independent Labour Party to fight the financial and landed capitalists. With that the class peace which characterizes colonial democracy was also broken, and a struggle for a new social form of democracy took its place. In Canada and New Zealand, where more favourable conditions existed, the period of free land and colonial democracy extended approximately until the World War.

Another form of bourgeois democracy, which differed from the original type of social democracy, developed in England after 1867. Marx had hoped that the granting of the franchise to the decisive groups of the English industrial workers would lead to the formation of a new political labour party. However, Marx and Engels were soon profoundly disappointed. In the election of 1868 all the Labour candidates were defeated, and when the English unions broke off their relations with the International after 1871, all hope for the revival of a modernized Chartist movement disappeared.

Until the World War the overwhelming majority of the English workers regarded the trade unions as their particular form of class organization, since the latter resolutely defended their trade interests. At the same time, however, the English workers were generally satisfied to elect the parliamentary candidates of the bourgeois parties. The bourgeois parties could depend upon the labour votes if they met the workers' demands half-way. In view of the decline of the Chartist Party, Engels had already intimated the possibility of such a development in 1858. He wrote that it appeared " as if the English proletariat is actually assuming bourgeois characteristics to an ever increasing degree; apparently this most bourgeois of all nations finally wishes to have a bourgeois aristocracy and a bourgeois proletariat besides the bourgeoisie itself. To a certain extent this is certainly justified in a nation which exploits the entire world! "

The class compromise upon which English bourgeois democracy rested could not be based upon free land, like the colonial democracy of America, since but few people owned landed property in England. Here the role of free land was taken to some extent by England's economic predominance. The extraordinary success of the English bourgeoisie in commerce, navigation, and colonial policy permitted the possibility of raising the standard of living of at least a part of the working class above the Continental level. Consequently at least this group of workers could assume bourgeois characteristics. The type of bourgeois democracy which England developed in the nineteenth century could therefore best be designated as imperialist democracy. The English Liberal Party, unable to cope with the problems of British world power which had thus become the basis of the political order, was necessarily doomed to impotence. (The causes underlying this situation will be discussed later.) The Conservative Party, which had been revived by Disraeli, became the actual bearer of imperialist democracy.

Disraeli developed his political theory of class compromise on the basis of British world power. In 1867, while Minister of a minority government, Disraeli passed the memorable electoral reform bill, which represents the first decisive step towards the attainment of political equality by the industrial workers. The elections of 1868 again returned a Liberal majority to the lower house, but at the same time, to the great astonishment of Marx and Engels, they clearly showed the advance of the Conservatives, particularly in the large cities. In 1874 Disraeli's Conservative Party obtained a majority in Parliament for the first time.

The meteoric career of the " Tory democrat " Randolph Churchill, and Joseph Chamberlain's entry into the Tory camp also occurred during Engels's lifetime. Nevertheless it is clear that Marx and Engels could not regard such a solution as final. They awaited the moment when the English workers would abandon the policy of class compromise and follow their own political path — that is, turn their backs on imperialist democracy and again fight for social democracy. In the Preface to the 1890 edition of the *Communist Manifesto* Engels proudly cites the declaration of the president of the English Trade Union Congress at Swansea in 1887; the latter had said: " Continental socialism has lost all its terrors for us! " Actually the development of the English working class in the direction of independent political action, such as Marx and Engels desired, proceeded at a much slower pace. For the present, at least, imperialist democracy was still stronger in England.

During the lifetime of Marx and Engels a third form of bourgeois democracy entrenched itself in Switzerland. The origins of the Swiss republics extended far back into the Middle Ages. A group of Swiss cantons, the so-called original cantons, had maintained a form of peasant democracy from the fourteenth to the nineteenth century; but this democratic peasant commonwealth had become completely inert and torpid. Since the sixteenth century it had lost all contact with the progressive forces of Europe, and these peasant communities were actually ruled by a few aristocratic families. During the seventeenth and eighteenth centuries a small group of patricians had also seized power in the other parts of Switzerland.

Between 1815 and 1848 the patrician-conservative groups in the Swiss cantons engaged in a struggle with the modern bourgeoisie for political control. In this struggle the privileged Catholic peasants of the original cantons supported the old order. On the other hand, the peasants of the other cantons had been deprived of their political rights and were the natural allies of the modern bourgeoisie. In Switzerland the labour movement was still in its beginnings; nevertheless in the French-speaking cantons the influence of French social democracy and of the various socialist schools of Paris was becoming noticeable. Following the example of the Revolution of 1830, the underprivileged masses also revolted in the most important cantons of Switzerland. The rule of the patricians collapsed and the leading cantons became bourgeois-democratic republics with general suffrage. Since the progressive bourgeois party depended on the help of the broad masses of peasants, it could not deny them the franchise. However, the patrician conservative party did not abandon hope as long as the resistance of the original cantons remained unbroken. In 1847 a civil war broke out. In this war of secession the larger modern cantons, Bern, Zur-

ich, and others, easily defeated the original cantons. Marx
and Engels unconditionally supported the modern bourgeois democrats of Switzerland and they sharply condemned
any romantic glorification of the original cantons, whose so-
called peasant democracy was only a cloak for fossilized sepa-
ratism and narrow-minded reaction.

After 1847 no further obstacle existed to prevent the development of Switzerland as a modern federal state. The
individual cantons first constituted themselves as bourgeois
parliamentary republics. After the sixties, however, important constitutional changes were carried out, first in the individual cantons, later also in the federation. Parliamentary
government was supplemented by the direct vote of all the
citizens, who alone decided on new legislation. Switzerland
remained outside of all the controversies of European politics and its army served only to defend its borders. While
the masses prospered under exceedingly peaceful conditions,
bourgeois democracy in Switzerland was able to consolidate
its position within the narrow borders of the cantons. During the lifetime of Marx and Engels the self-reliant and
wealthy middle class decided Swiss policies. The number of
industrial workers grew, but there was as yet no prospect
that they would seize power. Marx and Engels recognized
that Swiss institutions were suited to the limited space of
these rich and peaceful cantons. At the same time, however,
they cautioned against any mechanical transfer of Swiss political institutions to countries of a different type where a
strong proletariat existed.

11. The Decline of the Democratic Idea after 1871

After 1871 Switzerland alone among all the countries of the
European continent was in the fortunate situation of being
able to evaluate deliberately the various forms of bourgeois democracy. In all the other countries the broad
masses were restricted in their freedom of expression, dis-

couraged by defeats, and oppressed by powerful military or bureaucratic forces. The defeat of the working class in Europe was rendered graver by the fact that the masses had even lost the slogans and the aims for which former generations had fought. The nature of revolutionary democracy was no longer known and the significance of the " people " for the democratic movement had been forgotten. The European working man prior to 1848 resembled an illiterate, who knew that he could neither read nor write, but who at least wanted to eradicate these defects. After 1871, however, the masses could only be compared to an individual who can neither write nor read, but who hasn't even the slightest idea that such arts exist.

Not only the labouring masses but also the European ruling classes after 1871 had forgotten about revolutionary democracy. The English Liberal historian Justin M'Carthy, for instance, in his *History of Our Own Times,* the first four volumes of which appeared in 1879–80, speaks of Chartism with pitying superiority and takes this opportunity to express the following reflections: " We have in our time outlived the days of political abstractions. The catch-words which thrilled our forefathers with emotion on one side or the other fall with hardly any meaning on our ears. We smile at such phrases as ' the rights of man.' We hardly know what is meant by talking of ' the people ' as the words were used long ago when ' the people ' was understood to mean a vast mass of wronged persons who had no representation and were oppressed by privilege and the aristocracy."

However, M'Carthy informs his reader that these principles and catchwords which have now been superseded formerly meant something. " So it was with ' the people ' and ' the rights of the people ' and ' the rights of labour,' and all the other grandiloquent phrases which seem to us so empty and so meaningless now." An objective investigation of conditions on the European continent would certainly have proved that in 1882 the great majority of the working class was probably just as unemancipated, oppressed, and exploited as in 1848. The demands of 1848 had not become empty and unnecessary phrases, but people, at least outside of Russia, no longer took them seriously.

In 1882 Friedrich Engels published the first German edition of his famous book *Socialism — Utopian and Scientific*. Even though Engels diverges greatly in his political and historical judgments from the opinions current among the liberal bourgeoisie, yet he agrees with liberalism in disparaging the historical role of revolutionary democracy. Engels derives the fundamental ideas of modern socialism from the eighteenth-century French philosophers of the Enlightenment, then from the classical German philosophers of the nineteenth century, and finally from the great utopian socialists. According to Engels, the concrete facts upon which modern socialism arose were furnished by the development of industrial capitalism. All this is correct as far as it goes, but at the same time it is one-sided, because Engels does not do justice to the historical role of revolutionary democracy.

In this work Engels presents an exceedingly clear and striking characterization of Robespierre's period. " If the conflicts arising from the new social order were first engaged in the process of development, the means for their solution were even more immature. If the poor masses of Paris had been able to seize power momentarily, during the Terror, and to lead the bourgeois revolution to victory, even against the bourgeoisie itself, they would only have proved how impossible it was for them to establish a permanent government under the conditions of the period. The proletariat, which was just about to separate itself from these poor masses and to found a new class, was completely incapable of any independent political action and exhibited itself as an oppressed suffering group, which, due to its inability to help itself, could only be aided condescendingly by members of other classes."

In this passage Engels has presented with his usual mastery the weakness of the movement of 1793 and the causes of its rapid defeat. Nevertheless the fact that the poor masses had been able to seize power, even if only for a historic moment, in France during 1793–4, was enormously important. The entire subsequent history of all the popular European movements has been influenced by this "moment." In 1882, when Engels wrote his book, he himself was still the same revolutionary democrat that he had been from 1848 to 1871, but now he underrated the historic achievements of the so-called Reign of Terror as well as of the Revolution of 1848. His glance was directed towards the future, towards the coming socialist revolution, which the proletariat, trained by the doctrines of Marx, would carry out. In 1882 Engels considered it unnecessary to demonstrate the historical bond which united his own socialist movement with the democratic past, since there were no longer any social classes anywhere in Europe, with the exception of Russia, which could have been moved by an appeal to the traditions of revolutionary democracy. Engels was convinced that the future of the working man was indissolubly tied up with the rise of a socialistic proletariat. The other oppressed social groups, the small peasants, the urban middle class, and so on, could do nothing else except join the proletarian movement. In 1882, therefore, historic revolutionary democracy appeared just as dead to Engels as it did to the above cited Liberal English historian.

In May 1917, with the vivid impression of the Russian Revolution still in mind, the great French historian Mathiez published an article on " Babeuf and Robespierre." In it he discusses the criticism of Robespierre by subsequent generations in France and establishes the fact that until 1870 all revolutionary democrats and socialists regarded him as their prototype. " It was only during our time, with the loss of the revolutionary tradition, chiefly after 1870 and coincident with the invasion of Marxism, that the French democrats and socialists, or at least some of them, allowed themselves to be misled by propagandist claims of a political rather than historical nature, with the result that they no longer understood Robespierre, whom their predecessors had admired. It is remarkable, however, that this tradition remained alive abroad, especially in countries where the study of our Revolution served as a means towards their own liberation."

In the last sentence Mathiez apparently was thinking of Russia, where the revolutionary parties had always been based upon the example of 1793. It is absolutely true that in France itself an unbroken revolutionary tradition existed only from 1789 to 1871. The fall of the Commune was also the end of revolutionary democracy. As soon as this political movement ceased to lead a concrete existence, the political and historical writers found it difficult to comprehend it. The politicians of the French burgeoisie regarded the Commune as an atrocity. The workers, to be sure, honoured the memory of the Communards as their class comrades, but when the French labour movement again revived around 1880, it no longer carried on the tradition of the past. Because Robespierre and his friends belonged neither to the bourgeoisie nor to the socialist proletariat, in the strict Marxist sense of the term, it became very difficult to understand the party of the Mountain after 1871. Mathiez was able to restore the historical memory of Robespierre only because he himself in his own person carried on the ideas of the revolutionary democratic tradition. Nevertheless for French politics and society as a whole the fact remained that as a living movement revolutionary democracy had come to an end in 1871.

During the same period the Chartist tradition had been completely forgotten in England. Similarly after 1871 the history of the Revolution of 1848 appeared like news from a strange world to the inhabitants of the German Empire. The German bourgeoisie, the intellectuals, and the middle class had long since abandoned their revolutionary feelings.

At best the national aspect of the movement of 1848 was still recognized; with inadequate means and without success the men of 1848 had aimed at the same goal which Bismarck had subsequently attained in such a glorious manner. The developments in Baden and the Palatinate are typical of the change in German public opinion. They had been the scene of the republican revolt of 1849 and the greatest strongholds of the old German democratic tradition. After 1871 the National Liberal Party, the representative of the bourgeoisie, which was loyal to Bismarck, had a definite majority in both states. In both Baden and the Palatinate the National Liberals were not opposed by the radicals of the Left but by the Centre, the party of the Catholic peasants and petty bourgeoisie. To be sure, the Berlin workers honoured the memory of the March dead, the barricade fighters who had fallen on March 18, 1848, in the same manner as the Parisian proletarians kept alive the memory of the Commune. Nevertheless the socialist workers of the German Empire had no vital connexion with 1848 and consequently the example of that revolution could teach them nothing concerning the present. In Italy and Hungary the tradition of 1848 remained alive even after 1871, but it was only the national side of the revolution, which continued to exist in the cults of Garibaldi or Kossuth, and not the democratic aspect.

The decline of the historic democratic movement in Europe was accompanied by a change in the opinion of general suffrage. Until 1848 its friends as well as its foes had taken general suffrage very seriously. It was considered as absolutely self-evident that the acquisition of general suffrage would initiate the unrestricted political and economic rule of the broad masses. In this connexion it is only necessary to recall the determination and the vehemence with which the struggles for the franchise were conducted in England and France before 1848. Yet experience with general suffrage in Europe after 1848 apparently disproved these beliefs. Especially in France the radical workers were unable to forget that the June struggles of 1848 as well as the suppression of the Commune of 1871 had taken place with the approval of an assembly elected by general suffrage. Napoleon III had employed general suffrage in order to bestow a semblance of popular approval on his shady Empire. In 1867 Bismarck had introduced general suffrage for the Reichstag of the North German Confederation, and in 1871 for the new German Empire. From the point of view of the revolutionary labour movement the results were extremely wretched. The German people continued to present Reich-Chancellor Bismarck with the majorities which he desired. As far as any larger opposition parties existed in the German Reichstag, they represented the interests of the liberal capitalists or of the Catholic petty bourgeoisie.

Now general suffrage no longer appeared to be such a menace to the monarchies and the wealthy upper classes. On the other hand, the radical labour groups doubted that it would ever be possible to defend the true interests of the working people with the help of general suffrage. In so far as democracy and general suffrage were considered as necessarily associated factors, this period marks the beginning of a shallow, vapid interpretation of the concept of democracy, accompanied by its decline, which has continued up to the present. Democracy was no longer regarded as active self-government by the labouring masses for the purpose of effecting their political and social emancipation, but only as a capitalistic form of political organization, which is characterized by the existence of a parliament elected by general suffrage, but which otherwise has no positive value for the masses.

Anyone who judges the historical facts of the nineteenth century objectively must undoubtedly come to the conclusion that the social significance of general suffrage was greatly exaggerated before 1848 and just as greatly underrated afterwards. The temptation to consider general suffrage as something which would automatically work wonders was too great to be resisted. When the miracles failed to materialize, as is easily understood, the entire arrangement fell into discredit. Actually general suffrage cannot work wonders, but can only function within the limits permitted by the social structure existing in a country. If a completely ignorant group of people, unable to read or write, having no understanding of political concepts, and kept in a state of ideologic and economic subjection, suddenly receives the franchise, it is incapable of deriving any advantage from it. In this connexion we need only recall the sorry abuse of the Negro's franchise in the United States after the emancipation of the slaves. For this very reason the question of the franchise was of minor importance in countries like Spain and Italy, on the Balkan Peninsula, and in South America during the nineteenth and twentieth centuries. The ignorant and dependent rural and provincial masses voted just as their rulers desired anyway. In such countries the granting of general suffrage is followed at best, if the elections are free, by the victories of a few workers' deputies or representatives of the progressive bourgeoisie in a few large cities and industrial regions. Otherwise nothing changes in the social structure of the country as long as the masses are unawakened by a social revolution.

General suffrage has just as little value in more developed countries if the government is in a position to falsify the election results at will or to nullify the propaganda of the opposition by means of police suppression. France under Napoleon III furnishes the classic example of such employment of general suffrage. Finally, even in a country with a well-educated population and with free elections, general suffrage is of no great value if decisive forces in the public life of the country are independent of parliament. In the German Empire after 1871, for example, the King of Prussia, supported by his army and his officials, was much more powerful than the German Reichstag. Where such obstacles do not exist, general suffrage is the inevitable instrument by means of which the labouring masses exercise their political rights.

12. Socialists and Anarchists after 1871

After 1871 the number of workers in Europe who were determined to work for the emancipation of their class was relatively small. In addition, this small group of workers was convulsed by violent internal struggles. On the one hand were the followers of Bakunin's ideas. They rejected all party politics of the usual type and any participation in parliamentary elections. On the other hand were the friends of an independent political labour party, whose chief aim was to gain a footing in parliament and to present the grievances of the workers there. Marx had actually disrupted the International because he was not interested in being the leader of small, weak labour parties which were incapable of carrying out a revolution. However, the dissolution of the International did not end the struggle between the Bakuninists and the so-called Marxists. While the anarchists who followed Bakunin attacked Marx vehemently, the small political labour parties continued to support Marx and Engels. Thus even after the end of the first International a certain community of interests continued to exist between Marx and the political labour parties.

The German Social Democratic Party was the relatively strongest labour party of that period. In 1875 the Lassalleans had finally combined with Liebknecht's followers. In the Reichstag elections of 1877 the German Social Democratic Party won 12 seats out of a total of 397. This was little enough in view of the existence of general suffrage in an already strongly industrialized Germany. Yet the German Social Democratic Party was far stronger than the corresponding movements in Austria, Italy, France, and the smaller states. It is clear that in view of such an unequal distribution of power the European labour parties could not think of a revolution, but were satisfied to increase their membership by means of legal propaganda, enter parliament, and obtain economic improvements for the workers.

Nevertheless this peaceful, modest work for the trade interests of the workers did not satisfy a small number of men, who were scattered all over Europe and in whom the memory of the revolutionary past remained alive. They sympathized with the oppressed European masses and they felt that they had been betrayed by the political parties. Everywhere their hatred was directed especially at the legal social-democratic parties. As so often happens in political psychology, they confounded cause and effect and reproached the social democrats for the weakness of the labour movement and the unfavourable times. These impassioned radicals declared that the legal labour parties were no more than election machines. The workers are deceived so that a few leaders may occupy seats in parliament and make political and private deals with the ruling class. Not parliamentary elections but revolutionary deeds are necessary.

The isolated fanatics of revolutionary action found that a group possessing leaders who theorized, newspapers, and so on, and which shared their aversion to the social democrats and legal parliamentary work, already existed. These were the anarchists, the disciples of Bakunin. In general the wild advocates of action knew little about theory, but they joined the anarchist groups and persuaded themselves that the anarchist *Weltanschauung* was their own. Anarchism as a method of social criticism had nothing to do with bomb-throwing and terrorism. Still the political assassinations which occurred in Germany, France, Italy, America, and other countries during the last third of the nineteenth century, were the work of men who called themselves anarchists. Ever since terrorist social revolutionaries entered into the anarchist societies, an extremely biased picture of anarchism has been established in the public mind.

The completely purposeless, individual terrorist acts which were performed by so-called anarchists, had no political success. The masses detested these methods, and the governments used the anarchist deeds as an excuse to persecute the entire labour movement. Thus two anarchist attempts to murder Emperor Wilhelm I in 1878 furnished Bismarck with a pretext for the introduction of his laws against the German Social Democratic Party. The most important indirect effect of the anarchist terroristic acts, however, was the widening of the gap between the anarchists and the adherents of the political labour parties. In their opposition to the methods of bomb-throwing and assassination the social democrats attached themselves even more zealously to parliamentary and legal activity. The justified rejection of such acts of terror produced a feeling among the social-democratic workers that any employment of violence in a political struggle is absolutely to be rejected. Participation in parliamentary elections became the symbol of exclusively peaceful tactics, which promised success only within the bounds of the law. Thus as a result of the impassioned defensive struggle against anarchism the labour parties were trained in a completely anti-revolutionary spirit.

As a result of the conflict between the legal labour parties and the terroristic anarchists, Marx and Engels were placed in a strange situation. Both men were absolutely opponents of anarchism, of genuine anarchism with its repudiation of political action as well as of pseudo-anarchism with its bombs. Marx advocated a great popular revolution, but he considered isolated assassinations as serving no purpose. Besides, the work which Marx and Engels had performed within the International had been criticized uninterruptedly and not very objectively at times by the anarchists. The legal labour parties, on the other hand, stood by Marx and Engels and affirmed that they wanted to transform their ideas into reality. Marx and Engels absolutely approved of the participation of the workers in parliamentary elections.

They were in agreement with all reforms intended to improve the conditions of the working class. In this manner, even after the dissolution of the International, Marx and Engels were forced into a united front with the legal labour parties.

Under these circumstances it was a simple matter to overlook the profound differences which existed between Marx and Engels and the German Social Democratic Party. Until their deaths Marx and Engels were primarily revolutionaries. To be sure, they did not attempt to force the workers into adventurous undertakings, but their judgment of a political situation was based only upon the revolutionary possibilities which it offered. The conception of a revolution as a practical political possibility was gradually forgotten by the Continental labour parties. They were concerned only with daily, legal activities. The idea of a socialist state vanished into a nebulous future. For the European socialists, participation in the daily struggles of the workers against the employers, emphasis on the specific class position of the proletariat, participation in parliamentary elections, and rejection of false anarchist doctrines were considered identical with "Marxism." Until his death in 1883 Marx severely felt the lack of a revolutionary purpose in the labour parties, and he never ceased his pitiless and trenchant criticism of both the theories and the practice of these labour parties. Yet the union between Marx and the labour parties for the purpose of fighting anarchism remained a fact. Later, during the period of the Second International, this convergence of Marxism and the labour parties of the European workers became a fact of extraordinary historical importance.

13. *Reaction in Europe after 1871*

During the period from 1871 to 1889 the conservative forces, the defenders of property and authority, retained power almost everywhere in Europe. The old centre of power of the

European counter-revolution, Russian tsarism, was joined by a new and even stronger power, the German Empire. After 1871 the house of Habsburg no longer occupied the major European position which it had during the age of Metternich. Nevertheless, despite the defeats of 1859 and 1866, the Austrian Empire under Franz Joseph also succeeded in re-establishing a firm authority. Next to St. Petersburg and Berlin, Vienna remained the third great centre of conservative Europe. In Italy the dream of the patriots and the revolutionaries, national unification, had indeed been essentially realized since 1871, but the consequent centralization of the political power of the state certainly brought no advantages for the Italian labouring masses. Above all, the distressed condition of the rural population did not change under the ministers of the Italian Kingdom, but remained essentially the same as under the government of the Kingdom of Naples and of the Papal States. In France the Third Republic was characterized by the horrible massacre of the Paris workers in 1871. Even after the French bourgeois republicans, as a result of strenuous struggles, had succeeded in removing.the danger of a Bonapartist restoration, first under MacMahon and later under Boulanger, the Republic still remained weak and the condition of the labouring masses depressed. Similarly during the period from 1871 to 1889 self-government by the working people could not be achieved in a single one of the smaller European states, with the exception of Switzerland.

Under the new Empire Germany was industrialized with extraordinary rapidity. In former historical periods every development of industry, and of urban economy in general, had simultaneously increased the political power of the bourgeoisie and repressed the influence of the feudal elements. For the period after 1871 this principle, at least in its simple form, no longer holds true. The reasons for this extraordinarily significant historical change will be discussed in greater detail below. Bismarck founded his German Empire on a compromise between the Prussian feudal nobility, the ruling houses of the smaller federal states, and the liberal bourgeoisie. The overwhelming majority of the German bourgeoisie approved of Bismarck's Constitution and his governmental system. At the same time the German bourgeoisie lacked even the most modest parliamentary rights. The King of Prussia commanded the army and the mighty Prussian administrative apparatus and also ruled the Reich in agreement with the minor princes of the federation. The Reichstag was just as incapable of overthrowing the Reich government by a vote of non-confidence as the Prussian Diet was of displacing the Prussian government. Nevertheless the German bourgeoisie was generally satisfied with these conditions, as long as Bismarck personified the national greatness of Germany, secured a leading position in the world for the new Empire, and fulfilled the wishes of the bourgeoisie in all economic and practical questions. The liberal opposition to Bismarck's partially absolutist methods remained extremely weak.

The strongest party which opposed Bismarck was the Centre, composed of the various separatist and Catholic opponents of Prussian centralism. The Centre Party was supported by the Catholic peasants of western and southern Germany, by the anti-Prussian families of the old German aristocracy, and by the Christian workers' societies. Yet neither the Centre Party nor the Left liberals would have been ready for a struggle with Bismarck for the principles of revolutionary democracy. In the Protestant sections of Germany the peasants and the petty bourgeoisie voted either for the conservatives or for the liberals, and even among the workers the Social Democratic Party made but slow progress.

Under these conditions even the outlook for the success of bourgeois democracy was extremely slight in Bismarck's Germany. Still the small Social Democratic Party was an unpleasant and disturbing factor for the Chancellor. Bismarck had followed the revolt of the Paris Commune with the greatest interest. This was followed by the rise of a revolutionary wave in Russia. Consequently when anarchist acts occurred in Germany, Bismarck considered it possible that the waves of social revolution from east and west might also sweep over Germany. He therefore wanted to nip any socialist or anarchist movement in the bud by enacting repressive legislation. Furthermore, Bismarck did not desire the existence of a larger German labour party for reasons arising out of his own political tactics. The opposition of the Centre Party and the Left liberals was not dangerous for Bismarck as long as those groups remained isolated. If in addition to them a great democratic labour party developed as a third factor, however, the resulting opposition bloc could easily unite the majority of the German people. By destroying the Social Democratic Party, Bismarck wanted to anticipate any such development. At first the Socialist Law of 1878 made any public activity of the Social Democratic Party impossible in Germany and hindered its growth. However, the coherence of the Social Democratic workers in the factories was already so great that no police persecution could disrupt it.

The Habsburg Empire, comprising the great unified economic region of the Danube basin, was able to consolidate itself anew after 1871. The development of capitalism, which could be observed in almost all of Europe during this period, also became noticeable in the Danubian countries. Modern large industry and banking capitalism developed chiefly in Bohemia, in Vienna, and in Budapest. After 1867 the Habsburg Empire split into two independent states, Austria and Hungary, which were held together by a common ruler, army, foreign and tariff policies. In addition the interests of the aristocracy at court as well as the desire of the capitalists to maintain a united state proved to be connecting links between the divisions of the Empire.

In the Kingdom of Hungary the landed nobility and the bourgeoisie had political power. The labouring masses were excluded from the franchise. Although the Slavs and Rumanians who lived in Hungary comprised almost one half of the entire population, they were ruthlessly hindered in their natural development. The ruling oligarchy very skilfully utilized the ancient organization of the Diet, which had been retained since the Middle Ages. Depending on the situation, the ruling class could employ its machine against the King in Vienna or the labouring masses at home. Hungary would have been able to furnish an ideal spot for a democratic revolution if it had been possible to unite the forces of the rural and urban proletariat with those of the suppressed nations. However, as a result of the weakness and the division of the democratic forces within the country, the ruling class succeeded in maintaining its absolute authority until the World War.

In the Austrian half of the Empire the wealthy bourgeoisie was generally German. The aristocracy, however, contained Czech and Polish families besides the Germans. While oligarchic self-government in Hungary again had a free hand after 1867, an imperial bureaucracy ruled in Austria. Consequently a conflict of interests existed here between the liberal bourgeoisie, which desired a parliament after 1867, and the bureaucratic-aristocratic forces. Since Austrian liberalism in general represented the Germans, the Catholic conservative party, on the other hand, sought to encourage the Slavic peoples. The Polish nobility in Galicia was happy to find at least a minimum of cultural and linguistic independence within the Habsburg Empire and zealously supported the conservative party. At first the Czech national movement was also conservative and loyal to the Emperor. In Austria until 1879 German liberalism was generally in control; then the important conservative Prime Minister Taaffe obtained power. Taaffe attempted to replace the predominance of the Germans and bourgeois liberalism by another system, which aimed to achieve a compromise between the various classes and nations. The bureaucracy and the nobility should be the leaders of the state. At the same time

Taaffe also advanced the economic interests of the bourgeoisie and met the justified desires of the non-German nations. Until 1889 the popular and democratic forces in Austria were just as weak as in Hungary. The workers had no franchise and were repressed by the police. Nowhere were the poor rural masses organized for a struggle against the landowners.

Italy, of all the major European powers, made the slightest economic and political progress. The fact that the modern bourgeois northern part of the country was joined to the completely backward central and southern sections of Italy proved to be fateful for the new Kingdom. The north would only have been able to maintain its rule if at the same time a great social revolution had swept away the large landowners and the local cliques of the south and raised the dull rural masses to the level of citizens. Nevertheless a revolution of this type, which Mazzini had already envisioned to a certain extent, could never have been carried out by the capitalist bourgeoisie of northern Italy, united as it was with the dynasty, the bureaucracy, and the officers of Piedmont. The result was that during the seventies the southern reactionaries were already able to assert their predominance over the modern north. To be sure, the southern politicians also paid lip-service to Italian unity and the parliamentary state and called themselves " liberal " or " radical," depending on circumstances. However, in Italy, as in many other modern countries, party names are rather unimportant, and frequently their only purpose was to disguise the actual social forces. With the help of the officials, the landowners, and the local politicians, the party, which ruled in Italy after the end of the seventies, manipulated the elections in accordance with the best Bonapartist traditions. The income of the state was used to advance local interests. The power of the landlords was maintained at all costs. Attempts at revolt by the wretched rural masses were ruthlessly suppressed. Under such circumstances it was impossible for the state to encourage modern industry. Italy remained technically backward, and even its military organization was not capable of meeting any serious test. Opposition to the general incompetence and maladministration prevailed particularly among the academic youth, among whom the traditions of Garibaldi and Mazzini continued to survive. These groups dreamed of a stronger and better Italy and of the liberation of their "unredeemed brothers" in Trieste and the Trentino, who were still under the rule of Austria. Under these conditions the opposition of the working class was very weak. The most outstanding representative of the ruling system was the Prime Minister Crispi. In internal politics Crispi's group represented the predominance of the southern politicians and their backers, together with the brutal suppression of any opposition, while in foreign affairs it supported Bismarck and, in contrast to all Italian national traditions, even joined forces with Austria in the Triple Alliance.

During the seventies Spain passed through a period of confusion and civil war. Various factions of the clerical and feudal monarchists fought for power against the bourgeois republicans. Ultimately the historic Catholic, feudal monarchy was re-established. Attempts at revolt by the rural masses, influenced to some extent by anarchist slogans, were suppressed. The monarchy in neighbouring Portugal maintained a similar conservative character. In Holland and Belgium the wealthy bourgeoisie in alliance with the monarchy retained power during the entire latter part of the nineteenth century and refused any political concessions to the poor masses.

The political development of the Scandinavian countries during the second half of the nineteenth century varied greatly. In Sweden the old Constitution with its Diet was transformed without any serious crises into a liberal, parliamentary state, while the crown retained a decisive position as the mediator between the classes and parties. In Denmark, on the other hand, serious constitutional conflicts developed after 1870 and lasted for many years. The crown, supported by the bureaucracy and the upper classes, resisted the advance of the broad masses, who desired the development of a parliamentary democracy. However, the most intense struggles occurred in Norway. The Norwegian bourgeoisie and peasants fought for national independence against the foreign Swedish dynasty, which the Congress of Vienna had forced upon them in 1815. During the eighties the King was compelled to accept a parliamentary government. Gradually a new and vital liberal democratic movement developed in which the bourgeois-radical party was able to represent the nation and at the same time to mobilize the forces of the peasants and later also of the workers. Marx and Engels paid little attention to events in Norway, which were entirely outside of the decisive centres of social activity.

During the last years of his life Mazzini, having reviewed conditions in Europe in order to find a place where the national and democratic revolutionary movement could experience a revival, concentrated his hopes on the Balkans. Around 1871 it appeared as if all the conditions for a great national revolution were present there. In one form or another the Christian people of the Balkan Peninsula were still under the heel of Turkish feudalism. Only some of the Greeks had achieved an independent political existence in their small kingdom. Until 1878 all the Bulgars lived under Turkish rule. Some of the Serbs were directly subject to the Sultan, while others lived in the principality of Serbia, a Turkish vassal state. Rumania was likewise a Turkish vassal principality until 1878. In Rumania the native aristocracy, together with the princes, ruled the dependent peasants. The Serbian princes and their officials likewise denied their peasant and petty-bourgeois subjects any freedom of expression. In the Turkish provinces the Slavic population was terribly exploited and mistreated in every way. The South Slavs, who belonged to the Habsburg monarchy, lived at least in a civilized state, but they too lacked any possibility of an independent political existence.

Consequently the South Slavic patriots, who wanted to reawaken their people and improve their condition, had to contend with three opponents: with the Turkish Empire, the Habsburg monarchy, and last but not least the bureaucrats of their own principality of Serbia. During the sixties South Slavic students came into contact with the European progressive movement in Switzerland and also in other foreign countries. The connexion with the Italian revolutionary movement, which adhered to Mazzini's ideas, became especially important. The Greater Serbian Youth Organization, the Omladina, which arose during the sixties, wanted to emulate Garibaldi's example in the Balkans. The young Serbian intellectuals hoped that they would be able to become the leaders of the oppressed peasants and artisans, expel the foreign rulers and their own Serbian bureaucrats, and then establish a great South Slavic democratic nation. Ideas of peasant co-operative socialism were also prevalent in the Omladina.

The seventies brought the revolts of the rural Slavic population of Bosnia and Bulgaria against the Turkish rulers. They led to the Russo-Turkish War of 1877, and to a rearrangement of the Balkans at the Congress of Berlin in 1878. The Congress of Berlin and the events which followed were successes for the Balkan nations. The principality of Bulgaria was created, Serbia and Greece were enlarged, and Rumania and Serbia became independent. The inhabitants of Bosnia were likewise delivered from Turkish rule and were placed under the control of Austria. The greatest evil which the Congress of Berlin left unchanged was the maintenance of Turkish rule in Macedonia. The result was that the predominantly Bulgarian population of the country remained in its old misery, while all the efforts of the national Bulgarian Revolutionary Party in Macedonia were of no avail until 1912.

Before the World War only the most modest beginnings of a modern capitalistic bourgeoisie existed in the Balkan countries. A feudal Christian aristocracy was present only in Rumania. Apparently, then, no obstacle should have hindered the development of popular constitutions and typical democratic peasant states in Serbia, Bulgaria, and Greece. The educated patriotic youth might have been able to lead the broad masses. It would have been the common task of the Christian Balkan nations to expel the Turks from Macedonia at a favourable opportunity. The example of a successful democratic development south of the Danube would also have given the Rumanian peasant movement the necessary impetus.

Actually, events took an entirely different course. Up to the World War not a single one of the Balkan states succeeded in creating stable conditions and in finding a form of government which would have represented the will of the working people. Without a doubt one cause for this failure was the extraordinary economic and intellectual backwardness of the masses, the legacy of four centuries of Turkish oppression. The decisive factor, however, which contributed to the decay of the popular democratic forces in the Balkans was the alliance of the South Slavic movement for liberation with Russian tsarism. The Balkan people could not deal only with the Turks or with the Habsburgs, because for centuries the Balkan Peninsula had been a focus for the international policies of all the major powers. If a revolutionary democratic movement had been successful in western Europe after 1871, it would also have aided the young Balkan nations. But the victory of reaction in the rest of Europe also exercised a paralysing effect on the Balkans. Mazzini's friends could not even help themselves in Italy. The Italian democratic movement was even less capable of helping the radical youth of the Balkans, and after 1871 the Italian Kingdom was by no means able to place itself at the head of the oppressed peoples of the east. Consequently the only alternative left for the Christian Balkan nations in their struggles for liberation was to turn to Russia, with whom they were united by ties of kinship or by a common faith, for support.

Still, a people which owed its liberation to the Tsar could not actually become free. The sad history of the principality of Bulgaria after its establishment by the Congress of Berlin furnishes the commentary to this sentence. Russian tsarism did not want any independent peasant democracies on the Balkan Peninsula, but only vassal states which would obey every hint from St. Petersburg. The tiny, still very primitive, tribal principality of Montenegro, which was able to maintain its existence only by means of tsarist gratuities, furnished an ideal pattern for such a state. In Bulgaria, Russian agents and tsarist officers permitted no pacification of the country and ultimately made it impossible for the popular Prince Alexander von Battenberg to carry on his government. The government of his successor, Prince Ferdinand was likewise conditioned by the rivalry of the Russophile and the anti-Russian cliques. During the seventies and eighties, the Serbian Radical Party, which had developed out of the Omladina, fought courageously against the maladministration of the princes. Nevertheless the demands of national policy forced the radical leaders further into the arms of tsarist Russia and at the same time drove them to compromise with the native rulers. Pašič, the most important leader of the Serbian radicals, had begun his political career as a revolutionary student in Switzerland during the sixties. At the outbreak of the World War and even prior to that, during the Balkan Wars, he was the Prime Minister of the Serbian King and simultaneously the most important confidant of the Tsar.

During the entire period prior to the World War the Balkan dynasties or politicians were faced with the alternative of Austro-Hungarian tutelage as soon as they wanted to shake off the influence of Russia. Nowhere was the will of the peasant masses a decisive factor. Power was in the hands of the princes, the bureaucrats, the officers who eagerly participated in politics everywhere, and the professional politicians, who employed the necessary means to ensure their election to Parliament. Russian and Habsburg agents were to be found in the background. Especially after 1878 the influence of Germany, as well as of England and France, became apparent, the latter two particularly in Athens. The Balkan states were pawns in the game of the major powers.

Russian foreign policy was one of the strongest forces of the international counter-revolution. Meanwhile, however, the authority of the Tsar had been seriously shaken in his own country. Since 1870 Russian foreign policy had been governed chiefly by a desire to find an outlet for internal unrest. On the other hand, the patriotic Russian intelligentsia constantly drove the government forward, in the belief that tsarism would ultimately founder on the rocks of foreign policy. In a certain sense the Russian Pan-Slavists and revolutionaries furthered the same ultimate goal, since the diplomatic defeat which the Tsar sustained at the Congress of Berlin in 1878 weakened the authority of the government and furnished a powerful impetus to all the revolutionary tendencies in the country.

The forces which opposed tsarism in Russia around 1880 had almost nothing in common with the popular movements of central and western Europe. On the other hand, they exhibit an astonishing similarity to the revolutionary situation of 1848. In Russia power was concentrated in the hands of the feudal class of large landowners, bureaucrats, officers, and priests who gathered around the Tsar. A modern bourgeoisie as well as a modern proletariat was first developing. Actually the force which opposed tsarism was still the oppressed " people," composed primarily of the enormous mass of Russian peasants. The so-called emancipation of the peasants, which Alexander II had carried out, had not been able to solve Russia's agrarian problem, for even after the abolition of serfdom the greatest part of the land remained in the possession of the Tsar, the nobility, and the Church. The masses of poor peasants without land were as oppressed as ever. The radical young intellectuals of Russia recognized that it was only necessary to organize the enormous peasant masses of the country in order to get rid of tsarism.

Around 1880, therefore, the Russian revolutionary movement was not supported by either the liberal bourgeoisie or the industrial proletariat. It was rather a general, broad movement of the oppressed people against the ruling class, and consequently its aims were very vague. The two characteristic figures of this period of the Revolution are the student and the peasant. Since all legal means of propaganda for democracy were impossible in Russia, the revolutionaries resorted to violence. General revolts as well as isolated acts of terror occurred. In 1881 Alexander II was murdered by Russian terrorists. Marx overlooked neither the confused theoretical basis nor the doubtful tactics of the Russian revolutionaries. He realized, however, that he was dealing with an actual great popular movement whose goal was the establishment of a revolutionary democratic state. Marx was therefore unable to remain aloof from the Russian Revolution. At that time certain remnants of peasant communal property still existed in Russia. The significance of these vestiges was greatly exaggerated by the popular revolutionaries. They believed that it would be possible to establish a socialist-democratic peasant state based upon agrarian co-operatives after the fall of tsarism. In this way Russia would be able to skip the stage of industrial capitalism, which otherwise appeared to be a necessary stage in the development of every modern country. Despite the dubiety of this theory, Marx nevertheless supported it in order to create a connecting link between himself and the Russian revolutionary movement.

In 1882 a Russian translation of the *Communist Manifesto* appeared in Geneva, prepared by the well-known revolutionary leader Vera Zasulich. Marx and Engels wrote a new Preface for this edition in which they say: " At the time of the Revolution of 1848-9 not only the European monarchs but also the European bourgeoisie regarded Russian intervention as the only instrumentality capable of rescuing them from the proletariat, which was first becoming aware of its power. They proclaimed the Tsar as the leader of European reaction. Today he sits in Gatchina a prisoner of the Revolution, and Russia is the vanguard of the European revolutionary movement. The purpose of the *Communist Manifesto* was to proclaim the inevitable, imminent decline of modern bourgeois property. In Russia, however, we find that alongside of the capitalist order, which is developing with feverish rapidity, and the bourgeois ownership of land, which is just arising, the greater part of the land is still the communal property of the peasants. Now the question rises whether the Russian peasant community, which is indeed already a very decayed form of the original communal ownership of land, can undergo a direct transformation to a higher communistic form of landownership, or whether it must first pass through the same process of dissolution which took place in the historical development of the West? The only possible answer to this question at the present time is the following: If the Russian Revolution becomes the signal for a working-class revolution in the West, so that they supplement each other, then the present Russian form of communal landownership can serve as a starting-point for a communistic development."

If Marx had been nothing more than the spokesman of the industrial workers, then the development of Russia would have been just as unimportant for him as, for instance, the evolution of conditions in Ireland. Actually the industrial workers were not important for Marx as a trade group, but only as the one class which, in consequence of historical development, was qualified to lead the modern popular revolution. Nevertheless the Russian students and peasants who were preparing to destroy tsarism furnished a much stronger driving force for an international revolution than any peaceful trade unions of western Europe. In 1882, when Marx and Engels wrote this Preface to the *Communist Manifesto,* they regarded Russia as the outpost of the European revolution. During the last decade of his life Marx set his hopes chiefly on developments in Russia. As a result of the collapse of the Commune the European labour and democratic movements had entered a blind alley. A new impetus could only come from the east. If a democratic revolution actually triumphed in Russia, and a kind of socialist peasant state arose upon the ruins of the old feudal order, it would also reawaken the masses in central and western Europe.

The social democrats in central and western Europe were unable to appreciate Marx's and Engels's mode of reasoning. They couldn't really imagine that a revolution would actually succeed in Russia, and that the movement in their own countries would again assume revolutionary forms. In November 1882 Engels wrote to Marx: " Enclosed find a letter received from Bebel today. The ' mystical thing' that he cannot understand at once, and which can free them from the Socialist Law, is naturally the outbreak of the crisis in Russia. It is strange that none of these people can get used to the thought that an impulse should come from there. And this despite the fact that I explained it to him more than once." Next to Wilhelm Liebknecht, Bebel was already the most popular leader of the German Social Democratic Party at that time. As individuals Marx and Engels found Bebel more congenial than Liebknecht.

Nevertheless developments in Russia did not proceed as rapidly as Marx and Engels had still hoped in 1882. During the eighties it appeared as if the reactionary police state of Tsar Alexander III had again become stronger. A Russian uprising could neither free the German workers from the oppression of the Socialist Law nor help the French workers in overcoming the consequences arising from the defeat of the Commune.

14. *France after the Commune, and Boulanger's Attempted Dictatorship*

After 1871 the French democratic movement was apparently at its lowest ebb. A bloc of capitalists, landowners, officers, and officials ruled the country. The labour movement was completely destroyed. The peasants and the provincials were confused and frightened, and obeyed the commands of the upper class. The bourgeois democrats of Gambetta's group were completely impotent. The ruling class, supported by the conservative majority of the National Assembly, the army, the police, and the courts, felt secure in its powerful position.

All this was completely clear and evident. Still the ruling bloc, which had conquered the Commune, had not yet solved the question concerning the future constitution of France. The majority of the educated and wealthy classes did not want to attempt the dubious experiment of a republic. Instead a strong supreme authority should be established in the state in order to nip in the bud any attempt to restore the Commune. Nevertheless it was not easy to find such a firm authority upon which the French ruling class could actually rely. Since Sedan, Bonapartism was morally bankrupt. No one could seriously consider recalling the family of Napoleon III to the throne. Some other popular general who might have been able to play the dictator was not present after the defeats sustained by the French army in 1870-1.

Therefore the most convenient solution seemed to be the

recall of the legitimate line of the Bourbons to France. Yet
a restoration of this type was likewise unpleasant for the
French capitalist class. If it was actually desired to re-estab-
lish the authority of the legitimate royal house for the purpose of curbing the masses, it would not do to select any
prince; it would be necessary to crown the man who actually
had a hereditary right to be king of France. The legal heir
to the French throne, however, the Count de Chambord, was
still completely steeped in mediæval and feudal views. His
ideal was France prior to 1789. In France, however, genuine
feudalism — the rule of the historic landowning aristocracy
— was extremely weak. The monarchist bourgeoisie was
not interested in submitting to the nobility; it desired rather
to utilize the king as a bulwark against the labour movement. This difference of opinion ultimately found its expression in a controversy over a symbol. The Count de
Chambord wanted to accept the royal throne only on condition that the old white banner of the Bourbons would likewise be reintroduced. Still the ruling class was unwilling to
abandon the tricolour, the colours of modern France since
the Great Revolution, and at best the French army too had a
Bonapartist but no really vital Bourbon tradition.

Consequently the Count de Chambord refused the royal
dignity, if it was to be combined with the recognition of the
tricolour " flag of the Revolution." During the seventies,
then, the French ruling class had no candidate for a monarchy or a dictatorship. In view of these circumstances one
group of French capitalists and their political friends considered it best to abandon all negotiations with the monarchists and instead to establish a conservative republic. It is
characteristic that Thiers, who had been the chief advocate
of a bourgeois-capitalist monarchy for so many years, also
tended to favour a republic after 1871. Nevertheless the
majority of the French capitalists and of the members of the
upper class as a whole did not follow Thiers's advice. If no
king or dictator was available at the moment, it was deemed

advisable to place someone at the head of the state who would temporarily occupy the position for the future ruler. As a result of such considerations, the majority of the National Assembly overthrew Thiers in 1873 and elected Marshal MacMahon President of the Republic. Politically the Marshal represented a provisional form of Bonapartism. In no case was it an attractive and congenial arrangement for the masses, nor could the ruling class regard the Mac-Mahon government as anything but a poor, makeshift solution.

In 1875 the National Assembly passed a group of provisional constitutional laws. The purpose of this legislation was to furnish the basis for a disguised form of Bonapartism. A president, elected for seven years by a joint session of both chambers, was to be the head of the state. The president should collaborate with the Chamber of Deputies and the Senate. The Chamber would be elected by general suffrage. It is characteristic of the decline of general suffrage in the opinion of the general public that the French counter-revolution of 1875 considered a restriction of the franchise superfluous. Only four years had elapsed since the defeat of the Commune. The vanguard of the French working class was destroyed. No socialist or proletarian agitation was possible in France. Supported by the large standing army, the judiciary, and the large centralized police and administrative apparatus, the ruling class felt perfectly secure. Now the comedy of general suffrage could function just as well as in the days of Napoleon III. If the police suppressed any serious opposition, the elections would necessarily turn out " well." However, should the people vote the wrong way contrary to all expectations, the upper class need not become frightened on that account, as long as it had all the instruments of power of the state and society at its disposal.

Alongside of the chamber of deputies was the senate. One quarter of the senators were elected for life. The parish boards elected the others for a term of nine years by means of a complicated electoral system. Anyone who obtains an office for nine years without the possibility of being removed is actually independent of the will of the electorate. The French senate was intended to be a stronghold of the conservative interests and has remained so up to the present day. The president was to appoint the French ministers, while the latter were to co-operate with both houses of parliament. It was as yet entirely unclear whether the ministers required the confidence of parliament or whether they could remain in office without it. With the consent of the senate the president could dissolve the chamber of deputies. In this way at least the possibility was considered of a conflict arising between the government appointed by the president and the majority of the chamber. Apparently it was by no means self-evident for the legislators of 1875 that the will of the government must always coincide with that of the majority of the chamber.

A strong president, allied with the majority of the senate and supported by the power of the state, would have been able to rule in a completely Bonapartist fashion by means of the Constitution of 1875. This was the purpose of these laws and MacMahon wanted to apply them towards this end. It was only later, under entirely different circumstances, that the constitutional laws of 1875 were altered — not literally, to be sure, but in their application — so that they were able to become the basis for a parliamentary republic. The special weakness of the Bonapartism of 1873 and 1875 lay in the circumstance that such a constitution demanded an outstanding personality at the head of the state. A dictator must either be a great man, like Napoleon I, or attempt a skilful imitation of a great man, as Napoleon III had done. Marshal MacMahon had an honourable record as a soldier, but despite everything he belonged to the defeated generals of 1870, and no one could either support or oppose him with great zeal. The broad masses regarded him as temporary regent of the Count de Chambord. The French peasants and provincials had voted conservative in 1871 because they wanted peace and they detested the Commune, or at least the caricature of the Commune with which they were deceived, but they had no inclination to return to any regime of the nobility and the priests, as in the " good old " days.

In 1876 the elections to the Chamber of Deputies produced a majority for the bourgeois republicans, and an open conflict soon developed between the Chamber and the President. MacMahon retained a monarchist government in power, although the majority of the Chamber expressed a lack of confidence in the ministers. With the consent of the Senate, MacMahon dissolved the Chamber of Deputies and again appealed to the nation. The police and the administrative machine worked zealously to influence the new elections in favour of the conservatives. The constitutional struggle led to Gambetta's reappearance in the foreground of the political stage. His judgment of the situation was extremely sober. With the impression of the defeat of the Commune still so vivid, it would be almost a miracle if French democracy — even only as bourgeois democracy — were to triumph now. The workers of Paris were completely incapable of any action and their opponents had all the actual instruments of power. Consequently the republicans could only proceed cautiously. No demand could be raised which was not understood and approved by the peasant and provincial masses. Furthermore, the democratic republicans would have to take advantage of the split in the camp of the ruling class.

The campaign program of Gambetta and his friends was very simple in 1876 and 1877: removal of MacMahon's dictatorship and return to constitutional conditions under which the will of the popular majority would be respected. On this basis Gambetta could join forces with the moderate capitalistic republicans. A united front was formed, comprising all the adherents of constitutional conditions and including the republican faction of the bourgeoisie, the peasants and provincials, and the industrial workers. Gambetta supported the republican bloc with the entire force of his national reputation and oratorical ability. The republicans carefully avoided any acts of violence, demonstrations, or attempts at revolt.

The elections of 1877 once again produced a republican majority. The decisive moment had come. As things stood, MacMahon and his conservative friends would have been able to triumph without much trouble. It was only necessary actually to use the instruments of power which they controlled. Six years after the Commune it is extremely improbable that the republicans would have been able to meet a new dissolution of the Chamber of Deputies with a revolt. However, the conservative upper class lacked any desire to act. The bourgeois-capitalist adherents of the conservative bloc had but little inclination to conjure up a civil war and the complete disintegration of economic life for the sole purpose of retaining MacMahon as President. Just because the republicans avoided an open armed struggle and thus delayed the crisis, they exerted an especially strong influence on the monarchists. The popular movement led by Gambetta appeared so extensive and serious that it could apparently only be overcome through a civil war. The civil war would be avoided as soon as MacMahon appointed a ministry composed of moderate republicans.

The conservative block decided to retreat. In 1877 MacMahon declared that he would submit to the will of the majority. He appointed a new ministry, composed of moderate republicans. The majority of the Chamber was satisfied with its astounding success and avoided any further advances which might again have endangered the situation. It was only in 1879 that MacMahon resigned, because he did not want to collaborate any longer with republican ministers. The leader of the moderate republicans, Grévy, was elected President in his place. The attempt to rule in Bonapartist fashion with the aid of the Constitution of 1875 had failed. After that it remained the custom in France for the president of the Republic to appoint only ministers who had the confidence of a majority of the Chamber. If the Chamber refused to give the prime minister a vote of confidence, he had to resign.

After 1879, with the disappearance of MacMahon, the French Republic had become a state ruled by a parliament. The victorious republicans hastened to reintroduce the other bourgeois liberties which are part of a liberal state. Freedom of the press and of assembly were restored, so that radical opposition parties once again had an opportunity to carry on open propaganda. Nevertheless the crowning act was still lacking — an amnesty for the Communards. In 1879 Blanqui, who had again been imprisoned since 1871, was elected to the Chamber from Bordeaux. He was then released by the government. This was an act of poetic justice, a symbol that at least the bourgeois Republic had triumphed in France. In the Chamber it was chiefly the aged Louis Blanc who, as a member of the republican Left wing, advocated an amnesty. Gambetta's influence finally resulted in a favourable decision. All the Communards who were still alive and outlawed were amnestied. As a result it again became possible to build up a radical and socialist labour movement in a legal manner. Even Rochefort could now resume his political activity.

The victory which the French bourgeois republicans had won from 1876 to 1879 was almost a miracle. Since the strongest factor in the ranks of the democrats, the Parisian workers, had been crippled since 1871, Gambetta could rely only on the vacillating peasant and provincial masses in his struggle with the ruling class and its military and police machine. Nevertheless the fact should not be forgotten that the republicans did not owe their triumph to their own strength, but only to their extremely skilful tactical exploitation of the circumstance that their opponents shrank from extreme measures. For this reason the republican victory

was incomplete and it was impossible at first to establish a
stable bourgeois democratic regime in France.

On the whole the forces of the old order in France were
the same after 1879 as before. There were the large standing
army, with its officer corps, the centralized administrative
apparatus, the powerful capitalists with all their influence,
and finally the Senate, which had the same rights as the
Chamber of Deputies. Upon attempting any radical inno-
vations, a reform government supported by the majority of a
chamber elected by direct popular suffrage would immediately have come into conflict with the Senate. It was de-
batable whether a French government required the confidence of the senate besides that of the chamber of deputies
in order to carry on a constitutional existence. However,
even if a ministry ignored the lack of confidence of the senate
and continued to remain in office with the support of the
chamber, the senate could still paralyse the political system
if it desired. If the senate consistently rejected every government proposal, either the latter would have to resign or the
conflict would have to be settled by revolutionary means.

The three vital bourgeois democracies which were able
to develop during the nineteenth century, the United States,
Switzerland, and Great Britain, all have a highly developed
system of local self-government and also lack a large standing
army. The United States and England had no general conscription, but only small professional armies, while Switzerland had its militia system. Historical experience justifies
the conclusion that a larger standing army, with its corps of
professional officers, will always be a state within a state.
Up to the present no bourgeois democracy, with its parliamentary institutions, has been capable of completely controlling such a large army, with the result that the army has
furnished a basis for anti-democratic tendencies. The same
is true of every great centralized administrative apparatus.

In 1879 France, by dint of great efforts, had just become a
liberal state with parliamentary government. A transition

to democracy was possible only if the standing army were replaced by a militia system, the centralized administrative machine by free self-government, and the predominance of the Senate shattered. Only then would it have been possible to carry out the economic reforms required by the interests of the broad masses, social legislation for the workers, and a tax policy which would spare the poorer classes.

Was such a rapid, progressive development towards a bourgeois or even social-democratic state possible in France after 1879? The prospects for any progress in this direction were not very favourable. It was only in the nineties that the working class was again able to appear as an independent political factor. In the meantime it would have been necessary to depend upon the peasants and the provincials to be the actual fighting forces of the democratic movement. The mass of the rural and urban petty-bourgeoisie in France was sincerely republican in sentiment and rejected any government of the nobility and the bankers. Nevertheless the French middle classes were divided into the most diverse groups. It would have been extremely difficult to unite the chequered confusion of the rural and provincial population upon a uniform program of social reform. Up to what point would the republican middle classes follow a radical reform government and when would they refuse to support it? Upon such an uncertain foundation no social democracy could be established in France.

It is therefore comprehensible that after 1879 the moderates among the French republicans, led by Grévy and Ferry, who were friendly with the capitalists, had the upper hand. Even Gambetta joined the moderate group, at least on practical daily questions. Yet a smaller radical group of republicans refused to acquiesce in this pessimistic view of the situation. They demanded an unwavering advance on the road towards social democracy. The most significant leader of this group was Clemenceau. The program upon which Clemenceau's Radical Socialist Party campaigned in the elections of 1881 is exceedingly remarkable. It shows that at that time Clemenceau and his friends recognized the shortcomings of the French Constitution and French society perfectly well and indicated the path by which France would at least have been able to become a bourgeois democratic state.

The Radical Socialist Party made the following demands: a revision of the Constitution, in order to get rid of the president of the Republic and the senate; separation of Church and State, and secular schools; shortening of the period of military service and gradual replacement of the standing army by a national militia; popular election of judges; communal autonomy, so that the community " will become the master of its own administration, its finances, and its police, within limits, of course, that are compatible with the maintenance of national unity; elimination of the indirect taxes which oppress the masses, and their replacement by direct income, property, and inheritance taxes. The social demands included: a shorter working day, prohibition of child labour, old-age pensions and compensation insurance for the workers, development of an arbitration system in industry, a secure legal position for the unions, participation of the workers in the establishment and execution of factory legislation.

This was by no means an extreme program. It shows all due respect for bourgeois private property. Nevertheless its accomplishment would have raised France to the stage of a bourgeois democratic country, such as England and Switzerland were at that time. The Radical Socialist program of 1881 futhermore exhibits a far-reaching relationship to the actual ideas of the Paris Commune of 1871. The election proclamation of Clemenceau's party in 1881 contains the sentence: " Our program is the summation of those reforms with which the republican party has always pursued the goal of destroying the monarchical principle, which still exists in such powerful form in our institutions, and thus of preparing the way for the great social transformation which will be the consummation of the French Revolution." Entirely in the spirit of 1848, the proclamation concluded with the words: " Long live the democratic and social republic! "

For the moment, to be sure, the actual prospects of realizing a program of this kind were very slight. The radicals or Radical Socialists won but very few seats in the elections of 1881. The newly founded Socialist Labour Party had no representative at all in the Chamber. Since the overwhelming majority of Parliament belonged to the conservative and capitalist groups, it would have been most natural for a strong government of conservative republicans to have been formed. In practical daily questions it would have been able to co-operate with the monarchist groups. The existence of a moderate government of this type was apparently secure for a definite period. In case the radicals later increased in strength and obtained a majority, then they would have had to build a stable government in turn.

Nevertheless the development of France after 1879 took a very different course. It proved impossible to form a stable parliamentary government which would have run the country according to definite principles for a number of years. Instead, after 1879 the Republic reeled from one ministerial crisis to the next, and until the present day it has been impossible to establish an actual political equilibrium in France. One cause for this remarkable insecurity of French political conditions was the attitude of the educated and wealthy classes towards the government. In 1879 the old ruling class had tolerated a transition to a parliamentary state because it knew of no other alternative at the moment. But only a small minority of the wealthy French bourgeoisie actually reconciled itself to a republic because of conviction or expediency. As a whole, so-called society regarded the existence of the Republic as a personal insult. It was a feeling similar to that which the German upper classes exhibited towards the Weimar Republic after 1918.

The French upper class did not want to endure the exercise of political power by the uneducated masses, or at least by the republican politicians who were delegated by them. Consequently from the very beginning the moderate republicans of France found themselves between two fires. They were attacked simultaneously by the radicals of the Left, who accused them of betraying the republican program, and by the old monarchist-conservatives of the Right, who refused to reconcile themselves to a republic.

In the first place, it was this hostile attitude of the upper classes that prevented the creation of a stable republican government. The second element of insecurity came from the middle classes themselves. The republican peasants and petty bourgeoisie usually voted for the radicals, but generally they themselves didn't know how far they should carry their republican zeal. This uncertainty of the voters automatically transmitted itself to its representatives. After 1879 the French bourgeois Republic was not a definite government of the capitalistic upper class, since the majority of the latter refused to recognize the Republic. At the same time it was not a government representing the broad masses. Before a social-democratic state could have been established in France it would first have been necessary to realize all the reforms that Clemenceau's program contained. But there was also no compromise between the classes, for both sides lacked a desire for such an agreement. Consequently only a makeshift solution remained possible: the bourgeois Republic exhibited itself to the public as the government of the professional republican politicians.

After every new election the republican deputies found themselves in the same embarrassing situation. They had received the votes of their electors because they had been fiery opponents of monarchy and reaction. Now the promises of the politicians were to be realized: a strong, Left republican government is established with a fine program of reform. As soon as steps are taken to carry out the reforms in the form of laws, however, insurmountable difficulties appear — the resistance of the capitalist and militarist elements, the opposition of the Senate, and so on. In addition the government never knows how far it can actually rely upon the masses if it undertakes any energetic steps. The particularly timorous and cautious members of the government majority begin to desert it during the voting. Finally the day comes when the government no longer has a majority and must resign. Now a new and colourless republican government is formed, which renounces any daring reforms and restricts itself solely to the defence of the existing Constitution and the dispatch of routine business. The exhausted Chamber permits a government of this type to remain in office for a certain period, but then a spirit of opposition again arises on the Left. The realization grows that the government is doing nothing to carry out the necessary republican reforms. The dissatisfaction of the radical deputies grows and finally the government is overthrown. It is followed by a new one, and the cycle is repeated. In other words, after 1879 the class equilibrium of the Third French Republic was always labile, and not stable like that of England or Switzerland. The small group of professional republican politicians and republican capitalists is under fire from the radicals and the conservatives, is thrown back and forth, and appears ready to collapse. Nevertheless it ultimately retains its position because the Right is never strong enough to establish an open capitalistic and military dictatorship, and the Left is not strong enough to create a social democracy.

The remarkable shifting conditions of the Third Republic also contributed to the disproportionate importance which two special problems acquired in France. One was the position of the Catholic Church, and the other the question of the technical method to be employed for general suffrage. In general the religious situation in France has remained unchanged from the Great Revolution to the present day. A considerable majority of the nation was indifferent to religion, and a minority was actively Catholic. The changing policies of various French governments towards the Church did not change this situation. Thus the friendly attitude of Napoleon III did not suffice to lead the majority of Frenchmen back to the faith, nor was the intense struggle which several republican governments carried on against the religious orders and schools after 1900 able to destroy the Catholic minority. Nevertheless after 1871 the position of the Church in France had a peculiar social and political significance. Open profession of the Catholic faith and the education of children in religious schools were to a certain extent indications of adherence to the conservative section of society. On the other hand the professional republican politicians and the republican faction of the bourgeoisie were united in rejecting the Church. The Masonic lodges furnished an intellectual bond for the active republicans. Apparently, then, the struggle of " Church versus Free-masonry " appeared as a necessary supplement to the struggle of " monarchy against republic."

The Third French Republic had proved incapable of destroying the vested centralized bureaucracy. Since the normal form of self-government was too weak in contrast to bureaucratic officialdom, a strange substitute for self-government developed. The republican deputies considered it their duty to remain in constant touch with their constituents and to receive all complaints of a local nature. Consequently a great degree of mutual confidence developed between the republican voters of each small electoral district and their representatives. If the voters felt oppressed by the bureaucrats, they complained to their representative, who helped them as much as he could by putting pressure on the minister. This method certainly had its dubious aspects. The intervention of the parliamentarians in the routine administration caused uninterrupted disturbances. At the same time this kind of local, backstairs politics in matters of tax payments, assignment of government contracts, filling of positions, and so forth, furnished a fertile soil for corruption. Yet the petty daily task of the republican deputies was a necessary evil and a substitute for the lack of a really free system of self-government. As a result the opponents of the Republic incessantly attacked the system of small electoral districts as the root of evil and corruption. It was not desired to abolish general suffrage itself, but rather to create large electoral districts with voting by lists, proportional representation, and the like. All these projects had the same purpose — to destroy the direct connexion between the individual republican deputies and their constituents by eliminating the small election districts. Once this goal was achieved, the population was again entirely in the power of the bureaucracy, and the bourgeois Republic had lost the only way in which it could still attain a certain degree of popularity.

Towards the end of 1881 Gambetta became Prime Minister. He regarded the possibility of rapidly introducing major reforms with great scepticism and consequently drew the enmity of the radicals in the Chamber upon himself. Gambetta wanted to establish a strong republican government. He demanded absolute trust in himself in order to be able to direct the state with a firm hand. He opposed the accessory government of the deputies. The government paid no attention to the complaints brought forward by the deputies regarding matters relating to their constituencies. Gambetta even resorted to the fateful remedy of abolishing the small electoral districts and introducing voting by lists. As a result of his personal headstrongness Gambetta fell out with the republican majority which absolutely rejected such electoral reforms. Gambetta was overthrown. His Ministry, which had been awaited with such great expectations, ended with an astonishingly rapid failure. Yet despite his parliamentary defeat and his tactical mistakes, Gambetta remained the strongest personality among the bourgeois republicans, and the next crisis would have brought him to the top again.

Gambetta's sudden death in 1882 was an extraordinarily serious blow to the republican cause. It can hardly be imagined that the Boulanger movement or the Dreyfus affair would later have taken the same course if Gambetta had still been alive.

The French government was now in the hands of the moderate republicans, whose leadership Ferry assumed. Ferry drew up a realistic program for a capitalistic republican policy. He postponed all social and constitutional reforms, which would only have led to new crises. Instead he devoted all his energy towards the extension of French power abroad. Ferry recognized that for the present a war of revenge against Germany was impossible. He came to an understanding with Bismarck. Having protected his rear with the aid of Germany, he proceeded to carry out a large-scale policy of colonial conquest. Ferry deserves credit for: the French conquest of Tunis, the expansion of the French Empire in Indo-China from the modest beginnings which Napoleon III had left there, as well as the extension of French power in the Sudan and on Madagascar. Ferry and his friends thought of France as the head of a great colonial empire which would extend over all the continents; in a certain sense a smaller replica of the British Empire. French industry would find new sources of raw materials and new export markets in the colonies. The result of such a systematic French imperial policy would certainly have been a return to a system of high protective tariffs.

By his policy of national successes and economic development Ferry hoped to win over the monarchist, conservative circles of the bourgeoisie to the Republic. He was unable to accomplish this aim, however. At this opportunity it again became evident that a national policy is never an isolated phenomenon, but is always connected with the class and party differences of a country. Any party or class will be inclined to recognize as "national" only such a policy as is to its own advantage. During the nineteenth century the greatest national successes were obtained for France by two men, who received but little thanks, Charles X, the conqueror of Algiers, and Ferry, the founder of the modern French colonial empire. The French bourgeoisie did not recognize the deeds of Charles X, however, because the King wanted to strengthen the authority of the nobility with his colonial conquests. Now the French conservative bourgeoisie was just as little inclined to admit that Ferry's colonial enterprises were actual national successes. The number of firms that profited from the colonies was still small. For the present the majority of French citizens were not interested in colonies and regarded Ferry's policy as a capitulation before Germany; the French republican ministers permitted themselves to be enticed by Bismarck into all kinds of adventures in Asia and Africa, while the Prussians were able to strengthen their power in Alsace-Lorraine!

While the French bourgeois Republic, despite its foreign triumphs, was unable to win over the majority of the wealthy class, at the same time it also lost the confidence of the broad masses. The French workers, peasants, and artisans considered that they certainly had a republic now, and perhaps even a democracy, if one wanted to give that name to a state with general suffrage. But what had the labouring masses gained? The workers had learned by repeated experience that in any conflict with the employers the power of the state was on the side of the capitalists. The military forces were called into action in almost every strike in France, and if the troops fired upon demonstrating workers, it was a very poor lesson in the blessings of republican freedom. The peasants and petty bourgeoisie arrived at the conviction that the rich upper class always knew how to thwart any just method of taxation, and that the burdens of the state were repeatedly placed upon the working people. Every few years the people elected its republican deputies, and yet nothing improved. It appeared, indeed, as if the professional politicians were really under one cloak with the capitalists.

Such a crisis of confidence is the fate of every political state which claims to be popular but which is nothing of the kind in reality. The voters felt betrayed because the French Republic granted the masses general suffrage without the achievements of a genuine bourgeois democracy. Such an equivocal condition of pseudo-democracy must ultimately make the democratic idea itself ridiculous in the eyes of the masses. During the eighties a minority of French voters turned to the radicals of the Left, who criticized existing conditions with great severity. However, a still greater group had even lost confidence in the republican opposition, and in a spirit of exasperation they turned to the conservative monarchists, or dreamed of some great man who would appear one day and disperse the corrupt politicians.

The first great wave of popular dissatisfaction was directed against Ferry's colonial policy. At that time France had no special colonial army, so that Ferry ruthlessly dispatched the soldiers recruited for routine military training to fight colonial wars in Asia and Africa, where thousands of young men died of tropical diseases. In addition there were occasional military defeats, which are inevitable in colonial wars. In 1885 when the French sustained an entirely unimportant local defeat in Tongking, popular resentment broke out against Ferry, the " Tongkingese." The exasperation of the masses excited the Chamber. A combined attack of the monarchist Right and the radical Left overthrew the government. With the resignation of Ferry the power of the moderate republicans was broken, and one ministry after another barely managed to maintain a precarious existence.

In 1885 the moderate republicans were so weakened and disorganized that they agreed to an electoral reform. The small election districts were abolished and replaced by large ones with voting by list. Thus the personal contact between the representative and his constituency was disrupted. The last tie which had still bound the population to the bourgeois Republic no longer existed. The course of the new elections to the Chamber of Deputies was extremely serious. Out of a total of 8,000,000 votes the monarchists received 3,500,000. If the votes of the Radical Party were added, it appeared that a majority of the French people opposed the ruling system. At the second ballot the Radicals combined with the moderate republicans to prevent the formation of a monarchist majority in the Chamber. They succeeded, but the crisis of the bourgeois French Republic continued to exist unchanged.

The War Minister of the next republican ministry was General Boulanger, considered one of the few reliable republican officers in the army. In order to strengthen the fighting ability of the French army, Boulanger unfolded an intense activity and definitely indicated that his labours were directed against Germany. In this manner he rapidly became popular, and his name became a symbol for the coming war of revenge. During the last years the moderate republicans had attempted to maintain correct relations with Germany, and to a large extent achieved their colonial successes with the aid of Bismarck. All the greater had been the determination with which all the opponents of the bourgeois Republic condemned the colonial policy and again demanded a strong anti-German course. Since Boulanger had once again permitted the flames of revenge to flare up, all the enemies of the ruling system united around him. The monarchists began to approach him. Perhaps the popular general would be the future French dictator, the man who would overcome the Republic and establish a new form of Bonapartism, in conformity with the spirit of the time. Under certain circumstances Boulanger's regime might also be a transitional stage on the road to a restoration of the monarchy. Large sections of the radical electorate, many workers, petty bourgeois, and peasants were also filled with enthusiasm for Boulanger and hoped that he would at least free them from the rule of the despised professional politicians.

Gradually the republican parties recognized the threatening danger of the popular Minister of War, who readily allowed himself to be carried along by the wave of national enthusiasm. Boulanger was removed from his post as Minister of War, became corps commander in the provinces at first, and was ultimately discharged from active service in 1888. Boulanger's popularity among the masses became even greater. He now appeared openly as a political leader, with a program of constitutional revision. A strong government, supported by the will of the people, was to be liberated from the bonds which corrupt parliamentarianism had imposed upon it. It was a new edition of the Bonapartist program.

The conservatives determined to place all their organizations and funds at General Boulanger's disposal. It was an extremely favourable situation. Owing to their own mistakes and weakness, the liberals and democrats of the country had lost the sympathy of the masses and any impulse to act. Consequently the representatives of the capitalists, the large landowners, the Church, and the army could appear as the true champions of the insulted and betrayed people. The popular general was the connecting link between the counter-revolution and the masses. As a result of the rise of Boulangism the Radical Party was in great distress. Boulanger attempted to retain his old Radical friends. Rochefort now developed into a herald of Boulangism. On the other hand, all of Boulanger's attempts to win over Clemenceau failed, for the latter recognized that Boulangism, in the form which it had gradually assumed, was only a cloak for the capitalist and monarchist counter-revolution. Clemenceau, and with him the official Radical Party, remained on the side of the Republic; on the other hand, the majority of the radical voters together with Rochefort transferred their allegiance to Boulanger.

The irony of the situation lay in the fact that the moderate republicans were being punished just because they had fought so timidly against the capitalists and monarchists. Because the French bourgeois Republic had opposed the Right so faint-heartedly, it was unable to establish a stable democratic state. As a result the masses were disappointed and felt themselves betrayed by the republicans; now the parties of the monarchists appeared, cunningly disguised, and offered to wreak the vengeance of the dissatisfied masses on the Republic and democracy. This policy was to be repeated many a time until the present day. The manner in which the national idea was exploited for the cause of the counter-revolution in France at that time is also worthy of notice. If Gambetta had still been alive then, no one would have dared to present the friends of the bourgeois Republic as enemies of the fatherland and agents of Germany. Now, however, Ferry, the alleged friend of Bismarck, personified the republican idea for large sections of the population. Every Frenchman who voted for Boulanger felt relieved, because with this act he simultaneously combined a demonstration against the Prussians.

After 1888 the large bloc for constitutional reform included all the monarchists, Boulanger's radical adherents, and all kinds of vacillating groups that were attracted by the magnetism of the coming dictator. In every case where a secondary election to the Chamber was necessary in one of the large electoral districts, Boulanger was nominated as candidate. By this means it was proposed to carry out a kind of plebiscite for the new Napoleon. Boulanger was the victor in many of these elections. When a secondary election also became necessary in Paris in January 1889, it was felt that the decisive moment was approaching. The Right and Left wing republicans united to support a common candidate; nevertheless Boulanger was elected, receiving 244,000 votes against 162,000 for his opponent. The result shows that the majority of the Parisian workers must have favoured Boulanger. The disgust which the masses felt for the bourgeois-capitalistic Republic and its politicians was so great that any change was preferable to the existing conditions. On the evening of election day it was generally expected in Paris that Boulanger, at the head of the enthusiastic masses, would drive out the republican government and establish his dictatorship. Boulanger would not have had to fear any serious resistance, since almost the entire army and the police force were on his side.

Nevertheless, to the profound disappointment of his adherents, the general did not venture to carry out a coup d'état. He was neither a great man, like Napoleon I, nor an adventurer, like Napoleon III, but only a patriotic officer of average talents. Only the peculiar situation between 1885 and 1889 and the remarkable confusion among the parties and classes in France at that time had made it possible for him to acquire such enormous importance. After the bankruptcy of the bourgeois Republic, while the contemporary labour movement was weak and a monarchy lacked popularity, France was ripe for a dictator. The first general who appeared to advantage on horseback, preached revenge, and was also persecuted by the politicians appeared to the people as the personification of their dreams. Yet at the decisive moment Boulanger shrank from the deed which was expected of him.

When the coup d'état did not materialize, the republican government took the offensive. When Boulanger was indicted for treason, he fled the country and thus lost the remainder of his influence. The profoundly disappointed masses again sank back into political indifference or returned to the old parties. The republicans were clever enough to nullify the fateful electoral reforms and to return to the old small electoral districts. In the Chamber elections of September 1889 the republicans maintained their majority. Yet the triumph of the Republic in France was by no means due to its own strength. In 1889, just as ten years previously, the bourgeois Republic had only been able to triumph because its opponents were unable to determine upon an open counter-revolution. After Boulanger's flight, just as after MacMahon's fall, it was impossible to really strengthen the Republic by developing a stable bourgeois democratic state in France. The bourgeois Republic had only won a breathing spell and waited for the next crisis.

In 1889 Bismarck ruled in Berlin with his Socialist Law, in St. Petersburg Alexander III reigned with his police, Taaffe governed in Vienna, Crispi in Rome, and Boulanger's shadow hung over Paris. From the point of view of democracy, it was a sad result. Despite all that, the industrialization of the European continent had made rapid progress during the last two decades. In spite of all political reverses, the class-consciousness of the proletariat necessarily had to reassert itself. In 1889 the Second International was founded in Boulanger's Paris and began a new period in the history of European democracy.

15. Imperialism versus Liberalism

The extraordinary progress of technology during the generation prior to the World War resulted in a new revolution in the conditions of production. The irresistible process of concentration in industry and the final victory of large-scale production in all the important civilized countries also produced a complete revolution within bourgeois society. The death-knell of liberalism of the older type was finally sounded. It was succeeded by that development of internal and foreign policy which is most conveniently designated as imperialism. Concomitantly the character and position of democracy also changed.

It is unnecessary to repeat in detail the well-known facts concerning the progress of technology and the concentration of capital during the period from 1880 to 1914. A few catchwords and dates will suffice to remind the reader of the general tendency of this movement. Technology during the second half of the nineteenth century is characterized by the growing utilization of electricity in new branches of industry, together with the increasing perfection of the steam engine. The last twenty years before the outbreak of the World War furthermore saw the triumphal march of the automobile and the invention of the first practical airplanes and dirigibles. The new technical possibilities lent themselves more and more to large-scale production. Banking capital aided the large factories with all the means at its disposal. Large individual factories were soon inadequate. Industrial trusts and cartels began to develop on a gigantic scale. Every crisis which periodically shook the capitalistic world brought ruin to innumerable weaker plants. The concentrated large enterprises were the victors. In the great civilized countries the decisive means of production were soon in the hands of a restricted number of enterprises. Capitalism based on free competition had been transformed into the rule of monopoly.

Modern monopolistic capitalism disrupted bourgeois society and sounded the death-knell of liberalism. The concept of liberalism as employed here implies a form of political and social organization in which the wealthy and educated citizens rule through the utilization of constitutional liberties. The older form of liberalism, which developed when modern bourgeois society arose, united internal political liberty with a strong foreign policy. This older liberalism is characterized by parliamentary government, in the form of a republic or a constitutionally restricted monarchy. It is furthermore distinguished by the existence of security of person and property from any official encroachment, freedom of speech and press, freedom of association and assembly. Nevertheless only the wealthy upper class has actual political power. The wealthy bourgeoisie employs the apparatus of the state to carry out a powerful foreign policy, resulting in colonial conquests. The army and navy are developed, and foreign competition is combated by means of protective tariffs and trade embargoes. In short, the older liberalism is the typical political form of early capitalism.

The liberals of this older type included the political groups that were in power in Holland from the sixteenth century to the great French Revolution, the English Whigs of the seventeenth and eighteenth centuries, and the younger Tories from the period of the French Revolutionary wars until 1832. Other genuine old liberals were the bourgeois parties of the great French Revolution from 1789 to 1793. They were followed by a social democracy under Robespierre from 1793 to 1794. Then came another old liberal government under the Directory until 1799. Napoleon's dictatorship and the restored feudal Kingdom of the Bourbons followed in succession. Under Louis Philippe the older liberalism again ruled in France from 1830 to 1848. Finally the Federalists in the United States, who controlled the fate of the new federal state from its establishment until the end of the eighteenth century, were also a genuine liberal party of the older type.

The second, younger type of liberalism was a product of the industrial development of England. The new liberalism corresponded to the older form in that it upheld constitutional liberties and the rule of the wealthy bourgeoisie. The difference between the two forms of liberalism lay in their attitude towards the state and the control of political power. Neo-liberalism is so profoundly convinced of the conquering power of modern industry that it believes itself in a position to abandon the use of the instruments of political power. Peace and free trade are its slogans. Free competition between the individual entrepreneurs should take its course without any interference, hindrance, or artificial aid. In this manner the progress of individuals, nations, and all mankind would best be served. England between 1832 and 1866 became the classic country of neo-liberalism. Its political supporters were the younger Whigs and the followers of Peel. The younger liberalism found a second home in the Kingdom of Belgium, which had been established in

1830. Because of the geographic position and the general political situation of its small state, the Belgian bourgeoisie was dependent on peaceful development. The Belgian ruling class had no desire for any conquests or a large army; it simply wanted to develop its industries in peace and under the protection of a parliamentary constitution.

In order to develop the concepts clearly, it is necessary to differentiate the younger liberalism from liberal democracy. Liberalism, in the narrower sense, operates with a restricted franchise, under which only the wealthy class participates in the exercise of political power. This was the situation in England from 1832 to 1866 and in Belgium from 1830 to the World War. Liberal democracy is present when the labouring masses also receive the franchise and the bourgeoisie is compelled to maintain its power by arriving at an understanding with the broad popular masses. Thus in England after 1866 the Liberal Party is transformed into a liberal democratic one. Switzerland after 1847 is a typical liberal democratic state.

After 1830 the younger form of liberalism was unable to obtain power in any of the great monarchies of the European continent. Yet it decisively influenced the German bourgeoisie. Since 1830 the rise of German industry had produced a large group of energetic and optimistic entrepreneurs who, like their English counterparts, believed in free trade and free competition. In alliance with the progressive intellectuals and the broad masses, the liberal capitalists also attempted to obtain constitutional conditions — likewise patterned after their English prototype — in Prussia and Germany. German liberalism did not succeed in defeating the ruling feudal monarchy. Nevertheless Prussia-Germany at least changed to a system of free trade, and from about 1860 to 1879 the neo-liberal ideas dominated the parliaments. After 1867 Bismarck sometimes acted as if he seriously desired to co-operate with German liberalism, even though the neo-liberal ideas of progress were in profound disagreement with the militaristic Prussian policy of power politics. Owing to its common language and culture the Austrian bourgeoisie generally advocated the same ideas as the Germans. To be sure, Austrian liberalism was also unable to overcome the feudal imperial regime of the Habsburgs, but during the sixties and seventies the German Liberal Party of Austria was at least in control of Parliament and was likewise in a position to influence Austrian politics and business considerably. During this period the parliamentary franchise in Prussia gave the wealthy class absolute power. However, Bismarck introduced manhood suffrage for the Reichstag of the North German Confederation after 1867 and for the German Empire after 1871. Nevertheless the liberal tradition was still so strong at first that the liberal parties retained their parliamentary predominance in Germany until the end of the seventies.

Neo-liberalism, based upon free trade, peace, and progress was never really able to gain a firm footing in France; for until 1848 the French bourgeoisie had generally been influenced by the older liberal ideas. The dictatorial and Bonapartist period then prevailed until 1879, when modern imperialist ideas began to assert themselves among the wealthy class in France. The last decade of the reign of Napoleon III, when the Emperor advocated free trade, espoused the cause of peace and disarmament in theory, and at the eleventh hour even appointed a parliamentary ministry, furnishes a kind of substitute for the missing neo-liberal period in the history of France. If this Napoleonic caricature is disregarded, the neo-liberal period is missing in French history. Neo-liberalism was just as little at home in the United States. The fall of the old liberal Federalists was followed by a period of social democracy, which lasted from 1800 to 1815. This in turn was followed by the peculiar colonial form of bourgeois democracy, whose offshoots extended approximately until 1890. On the one hand the wealthy bourgeoisie of America could not restrict the franchise, but was compelled to seek a compromise with the broad masses such as is characteristic of bourgeois democracy; on the other hand the industrial bourgeoisie of America remained unconditionally in favour of a protective tariff. An essential characteristic of the United States was the progressive colonization of more and more new land in the West. Thus the distinguishing feature of the development of America during the nineteenth century was the constant conquest of new land, and not peaceful competition within the boundaries of the old homeland. Consequently the democracy of the United States, based as it was on protective tariffs and conquest, never fitted into the scheme of neo-liberalism.

The movements of the Italian bourgeoisie during the nineteenth century, starting with the Carbonari, belong to the older liberalism; for the Italian bourgeoisie needed political power and armed force to obtain national unification and to secure the new Italy against its internal and external enemies. Dutch liberalism of the nineteenth century likewise belongs to the old liberal pattern. When Holland again became independent after the collapse of the Napoleonic Empire, the country was reconstituted as the Kingdom of Holland. Owing to a considerable increase in the power of the crown, the traditional self-government of the Dutch bourgeoisie was greatly restricted after 1815. Holland retained its large colonial empire in Asia even after 1815. The economic existence of the Netherlands depended on the possession of Java and other transoceanic colonies. However, the defence and the exploitation of the colonial empire required a consistent, energetic foreign policy which was incompatible with the ideas of neo-liberalism.

It is evident that during the nineteenth century the actual sphere of power of neo-liberalism was extraordinarily small. If the exact definition of neo-liberalism is taken as a standard, then only Belgium is left as an example of this movement. On the Continent the neo-liberal policies were constantly restricted by the great monarchies, and in England neo-liberalism was basically irreconcilable with the methods and demands of the British Empire. The neo-liberalism of the nineteenth century was only a transitional episode. It was an illusion of the early industrial capitalists, who believed themselves in a position to renounce the most essential characteristics of the capitalist economy, power and force. During the latter part of the nineteenth century the wealthy bourgeoisie in all the important modern countries abandoned liberalism for imperialism. Neo-liberalism, however, had an astonishing indirect effect. The capitalist bourgeoisie, in whose interest neo-liberalism had originally been invented, rejected these ideas; instead neo-liberalism in the form of liberal democracy was eagerly taken up by the workers and some of the petty bourgeoisie in their desperate quest for a theory which could help them in their struggle against imperialism.

The conversion of the influential industrial groups to imperialism is easily comprehensible. Picture the average small European manufacturer of the eighteenth and the early part of the nineteenth centuries. When a man of this type demanded " liberty " and was ready to make sacrifices for it, it was not because of any abstract idealism. Liberty and popular rights were very concrete necessities for the older European bourgeoisie. Liberty meant that that citizen should not be dependent on the whim of some royal police official. The citizen wanted to be protected against any arbitrary imprisonment or the confiscation of his property on some pretext furnished by the sudden appearance of a government decree. The European bourgeois demanded a constitution, legal security, and protection of person and property as safeguards against absolutism and the caprices of the nobility and bureaucracy. He wanted to free himself as far as possible from the burden of taxation. He considered any expenses for the maintenance of a monarch, a state church, a corps of officials, the nobility and army as unproductive and demanded their abolition. He wanted no general military service. His son had no inclination to be killed for some dynastic project, but intended to carry on the paternal business. As a rule the small manufacturer of the older period knew his workers personally. Many a time he engaged in controversies with them. He did not believe that they were ripe for the exercise of the franchise. He was angry if agitators incited his workers with co-operative and socialist catchwords. Nevertheless he regarded his workers as his personal assistants, who were not always very amenable to reason, but who still belonged to him and whose political interests were generally the same as his own — cheap bread, few taxes, no military service, and protection from arbitrary police power.

The great industrialist towards the end of the nineteenth century saw the world very differently. As head of a concern he employed perhaps ten thousand workers. Outside of the large cities, in the typical mining and industrial regions, the picture was especially impressive: The entire region belongs to the firm. The workers and the office employees live in houses owned by the concern. Every cent which is spent in the area is derived either directly or indirectly from the factory. The large industrialist commands both land and people, almost like a new feudal lord. The concept of liberty has an entirely different meaning for the modern great industrialist. He no longer has to fear any state officials. He deals with ministers on a basis of equality. His political worries are of an entirely different nature. For him " liberty " means that foreign agitators should have unrestricted opportunities to incite his subjects, the workers, to rebellion. Consequently, the modern capitalist grows more and more sceptical concerning the value of liberty and constitutional rights. He now demands a strong state, which actually exercises its authority over the masses and is always capable of suppressing a " Red " rebellion. The modern capitalist furthermore demands that the state should protect him from foreign competition, by means of tariffs, and open up new markets for him by a successful foreign and colonial policy. In return, when the state needs money for the army and police, it must be produced, and the firm must bear the necessary sacrifices, as a kind of insurance against internal and external dangers.

The neo-liberal entrepreneur wanted peace, reduction of administrative bureaucracy, security of civil liberties, and the undisturbed play of free competition. The modern monopoly capitalist, on the other hand, wants a state with a strong internal and external authority. The transition from the one to the other *Weltanschauung* took place gradually and differed according to conditions in the individual countries and the characters of the leading personages. This process has nothing to do with questions of morality. Many small employers of the older period were liberals, to be sure, but personally hard and narrow-minded; while some of the modern trust capitalists wanted to make mankind happy, in the manner of absolute monarchs, and transformed the greatest part of their enormous fortunes into philanthropic foundations. It is not the province of historical analysis to attempt to divide individuals into " good " and " evil " categories, but only to try to explain the psychology of society as a whole.

During the latter part of the nineteenth century the advance of imperialist ideas resulted in the disintegration of bourgeois society. Until then the wealthy and educated bourgeoisie as a whole had formed a united front, which became evident during all serious crises. At such opportunities the united power of the bourgeoisie and of public opinion, with which it was allied, usually influenced the greater part of the nation. As early as the sixteenth century the Dutch bourgeoisie had united, and was supported by the broad masses, in its struggle of liberation against the Spanish monarchy. During the seventeenth century the English bourgeoisie was just as united against the encroachments of Charles I and James II. In 1832 the overwhelming majority

of the educated and wealthy class of England favoured electoral reform. From 1832 to 1866 the liberals always had a
majority in the English lower house, if Peel's followers are
counted among the liberals.

The history of France shows the same picture. The same
overwhelming unity of public opinion opposed the absolutism of Louis XVI in 1789 and the policy of Charles X in
1830. In 1848 almost the entire French nation, led by the
educated classes (with the exception of a few small cliques),
fought against Louis Philippe. The same unity of liberal
public opinion appeared at the beginning of the Revolution
of 1848 in Germany, Austria, Hungary, and Italy. During
the Prussian constitutional struggle from 1863 to 1866 at
least nine tenths of the nation supported the liberal deputies. The groups that were isolated were Bismarck with a
small group of feudal aristocrats on the Right and Lassalle
with a small following of socialist workers on the Left. In
1830 in Belgium the people supported the revolution led by
the liberal bourgeoisie against the Dutch King with equal
unity.

To be sure, during the older period the financial aristocracy had already frequently separated itself from the general
bourgeois-liberal movement. The court bankers sided with
their monarchs, and until 1848 the great French banks supported Louis Philippe. However, a few bank firms do not
comprise bourgeois society, and the divergent tendencies of
such financial circles could not destroy the great unity of the
liberal popular movement. This situation changed completely as soon as the great European and American industrialists began to occupy a position in public life; for the
great manufacturers, in most cases, were able to convert the
lesser industrialists to their ideas. Although bourgeois society could endure the opposition of a few bankers, if need
be, it could no longer be a vital political body after the de-
sertion of industry. The industrialists not only united on
the basis of imperialism with the banks, but also attracted

a large section of the intellectuals to their side. Imperialist ideas influenced new and larger groups of the intelligentsia, especially the students. In most civilized countries it was exactly the intellectuals who turned their backs on the old slogans of liberty and progress and instead grew enthusiastic for national greatness, power politics, and authority.

The imperialist groups, composed of the manufacturers, the bankers, and an ever increasing section of the educated and intellectual public, sought support on the Right, as far as militaristic monarchies or aristocratic landlordism still existed in the individual states. Liberalism was gradually restricted to a few sections of the merchant group and the remaining intellectuals, who still retained firmly the old ideas of political and economic freedom. Bourgeois liberalism, devitalized and discredited in this manner, no longer has the power to retain even the poorer labouring classes. Coincident with the conversion of the industrial workers to socialism, the influence of liberalism on the European petty-bourgeois middle class constantly decreases. Peasants and urban members of the middle class become politically independent. Simultaneously the imperialist upper class also attempts to obtain a mass basis by exploiting nationalist ideas.

Approximately since 1880 imperialist politics appear in every country as *the* national policy. Consequently by opposing armaments, tariffs, colonies, and a strong foreign policy, the opponents of imperialism — liberals, democrats, or socialists — appear unpatriotic. This change was to have very serious consequences. By assuming the form of an exaggerated nationalism, by extolling its own people, imperialism can make use of all kinds of patriotic and even anti-Semitic movements. In a certain sense, imperialism outstrips the remains of the liberal movement. It passes the remnants of the liberal forces and takes possession of the popular masses. Peasants, demanding protective tariffs, the urban petty bourgeoisie, angered by modern department stores and Jewish competition, religious groups, opposed to irreligious

liberalism and seeking a new authority — all become allies
of imperialism in its struggle against the remnants of the
liberal party and socialistic and democratic tendencies. The
nationalistic academic youth forms a natural bond between
the imperialist lords above and the patriotic petty bourgeois
or clerical masses below.

Imperialistic capitalism generally disdained to form new
parties; instead it entered the existing political movements,
imbued them with its ideas, and transformed them in accordance with its needs. In this manner certain parties, which
had been founded for an entirely different purpose, became
the representatives of modern imperialism. This is particularly true of the Republican Party in the United States.
What a vast difference between the party of Lincoln and the
movement led by McKinley thirty years later! Since the Republican Party had been the victor in the Civil War and
had then become the chief mainstay of the state, it was supported by the majority of the capitalists. To be sure, there
was always a progressive Left wing among the Republicans,
just as there was a capitalistic wing, in sympathy with the
trusts, in the opposing Democratic Party. On the whole,
however, after the seventies the official Republican Party
represented high finance and the industrial trusts. The Republicans advocated high tariffs, the construction of a large
American navy, and colonial expansion in Central America
and the Pacific Ocean.

In internal politics they demanded free play for business.
They wanted no government interference in the affairs of
capital, and at the same time the employment of repressive
measures against the labour movement and any apparently
radical tendencies. The American imperialistic Republicans wanted to retain the traditional bourgeois-democratic
Constitution of the United States, but they undermined the
substance of democracy until only the empty shell remained.
Since the national, state, and local party machines controlled
the elections and the same machines obeyed the command of

the capitalists, so-called democracy was only a cloak for a dictatorship of imperialistic capitalism.

During the nineties an imperialist bloc developed in France. Here an unnatural condition existed, since the majority of the capitalists were the political allies of the monarchists. Only a minority of the industrialists supported the Republic. This was Ferry's group, which during the eighties by its colonial policy prepared the way for modern French imperialism. After the Boulanger crisis of 1889 had been weathered and the Republic rescued, as if by a miracle, the new conditions had to be taken into account. The most natural thing was an attempt to reconcile the hostile sections of French capitalism, to postpone the question of political organization for the present, and to render feasible the creation of a strong imperialist government, by united action of the French upper class. Pope Leo XIII aimed at the same goal and advised the French Catholics to recognize the Republic. The moderate capitalistic republicans replied with an assurance that they too desired peace with the Church. The result was that the republican capitalists joined the conservatives. The new Right-wing bloc was composed of royalists, the Catholic groups, the " progressive " republicans, the nationalist remnants of the Boulanger movement, and the anti-Semites. It was determined to retain the form of a republic, but to prevent any reform which smacked of popular democracy and, if necessary, to suppress the masses with the aid of the Senate, the army, and the bureaucracy.

During the nineties the President of the Republic Faure and Prime Minister Méline represented the new French course. The policy of the conservative bloc was clearly and successfully imperialistic. In 1892 France returned to a system of protective tariffs — an event of equal practical and symbolic significance. The French foreign policy which had been started by Ferry was energetically continued during the nineties in northern Africa, Madagascar, and Indo-China. With it the French conservative bloc also combined a new policy in Europe. The Franco-Russian alliance was intended to protect France against the superior power of Germany and appeared to offer a possibility that France might reconquer Alsace-Lorraine at a favourable opportunity. The recovery of these provinces appeared necessary to the French bourgeoisie not only for nationalist reasons, but also because the incorporation into the French economy of the important Lorraine iron industry and the Alsatian potassium plants and textile industry was an exceedingly enticing goal for the French imperialists. The Franco-Russian alliance furthermore opened the way for the French banks to negotiate the transfer of an enormous accumulation of capital into Russian bonds.

In Germany Bismarck gradually accommodated himself to the demands of the imperialistic age. In 1879 Germany reintroduced the protective tariff. During the eighties a successful policy of colonial expansion was started in central and southern Africa. In addition the German fleet was greatly strengthened under Wilhelm II. The transformation of the old National Liberal Party furnished a party basis for imperialist politics. The National Liberals had originally been the great party of the German bourgeoisie, which since 1866 had been ready to co-operate with Bismarck on national questions, but at the same time wanted to remain true to its liberal traditions. After 1878 the new economic phenomena and problems of imperialism led to the disintegration and dissolution of the old National Liberal Party. In 1884 the party was reorganized on the basis of the Heidelberg program. From 1884 until the World War the new National Liberals no longer had anything in common with the older ones except the name. They were the party of the imperialist bourgeoisie. They supported the tariff, naval, and colonial policies of the government, defended the rights of the employers against the workers, and in the interest of the imperialistic industrialists renounced all liberal constitutional reforms in Germany.

While the new National Liberal Party was developing out of the ruins of the old German liberal movement, an important section of the German academic intellectuals demonstratively turned its back on liberalism. Treitschke, a professor at the University of Berlin, became the herald of the new *Weltanschauung,* which combined aristocratic nationalism with hatred of the Jews. The eighties also saw the origin of an anti-Semitic petty-bourgeois movement led by the court chaplain Stöcker. During this period the most important leader of the new imperialistic National Liberals was the Reichstag deputy Miquel. He personified very vividly the historical transformation of important groups of the German bourgeoisie. As a young man Miquel had been a revolutionary democrat and communist in 1848. He then became a liberal deputy, director of a large bank, Mayor of Frankfurt am Main, and an important leader of the National Liberals in their evolution towards imperialism. Miquel ended his memorable career as Prussian Minister of Finance under Wilhelm II. The other group of the German bourgeoisie, which wanted to retain the liberal ideas of the past, was represented by Eugen Richter, the leader of the German Independent (*Freisinnige*) Party. With dogged determination Richter maintained his forlorn hope and fought against the movements of the new period — against imperialism on the Right and socialism on the Left.

By recognizing the existing Prussian military state as a basis for their actions and declaring their readiness to support the King of Prussia in a policy of imperialism, the German industrialists were able to arrive at an understanding with the aristocratic large landowners. The East Elbian nobility, just like the industrialists, were interested in the maintenance of protective tariffs and a strong state. Bismarck united the Conservatives and the National Liberals — the parties of the large agrarians and the industrialists — to a so-called cartel. At the Reichstag election of 1887 the cartel obtained a majority of the seats. Under Wilhelm II the growth of the Social Democratic Party resulted in a corresponding weakening of the National Liberals. In order to maintain a Reichstag majority, the government was compelled to include the Catholic Centre Party in the coalition of Conservatives and National Liberals. However, the narrow-minded arrogance of the Prussian nobility, which would have preferred not to divide its power with any other group in Germany, made it exceedingly difficult for the government machine to function. The imperialistic manufacturers and intellectuals, who were loyal to the Empire, were sometimes driven to despair by the narrow-mindedness of the junkers, by the political escapades of Wilhelm II and the ineptitude of his bureaucracy. There were moments in the history of Germany under Wilhelm II when the entire bourgeoisie, industrialists as well as merchants, imperialists and liberals, were compelled to unite in opposing the government. The unfinished state of German political conditions, under which a powerful modern industrial development was implanted in a backward feudal, agrarian political organization, constantly produced new crises.

Similar problems regarding the manner in which modern industrial imperialism should be combined with feudal, agrarian institutions were also evident in the development of Russia and Japan, in Austria-Hungary and Italy. Until the World War the power of the state was relatively strongest in Japan. The energetic personality of the Emperor Mutsuhito united the historical military nobility and the new industrial bourgeoisie. A parliament with very few rights supplemented the bureaucratic machine of the state. The army, the navy, and industry were energetically modernized and Japan embarked upon a policy of colonial conquest in Korea and China. Until 1914 the opposition of democratic or socialist groups was very insignificant in Japan. Much greater were the internal difficulties of Russian tsarism. In Russia the modern imperialist bourgeoisie also looked to the state for support. The traditional tsarist policy of expansion towards Constantinople, the borders of India, and the Pacific Ocean could easily be employed for bourgeois-imperialistic purposes. Intelligent statesmen, such as the Minister of Finance Witte, aimed at a firm alliance between tsarism, the landowners, and the imperialist bourgeoisie. However, the Russian bureaucracy and nobility were even more backward and duller than the corresponding groups in Prussia. In addition the advance of the revolutionary masses repeatedly agitated the Russian ruling class. Nevertheless, after the defeat of the Russian Revolution of 1905, a kind of compromise was concluded in the new imperial parliament, the Duma, between the tsarist bureaucracy and the capitalistic groups, for the purpose of promoting a common imperialistic policy.

After 1871 Austro-Hungarian foreign policy turned more and more towards the Orient. The occupation of Bosnia and Herzegovina by Austrian troops in 1878 was to a certain extent the Habsburg contribution to colonial politics. Beyond that, however, Austrian economic interests extended throughout the entire Balkan Peninsula. To a lesser degree, then, Austria-Hungary also had its form of imperialism — power politics, supported by modern industrial and financial capitalism, together with the growth of the army and navy, protective tariffs, colonial acquisitions and economic interests in backward countries, which were aided by the Austrian government. After 1867 the Hungarian government party, composed of the landowning aristocracy and the modern bourgeoisie of Budapest, became the political representative of the imperial idea within the Habsburg Empire. In Austria, on the other hand, it was impossible to create a really modern imperialist party until the World War. During the last twenty years prior to the World War, the active Austrian imperialists, the officers, high officials, aristocrats, and their capitalist friends, generally gathered around the successor to the crown, Archduke Franz Ferdinand. Yet the group around Franz Ferdinand opposed the powerful position of the Hungarians within the Dual Monarchy and wanted to replace Austro-Hungarian dualism, which had existed since 1867, by centralization. This disagreement prevented united action by the Austro-Hungarian advocates of power politics.

Since the eighties the old German liberalism had completely disintegrated in Austria. Upon the ruins of German liberalism Lueger founded his anti-Semitic petty-bourgeois and peasant Christian Socialist Party. In a certain sense, Lueger's Catholic and loyal imperial party supplied a substitute within the Austrian Parliament for the missing imperialistic party of the bourgeoisie. The German academic youth of Austria likewise turned towards nationalism and anti-Semitism. However, owing to the circumstance that the ruling Austrian officials since Taaffe's time were by no means German nationalists, but, rather, friendly to the Slavs — in a certain sense, supra-national and Catholic — the Austro-German academic youth found no real sphere of activity. It may be said that prior to 1914 the German youth in Austria were generally inhibited imperialists. Consequently the Pan-German and German nationalist movement in Austria, which chiefly influenced large sections of the middle class in the German parts of Bohemia, was very hostile towards the Habsburg system. At the same time the opposition of the Slavic peoples towards the existing Austrian state gained in strength.

During the nineties the struggle between the various nationalities and the resulting general confusion led to the paralysis of the parliamentary machine in Vienna, so that the clerical and imperial bureaucracy was compelled to govern in order to maintain the existence of the Empire. The case of Austria proves that an imperialist movement can only become popular and influence the masses if it is based upon a definite nation. In Austria an imperialist nationality of this type was lacking, since the German nationalist movement was irreconcilably opposed to the Habsburg imperial idea. The necessary consequences of German nationalism were the dissolution of the Habsburg Empire and the union of the Germanic part of Austria with Germany. Consequently in Austria those academic groups whose counterparts in other countries represented the imperialist movement were hostile to the state; for if the aims of the German nationalist movement were incompatible with the existence of the Habsburg monarchy, those of the Slavic peoples of Austria-Hungary were even more inconsistent with the basic idea of the Empire. After the settlement of 1867 only Hungarian nationalism could perhaps have been united with the Habsburg imperial idea, but even in Hungary there was a faction among the Magyar landowners and intellectuals which regarded the union of the Hungarian people with the Habsburg dynasty as pernicious. Within the Budapest Parliament they sharply opposed the loyal government party. This lack of an effective internal political and national basis also prevented the advance of Habsburg imperialism abroad.

In comparison with the Habsburg Empire the Kingdom of Italy had the undisputed advantage of national unity. On the other hand, however, the individual Italian regions differed altogether economically, culturally, and psychologically. The educated liberal bourgeoisie of the north had created the Italian Kingdom. In the long run, however, it was incapable of maintaining its predominance over central and southern Italy. The parliamentary upheaval of 1876 resulted in the overthrow of the so-called Rights, who had been in power until then, and their replacement by the Lefts. With slight interruptions the so-called Lefts then governed Italy until the World War.

Nevertheless party names and the external appearance of parliamentary events ought not to deceive anyone. Actually the modern bourgeoisie supported the Rights, while the Lefts represented the semi-feudal south, with its combination of landlords, petty bourgeoisie, and leaders of local cliques. The patriotic politicians of the south opposed the predominance of the moderate, liberal north. Some of the former were men who, in their younger days, had fought against the maladministration of the Bourbons in Naples and had supported Garibaldi. These advocates of the south likewise wanted their share of power. Consequently they fought against the prevailing capitalistic-bureaucratic system of the north, apparently as radicals. Yet as soon as the Lefts came into power after 1876, only two possibilities were open to them. They could either carry out a social revolution, for which the so-called radical leaders had but little desire, or they could exploit the existing social structure of the south for their purposes. They decided for the latter.

The prime ministers of the so-called Lefts in Italy, men such as Depretis, Crispi, and Giolitti, who from 1876 until 1914 generally decided the fate of the country, were neither the leaders of the broad labouring masses nor of the modern capitalistic bourgeoisie. They were the representatives of a skilfully constructed party and administrative machine which drew its actual strength from the pre-capitalistic, backward sections of central and southern Italy. The internal policy of the Lefts was chiefly concerned with maintaining the rule of the landlords over the wretched and illiterate rural labourers and small tenants at all costs. If the rural Italian slaves dared to revolt, they were mercilessly shot down. Furthermore the state revenues were often used to aid the interests of local adherents of the government. Thus from 1876 until the World War the parliamentary monarchy in Italy was only a façade for a corrupt system, which was a strange mixture of democratic ministerial speeches, the speculations of unscrupulous professional politicians, the bullets of the police, and the devious dealings of the Camorra.

It is clear that such a system of government was incapable of serving modern imperialism consistently. When the Italian Lefts came into power in 1876, no modern large-scale industry existed as yet. When modern large industries and banks then gradually developed in northern Italy, the economic leaders received but little assistance from the government. Public funds were not employed primarily to aid industry and transportation and to modernize the army and the navy, but rather for the local and other purposes of the dominant groups. Prior to the World War the imperialistic bourgeoisie was still too weak in Italy to carry out any fundamental changes. Nevertheless the pressure of the imperialists on the ruling politicians gradually grew stronger. In Italian politics prior to the World War, the representatives of the imperialist tendency were still to be found together with the remnants of the old Rights. These were men like Sonnino, who worked energetically for a reorganization of Italy and the concentration of all the national energies for imperialistic development. Prior to 1914, although head of the government for short periods, Sonnino was unable to achieve any fundamental changes in the system of government. Gradually the national youth and student movement, which was still inspired by Garibaldi and Mazzini, also turned towards imperialism.

The only possible foreign policy for Italian imperialism was the continuation of the struggle against Austria and the liberation of the last Italian provinces that were still in the hands of the Habsburgs. With the conquest of these " unredeemed " regions, Italy would have received not only South Tyrol, but also the large harbour of Trieste, a dominant position on the eastern coast of the Adriatic, and the possibility for active penetration of the Balkans. However, by entering the Triple Alliance and thus concluding an alliance with the house of Habsburg, the Italian Lefts renounced not only all intention of liberating the Trentino and Trieste, but also any active Adriatic and Balkan policy, since this was impossible with the consent of Austria. Instead the Left governments undertook several colonial expeditions in Africa. Crispi failed completely in Abyssinia, while Giolitti was more fortunate in Tripoli. Prior to the World War Italy's national imperialism exhibited itself in these colonial enterprises and in several agreements with France, which were contrary to the Triple Alliance. Corresponding to the unsolved internal conflicts, Italian foreign policy remained vacillating and equivocal until 1914. It was not until Italy's entry into the World War in 1915 that a decisive step was taken towards imperialism in internal and foreign affairs.

In Russia, Japan, Germany, and Austria-Hungary the imperialistic movements prior to the World War were definitely anti-democratic. In France the imperialists were the allies of the monarchists and the advocates of a dictatorship. In Italy the nationalists grew more and more sceptical of attaining their aims with the help of Parliament and elections. By means of violent demonstrations and by terrorizing the majority of Parliament, which favoured neutrality, the imperialists compelled Italy to enter the war in 1915. In the United States the imperialists employed the traditional democratic machinery, but by the use of ruthless political methods they forced their will upon the masses. Only in England did modern imperialism combine with an indigenous bourgeois-democratic movement.

During the period when Disraeli was carrying out his reorganization of the Conservative Party in Great Britain and had attached the labouring masses to his party by means of the electoral law of 1867, modern trust capitalism hardly existed as yet. The Conservative Party, which united the imperial idea with social progress, was nevertheless the only organization by means of which the modern imperialists could later gain political influence. The union of the English Conservative movement with capitalistic imperialism took place gradually, during the eighties and nineties. Thus because of his views on Ireland, Cecil Rhodes began his political career as an opponent of the Conservative Party, and it was only later that Joseph Chamberlain too abandoned the Left Liberals for the Conservatives. The new tendencies within the British Empire did not definitely manifest themselves until 1895, when, after a short liberal interlude, a new conservative government was formed, with Chamberlain as Secretary of State for the Colonies. The Conservative Party now espoused the great project of Cecil Rhodes, the creation of a united British Africa extending from the Cape to Cairo. Chamberlain devoted all his energy to the realization of the African plans and to the extension and co-ordination of the British Empire. After the turn of the century Chamberlain also began his propaganda for England's return to a protective tariff. Nevertheless the Conservative Party generally remained a firm advocate of bourgeois democracy, and Chamberlain always took particular pains to win over the English working masses to his ideas.

The years 1895 and 1896 represent the high-water mark of imperialism in the internal and foreign affairs of the major powers. In England the Conservatives were the victors in the elections of 1895, as has been said. During the same year Faure was elected President of the French Republic by the votes of the imperialist bloc. In 1896 after a dramatic election campaign the Republican candidate McKinley became President of the United States. In Germany towards the end of 1894 Wilhelm II had dismissed his vacillating Chancellor Caprivi. He was succeeded by Prince Hohenlohe, who pursued a decidedly imperialistic course. During 1895–6 the government coalition in Germany, consisting of the National Liberals, the Conservatives, and the Centre, was strengthened in the Reichstag. During the same period Germany embarked upon an unsettled policy of colonial acquisition, based upon the personal initiative of Wilhelm II. In addition the navy was enlarged, while at the same time plans were considered to pass a new repressive law against the socialist workers and to abolish general suffrage in the Empire. Contemporaneously in Russia the Minister of Finance, Witte, attempted to arrange an agreement between the Tsar and modern capitalism.

In 1895 Japan also made its first major imperialistic advance in the war with China. Russia, France, and Germany, however, opposed the victorious Japanese and compelled them to give up the greater part of their booty. Towards the end of 1895 Jameson, aided by Cecil Rhodes, attempted to overrun the Transvaal Republic of the Boers and by a bold stroke to seize it for the British Empire. The famous telegram of Wilhelm II to President Kruger of the Transvaal showed the desire of the German Empire to oppose the policy of the British in South Africa. At the same time Crispi carried out his unfortunate expedition against Abyssinia. Thus during 1895–6 imperialism was very active in the internal and foreign politics of seven major powers. Only Austria-Hungary was paralysed by its internal crisis. In Vienna at that time the Slavophil course of Prime Minister Badeni met with the strongest opposition from the German nationalists. Consequently the Habsburg Empire was completely incapable of participating in colonial expansion.

It is a remarkable fact, which proves the general validity of imperialism, that after 1880 even Belgium and Holland, the two minor European states which were most highly developed economically, exhibited similiar tendencies. In 1884 the Catholic Conservative Party obtained power in Belgium, and it maintained its position until the World War. During the eighties Belgium also began, at first as a personal undertaking of Leopold II, an extremely successful colonial policy in central Africa, which resulted in the establishment of the Belgian Congo state. After 1884 the Belgian Catholic Conservative government stubbornly opposed the demand of the socialistic workers for general suffrage. Belgium also exhibited the same tendencies as the major powers: continually increasing concentration of industry, colonial politics, decline of the liberal idea among the bourgeoisie, desire of the wealthy class for a strong government which would be capable of combating the socialism of the proletariat. Developments in Holland, where the rich bourgeoisie had to defend both its political power and the great colonial empire of the Netherlands, were very similar to those in Belgium. With growing industrialization, the number of industrial workers also increased, thus rendering the class struggle more acute. In Holland, too, the bourgeoisie gradually turned away from the liberal traditions. A new Calvinist conservative party appeared, whose name, the Anti-Revolutionaries, was sufficient indication of its bias. In 1887 the first government of the Right was formed in Holland. After the eighties the complete decline of liberalism became equally evident in all countries where a liberal movement of any significance at all existed. The power of the liberals in parliament collapsed alike in Holland, Belgium, and Austria. In England the elections of 1892 had not been decisive. Neither the Liberals nor the Conservatives had a majority. The decision lay with the Irish party, with whose aid a Liberal government had stayed in power from 1892 to 1895. During these years English liberalism was torn by serious internal dissensions. The Right wing of the party, led by Lord Rosebery, leaned more and more to the imperialist views of the Conservatives, while the Left wing, under Harcourt, defended Gladstone's traditions. When Gladstone resigned his office as Prime Minister in 1894 and was succeeded by Lord Rosebery, it appeared as if the Right wing of the party had gained the upper hand.

But if the English Liberals agreed with the Conservatives on the decisive questions of imperial and foreign policy, what justification was there for the continued existence of a separate Liberal party? The power exerted by imperialist ideas on the wealthy bourgeoisie was so great that more and more bourgeois groups turned to the new principles, and the sphere of action of traditional liberalism constantly decreased. In the two following English parliamentary elections of 1895 and 1900 the Liberals were seriously defeated, and at the turn of the century the Boer War split the party even further. A number of Liberals fought vehemently against this genuinely imperialistic enterprise, while another Liberal group supported the government for national reasons.

The decline of liberalism in Germany took place in a corresponding manner. In the spring of 1884 the Independent Liberal Party, led by Eugen Richter, the actual representative of the liberal tradition, still had 100 out of a total of 397 representatives in the Reichstag. When new elections were held in the autumn of 1884 the number of Independent Liberal representatives dropped to 65 and after the elections of 1887 to 32. In 1890, 64 Independent Liberals were elected, but three years later the party split because a group of German liberals wanted to support the Caprivi government; that is, they wanted to arrive at an understanding with the ruling system. In the elections of 1893 Richter's irreconcilable opposition group, the Independent Liberal People's Party, was able to elect only 25 deputies. The Independent Liberal Union elected 13 representatives, while a separate group of south-German liberals, the People's Party, obtained 11 seats. It is evident that around 1893 German liberalism was in a state of complete disintegration, and indeed chiefly because of the problems of imperialism. The Independent Liberal Union supported the greatly increased military budget of the imperial government, which Richter vehemently opposed. The Independent Liberal Union, in contrast to Richter's group, also voted for the naval construction program demanded by the government in 1895. In Germany, then, as well as in England, liberalism disintegrated at the same time and for the same reasons.

16. *Liberal Democracy and the Second International*

During the last third of the nineteenth century declining liberalism could only count upon the constantly decreasing groups of the bourgeoisie which rejected imperialism. Consequently liberalism was compelled to seek contact with that section of the masses which likewise opposed imperialism. In this manner liberalism united with the liberal democratic movement. At a time when the liberal parties still influenced the majority of the wealthy bourgeoisie and exercised parliamentary power in England, Germany, and Belgium, differences of opinion were already present in their ranks regarding the expediency of making the workers politically responsible by granting them the franchise. In England the extreme Left wing of the Liberals, led by Bright, had advocated an understanding of this kind with the workers; in 1848 similar endeavours had been made by the Left wing of the bourgeoisie in Germany and France. However, the defeat of the revolution on the Continent and the failure of all efforts for electoral reform in England until 1866 prevented this liberal democratic movement from attaining any practical significance. Only Switzerland after 1847 developed as a typical liberal democratic country. Switzerland wanted no conquests, had no military ambitions, and developed her economic interests in peace. Switzerland had manhood suffrage, together with the complete protection of civil private property — that is, just those social and political institutions which liberal democracy wanted.

Bismarck introduced manhood suffrage into the German Empire, and Disraeli did the same in England. After that it was impossible for the liberals either in England or in Germany to advocate restriction of the political rights of the workers. In these two great countries a practical liberal policy was only possible on the basis of general suffrage and an alliance between the capitalists and the workers. Consequently in the age of imperialism liberal democracy was the only conceivable basis for liberal politics. The program of the German People's Party of 1895 is a classic example of a liberal-democratic program of that period. The People's Party was still supported by the majority of the middle class and petty bourgeoisie of Württemberg, who were as yet untouched by the influence of monopoly capitalism. The tradition of this local form of German Left-wing liberalism was derived from the bourgeois south-German democratic movement of 1848. The program contains the following:

" The German People's Party is a party of political progress. It adheres to the democratic principles of liberty and equality and demands the equal participation of all citizens in legislation, administration, and administration of justice — in other words, popular self-government in the state. . . . The People's Party is a party of social and economic reforms. It recognizes that political and social questions are inseparable, and that the economic and social elevation of the working classes and the realization of political liberty are mutually interdependent. It strives for a peaceful settlement of all social differences, within a social order which guarantees liberty for the individual. The People's Party is a party of peace. The party recognizes that war and militarism are serious menaces to public welfare as well as to the interests of culture and freedom. It strives for the establishment of a league of nations for peace and liberty." The specific economic demands of the party were: " Increase of national wealth and protection of the poorer classes, promotion of free trade, no preferential treatment for large capitalistic groups and cartels."

The program of Eugen Richter's Independent Liberal People's Party agreed in all fundamental points with the views of the Württemberg People's Party. In England, at least the adherents of the Left wing of the Liberals would have been able to subscribe to these principles. During the nineties the liberal democrats had but little influence on the wealthy bourgeoisie in Germany as well as in England, to say nothing of the other countries. Liberal democracy became historically and politically significant at that time, only because the great mass of the industrial workers of Europe as well as certain sections of the petty bourgeoisie which were hostile to imperialism accepted the liberal-democratic slogans.

Since the eighties the rise of large-scale industry in all the important countries had been accompanied by an increase in both the number and fighting spirit of the industrial workers. Concomitantly the significance of the socialist workers' parties automatically increased in Germany, Austria, France, Italy, Holland, Belgium, and Switzerland. During the nineties the socialists in all these countries had become political factors worthy of serious consideration. As a result it was correspondingly more difficult for the socialist parties to find their way about in the new world of politics. At first the socialists in the industrial countries of Europe were only able to agree on a few tactical principles: organization of the workers in trade unions for economic struggles, and the organization of socialist parties for political activity; the use of parliamentary activity, in order to present the demands of the workers with as great determination as possible; propaganda for general suffrage in those countries where the ruling class still denied the workers this right; restriction of the labour movement to peaceful methods, rejection of individual terrorism and hopeless attempts at revolt.

Nevertheless these principles did not suffice to permit the socialist parties to take a definite stand on the manifold questions of daily political life. The European working class was compelled to grope its way forward laboriously and empirically. At the same time, for reasons which will be explained in detail later, they received practically no help from Marx and Engels. They were chiefly concerned with the following questions: What should be the attitude of the workers to the other large groups of the population, the peasants, artisans, and intellectuals? Connected with it was the question: What attitude should a socialist workers' party take with respect to the other parties of the country? Should they attempt to achieve partial successes through alliances with other parties and influence the state in this manner? Or should they reject such compromises? What was the relation of the socialist parties to the general questions of economic policy where they transcended the direct relations of employer and employee? What was the attitude of the socialists to the state and the fatherland in general? What position was a socialist party to take with regard to the questions of foreign policy, the army and navy, colonies, and the problems of imperialism which were acute then?

The answers to all these questions followed from the views which gradually developed among the socialist workers during the latter third of the nineteenth century. The leading socialist theoreticians of the period, men like Kautsky, attempted to unite only those views which were actually present among the workers with the general scientific doctrines of Marxism. It would be completely false and unhistorical, however, to maintain that Kautsky and his friends invented the principles of the Second International. On the contrary, the socialist labour movement during the period of the Second International from 1889 to 1914 is the historical product resulting from the evolution of the European proletariat. This type of labour movement necessarily resulted from the conditions which had developed up to 1889.

The class-consciousness with which the industrial workers of Europe were imbued led them to lay great emphasis on their specific position and on those factors which differentiated them from all other economic groups. The result was that although no socialist party injured the peasants or the artisans with its program, or initiated any movement against the middle class, still the practical activity of every socialist party was restricted chiefly to the industrial workers. To say the least, to the middle classes the socialist parties as labour parties appeared strange. As a result, in practical politics a gap, which was to have serious consequences, appeared between the labour party on the one hand, and all the other parties on the other which, as the so-called "bourgeois" parties, agreed in rejecting socialism. The simple socialist worker furthermore distrusted profoundly all groups of employers, all organs of the state, and all non-socialist parties. He felt, and was usually justified in doing so, that he was persecuted and slighted by all other parties and institutions. Consequently he demanded that his party maintain an attitude of irreconcilable protest against the existing bourgeois state. He rejected alliances with other political parties and so-called partial political successes. In this manner it was particularly the strong and genuine class-consciousness of the vanguard of the European working class that increased the political isolation of the socialist movement.

The socialist worker was profoundly sceptical of all speeches about the fatherland and its greatness, such as were common on all official occasions. He was convinced that the army of the capitalist state was used to repress the masses, and that only small groups of speculators obtained any advantage from the government's foreign policy of conquest. He was not interested in colonies. He did not want his sons to be killed for the policy of conquest of the ruling class. He demanded peace and understanding between nations, and felt himself attracted to his class comrades in other countries, who had to fight against the same opponents under the same conditions as he himself. The class-conscious European worker therefore greeted the re-establishment of the International with especial sincerity and joy, and he opposed the propaganda of the nationalists in his own country with his faith in international social democracy, which united the nations.

The study of scientific Marxism only tended to confirm the European labour leaders in their views. Here they found the material for a trenchant criticism of the prevailing capitalistic order. It explained to them why the workers were constantly being exploited by the capitalist system, and why it is impossible to change this fundamental fact without replacing the capitalistic social order by a socialist one. Marxism showed the European industrial workers the importance of their own class and pointed out the historical task of the workers at present and in the future.

In general these views correspond approximately to official radicalism, the most important current of thought within the socialist International from its founding in 1889 until the outbreak of the World War. At the same time it is very odd that on every single question of practical politics the official radicalism of the Second International found itself in sharp contrast with the teaching of Marx himself. The very division of the nation into a socialistic-proletarian and a so-called bourgeois mass, whereby every individual is considered "bourgeois" who is not a factory worker or who votes against the social democrats, is completely non-Marxist. Marx erected his doctrine upon the antagonism of the proletariat to the bourgeoisie, but not on the contrast of the socialists with the "bourgeois elements." The bourgeoisie, according to Marx, is only a small minority of the nation. It consists of the owners of the socially important means of production. The proletariat, as the leader of all the productive elements of the nation, is to solve the historical task of building a new society. Because of their class position the industrial workers are especially suited to lead this struggle. In the opinion of Marx the working class can free itself of certain prejudices much easier than the peasants and the petty bourgeoisie. But to consider the peasants and artisans in one group with the manufacturers and bankers, to label this entire group as " bourgeois," and to oppose this peculiar " bourgeois " world by a socialist one, have nothing to do with Marxism. Marx and Engels were never interested in the industrial workers solely as an economic group. It has repeatedly been emphasized in the course of this study that Marx and Engels devoted a large part of their work to the study of agrarian conditions, for instance in Ireland and Russia.

The attitude of Marx and Engels to the question of a

coalition between the workers' parties and the so-called bourgeois parties followed from these considerations. Marx always considered an alliance between his party and other parties admissible if it served the interests of the revolutionary movement. This is not only true of the Revolution of 1848. Marx's and Engels's criticism of the Lassalleans in 1863 and later is based chiefly on the reproach that the latter deserted the liberal bourgeoisie in its struggle against Bismarck and feudalism, by attacking only the capitalists and not the Prussian junkers. During the last years of his life Marx completely identified himself with the Russian revolutionary movement — that is, with a peasant movement led by intellectuals — although it had no connexion either with the proletariat or with proletarian socialism.

From these premises it necessarily followed that as soon as the workers' party, together with its allies, obtained power, or at least a majority in parliament, it would have to fulfil corresponding obligations. It was, for instance, evident that when Ledru-Rollin's party had received its share of power in France in February 1848, it also had to participate in the administration of the revenues. The only question was whether the party actually did influence the budget in accordance with its ideas. The so-called radicals of the Second International, on the other hand, rejected alliances with other parties and considered it inadmissible to approve the budget of a bourgeois state. During the period of the Second International the attitude of the official social democrats towards monarchism assumed forms that were just as odd. Marx had demanded a definite espousal of republicanism from the labour movement in Germany as an expression of revolutionary opposition to the ruling system of the Hohenzollerns. Nevertheless during the period of the Second International this serious problem degenerated to petty questions of tact: whether it was permissible for a social democrat to converse with an archduke, to accept his invitation, or even to attend his funeral.

For Marx and Engels the question "Free trade or protective tariff" was a problem of expediency. The first was just as much a form of capitalistic economic policy as the second. Yet the radicals of the Second International advocated free trade with dogmatic partiality; partly in order to lower the cost of living for the workers as consumers, and partly because they adhered to the current liberal theories. Marx and Engels always regarded war as a political instrument, capable of being employed for the revolutionary cause as well as for any other. The Second International, on the other hand, unconditionally advocated peace under any circumstances. Marx and Engels always affirmed the right of national self-determination and the right of major nations to exist. In contrast with this the radicals of the Second International by their polemics against the national policies of their own governments and their general avowal of the brotherhood of man produced the most serious misunderstandings, to say the least, in the minds of both friend and foe.

The decisive difference lay in the circumstance that Marx and Engels carried on a realistic revolutionary policy, which was compelled to take account of concrete facts, while the radicals of the Second International abandoned a popular revolutionary policy for a policy more directly concerned with the economic interests and protests of the industrial workers. It may be asked: Why did Marx and Engels calmly watch this development without protesting against the wrong trend of the European socialist parties? Until their death both men were incessantly active and full of fighting spirit. Marx followed the most important tendencies of the European social-democratic parties until 1883, and Engels, his strength unimpaired, lived for six years after the founding of the Second International and was venerated as their chief and leader by the members of the International. In 1848 Marx and Engels in the *Communist Manifesto* had presented their followers with a very realistic program, which considered the tactical conditions of each country and was a clear guide for the revolutionary workers. Why didn't the two men issue a new edition of the *Communist Manifesto* in 1880 with changes corresponding to the altered conditions? Why didn't Engels publish a corresponding book in 1890 as a political guide for the new International?

In 1872, while preparing a new edition of the *Communist Manifesto,* Marx and Engels wrote a short foreword, dealing particularly with the Paris Commune, and closing with the following statement: " The *Manifesto* is a historical document, which we no longer have the right to change. Perhaps a later edition will appear, accompanied by an introduction bridging the interval from 1847 to the present. The present reprint arrived too unexpectedly to permit us to do so." Nevertheless the new introduction was never written. For the editions which he later prepared in 1883 and 1890, Engels wrote short prefaces, containing very important ideas but no accommodation of the tactical problems of the labour movement to the present. The most popular Marxist work dating from the last years of Marx and Engels is *Socialism — Utopian and Scientific.* But even this book did not help the European workers by furnishing them with a tactical guide to the political tasks of the present. In the fourth edition, of 1891, Engels inserted a section on the trusts, which had become important in the meantime. This would have been a good opportunity to elucidate anew the tactics of the socialist labour movement in the age of the trusts. But Engels did not do it.

Several causes contributed to this peculiar attitude of restraint on the part of Marx and Engels. In the first place, both men never completely understood the actual character of the new European labour parties that developed after 1863. They felt that these parties did not act in accordance with their own ideas. Yet they regarded the mistakes of the workers' leaders and the petty-bourgeois backwardness of their followers as the cause of this deviation. Marx and Engels mercilessly criticized individual actions of Lassalle and

Wilhelm Liebknecht, yet this criticism hides the conviction
that basically the socialist parties still are, or at least should
be, revolutionary parties like those of 1848; that it suffices
to berate the erring leaders and to oppose the petty-bourgeois
prejudices of their followers in order to set matters right
again. But Marx and Engels failed to recognize that after
1863 they were not dealing with individual mistakes within
the socialist parties, but rather with a new type, and that the
average European labour party was basically different from
revolutionary Marxism.

After the catastrophe of 1871 Marx and Engels had to give
up all hope of early revolutionary developments in Europe,
with the exception of Russia. They considered it unnecessary for the present to give the small, weak workers' parties
any tactical instructions for a revolution which they would
not be able to carry out within the near future. Then came
the German Socialist Law of 1878. For twelve years the German Social Democrats were persecuted and oppressed by the
strongest European government of that period; yet the German labour movement remained intact. In 1890 Bismarck
was overthrown, the Socialist Law repealed, and it became
evident that the Social Democratic Party had increased its
strength during the years of persecution. Engels was filled
with the greatest admiration for the courage and loyalty with
which the German socialist workers had maintained their
ground. But once again his conception of the causes underlying this attitude of the German workers was incorrect.
During the nineties Engels, then an old man, made the same
mistake that he, together with Marx, had made fifty years
earlier. In his own revolutionary ardour he overestimated
the fighting power of the existing popular parties. Just as
Engels had overestimated the Chartists and Ledru-Rollin's
party during the forties, he now judged the German Social
Democrats incorrectly.

The respect which Engels had for the German working
class during the period of the Socialist Law was certainly

merited. Nevertheless the motives which moved the German workers were actually very different from those that Engels assumed. The German socialist workers were imbued with a firm and unshakable class-consciousness. They refused to be defeated by the capitalists and the police. They preferred to endure all kinds of persecution rather than desert their party and their class; but they had no thought of an imminent revolution in the near future, in the course of which the socialist workers, at the head of the German people, would drive out the Hohenzollerns. Engels, on the other hand, could expect no greater proof of the German workers' revolutionary spirit than their behaviour during the twelve years of the Socialist Law. After 1890 he believed implicitly in the vitality of German Social Democracy, and as the German party was the strongest and most important one of the new International, Engels was able to approve heartily of the International of 1889 and to co-operate with it.

A few quotations from Engels's letters may serve to indicate how little actual correspondence existed between his conceptions and the real conditions of German politics. In 1895, the year of his death, Engels wrote: "The constantly growing, unceasing spread of the party contributes to the difficulty of absorbing the newer elements as compared with the older ones. We already have the workers in the large cities — that is, the most intelligent ones. Those who join now are either workers from smaller towns or rural districts, students, white-collar workers, etc., or petty-bourgeois elements, struggling against destruction, and rural home workers who still own or rent a piece of land, and now, over and above that, even real peasants. And since our party is in fact the only really progressive one, the only party strong enough to force concessions, the temptation lies close at hand to spread propaganda for socialism among the indebted farmers with large and middle-sized holdings who are becoming rebellious, particularly in regions where these groups predominate."

Engels stated correctly that at this period German Social Democracy had already won over the majority of the industrial workers in the large cities. It was also true that until 1914 the Social Democratic Party also attracted certain petty-bourgeois and rural groups that were exasperated by conditions within the Empire and expressed their dissatisfaction by voting for the Reds. Nevertheless the relation of the Social Democrats to the German middle classes, and in general to all the other groups of the population who were not industrial workers, was indeed very different from what Engels imagined. Engels believed that it would be possible to bridge the gap between the socialist party and the middle classes; social democracy as the only actually progressive party of the nation might then be a real popular movement, capable of attracting ever increasing groups without great effort. Actually the rigid contrast of " bourgeois " and " social democratic " and the isolation of the socialist skilled workers, which could not be removed even by the occasional entry of middle-class individuals into their ranks, already existed at that time. However, the Social Democratic Party would only have been able to triumph in a revolution if it had been a party of the people, in the manner of 1848. Engels believed this to be the case, but the actuality of German politics was different.

In a letter written in 1884 Engels had already engaged in noteworthy reflections on the coming German revolution and the role which so-called pure democracy would play in it. He wrote: " This has been the course of every revolution; the most moderate party which is still capable of governing obtains power, but only because the vanquished regard it as their last hope of salvation. Now, it should not be expected that we will be supported by the majority of the voters — that is, of the nation — at the critical moment. The entire bourgeoisie and the remnants of the wealthy feudal class, a large section of the petty bourgeoisie, as well as the rural population will then gather around the bourgeois party, whose phraseology is extremely revolutionary, and I consider it very likely that it will be represented in the provisional government; indeed, it may even have a momentary majority. How the minority should not act at such a time was shown by the Social Democratic minority of the Paris February government of 1848. However, the latter question is at present only of academic interest."

In this passage Engels considers the possibility of a victorious revolution in Germany at a moment when the Social Democrats are not yet in the majority. The government would then fall into the hands of the pure democrats. At that time in Germany this meant the party of Eugen Richter. The Social Democrats would certainly participate in the provisional government; that is, Bebel would take part in the temporary republican government together with Richter, just as in 1848 in Paris Ledru-Rollin had co-operated with Lamartine. As Engels emphasizes, the Social Democrats, in participating in a future government, would have to avoid the mistakes which had resulted in the failure of the Social Democrats in France in 1848. But where were the concrete conditions for a revolution in Germany from 1884 to 1895? Actually not the slightest prospect existed that a popular revolt would drive the Emperor out of Berlin, that Richter and Bebel would enter the palace together and occupy the positions of Bismarck and Wilhelm I. Engels himself regards his reflections as " academic." Yet he was very serious about it. During the last decade of his life he repeatedly considered the possibility of a German revolution of this type. The only basis for such an eventuality was the revolutionary spirit which Engels assumed in the Social Democratic Party. The revolutionary wave which would emanate from the Social Democrats would then also involve the Progressive Party and might possibly make Richter and his friends the head of the German government.

At the same time Engels also considered the manner in which such a transitional government of the Left liberal bourgeoisie could be avoided. In the same letter he wrote: "Now events in Germany can certainly take a different course, due to military reasons. As matters now stand, an external impulse can hardly come from anywhere but Russia. If it should fail to materialize and the impulse arises within Germany, it can only come from the army. From a military point of view an unarmed nation is an almost negative quantity in comparison with a modern army. In this case, where our reservists between the ages of twenty and twenty-five, who drill but do not vote, go into action, the stage of pure democracy could be skipped. At the present, however, this question is likewise still academic, although I, as the representative, so to say, of the entire general staff of the party, am obliged to consider it."

Engels knew perfectly well that a barricade revolt against an intact modern army of the continental European type is hopeless. A modern European revolution can only triumph if the army itself revolts. The history of the revolutions of 1917 and 1918 in Russia and Germany confirms completely the correctness of this view. If the German urban and rural recruits could be influenced by revolutionary propaganda so that the majority of the army would be composed of Social Democrats, the Prussian army would collapse internally. The revolution would then produce a socialist government, and the Red soldiers would not have to tolerate a government of the liberal progressive party. If the events of 1918 are considered, it becomes evident that Engels's ideas were by no means fantastic. The German November Revolution actually approximated this course. However, in Germany in 1914 a conscious desire for revolution was completely lacking both within and outside of the Social Democratic Party.

It is now possible to answer the question which was raised at the beginning of this book: How far had the political concept of democracy changed between 1848 and 1884? For Engels in 1884 "pure" democracy meant Left bourgeois liberalism, the liberal democracy of Eugen Richter. In the meantime in Germany the barricade fighter of 1848 had been replaced by the Progressive Party as the representative of democracy. In France in 1884 the democrats were no longer Blanqui or Ledru-Rollin, but rather the members of the Radical faction in the Chamber. In England the democrats were no longer the Chartists, but rather Gladstone's group. The old social-democratic movement of 1848 had vanished from the political horizon of Europe. Its place was taken, even if very inadequately, by the various socialist parties and groups.

In 1848 the concept of democracy generally embraced the labouring masses, in so far as they fought against the wealthy upper class. In the meantime, however, the concept of democracy had been taken over into the camp of the wealthy bourgeoisie and now embraced the Left wing of bourgeois liberalism — namely, the parties and groups that had accommodated themselves to general suffrage and fought against modern imperialism in the name of liberty and free competition. While the older democratic movement had had a definite social content, now the social fighting slogans no longer belonged to the essence of bourgeois democracy. This new form of democracy desired class conciliation together with modest reforms. It had become a purely political form of democracy. It is in this sense that Engels in 1884 speaks of " pure " democracy. For the social revolutionary, therefore, pure democracy is on the other side of the barricades, although he may sometimes be compelled to conclude an alliance with the liberal democrats in his struggle against the imperialists and the militaristic monarchists.

From the beginning the relation between Engels and the Second International rested on a profound misunderstanding. The supposition that revolutionary Marxism and the modern labour parties had the same aims was tacitly recognized. Nevertheless this condition did not exist. The peculiar contradiction which runs through the entire history of the Second International had already appeared at its foundation. During the seventies English social legislation had reached a temporary conclusion and in Switzerland a factory law had been passed. During the eighties in Germany, Bismarck also initiated protective legislation for the workers, although still in a very cautious and inadequate form. In every country the industrialists opposed demands for social reform with the objection that social legislation increases production costs: it is imperative that the social reforms should not remain restricted to single countries, for otherwise the socially progressive countries would be surpassed in international competition by the more backward countries, capable of producing cheaply. As a result social legislation and the protection of labour became matters of international concern.

The working class endeavoured as far as possible to achieve the same level of social progress in all the industrial countries. In 1887, in accordance with this purpose, the congress of the German Social Democratic Party at St. Gall—the German socialists were compelled to meet in Switzerland as long as the Socialist Law made it impossible for them to do so in their own country—proposed the convocation of a general international labour congress. This assembly should promote common action by the workers in all countries towards the enactment of legislation for the protection of labour on an international scale. This congress met in Paris in 1889. The result was that the participating parties decided to remain in closer contact with each other. The congress drew up a practical program for the international protection of labour, which was to culminate in a legal eight-hour day. The first of May was designated as a labour holiday for the purpose of propagating this idea. These resolutions of the congress of Paris were very logical and in accord with the conditions of the period. It is characteristic of the situation at that time that an international governmental congress met in Berlin in 1890, at the invitation of the German government, to discuss the question of the protection of labour. Although Wilhelm II and his advisers were very far removed from the socialist leaders, yet they agreed with the latter in the conviction that the protection of labour was an international question which should be solved on an international scale.

In this respect the new International represented the interests and the character of the socialist parties and the labour movement in the individual countries of Europe. The chief task of the individual parties was to promote the trade interests of the workers in each country. The corresponding International should co-ordinate the efforts of the working class to improve its condition as uniformly as possible. In this manner successes which were achieved in one country could immediately affect the other industrial nations. It is evident that the Second International was very different from the First International. To be sure, the latter had also occupied itself zealously and successfully with the trade questions of the proletariat, but it had not been founded in the interest of social reforms; its purpose was rather to organize the workers of the most important countries for a common revolutionary democratic policy. The Polish question contributed to the rise of the First International just as the problem of the eight-hour day led to the establishment of the Second International. At the same time it should not be overlooked that the First International also occupied itself energetically with the problem of the working day, and that the Second International at all times expressed its sympathy for the oppressed nations. Yet the occasion for the creation of each International and the aims which they pursued were fundamentally different.

Nevertheless the Second International, too, was not only an association of proletarian parties for the purpose of advancing their international economic interests. The socialist parties whose delegates met in Paris in 1889 had also accepted the Marxist doctrine, at least formally. It was as a symbolic gesture that the International Workers' Congress

had been convoked in Paris on the centenary of the great
French Revolution, although the Paris of General Boulanger
no longer presented any great similarity with the Paris which
existed at the time of the storming of the Bastille. The tradition of Marxism and the Revolution contained its own obligations. Consequently the workers in the socialist parties
demanded something more from their new International
than simply uniform proposals for a struggle against child
labour, and so on, in the various countries. The workers
in all the larger countries gradually comprehended the character of the new imperialistic period in which they lived.
The growing armaments of the major powers and the danger
of war, which grew greater from year to year, agitated the
minds of men. Although the labour International could not
agitate for a world revolution under the conditions of 1889
and the subsequent years, still it was expected that the International should somehow prevent the approaching world
war.

The first year of the new International saw the repeal of
the Socialist Law in Germany and the astounding electoral
victory of German Social Democracy, which after twelve
years of persecution received almost a million and a half
votes in the Reichstag election of 1890, thus becoming the
strongest party in Germany. Engels also still lived to see the
Reichstag election of 1893, in which the Social Democratic
Party gained hundreds of thousands of votes. The Social
Democratic Party appeared to grow with the automatic cer-
tainty of a natural law. Apart from slight chicaneries, the
imperial government no longer dared to prohibit the labour
party. Engels believed that any government is lost if it permits a hostile movement, working to overthrow it, to carry
on its agitation within legal limits. Historically this opinion
is very true. When the absolute monarch of France was compelled to permit elections to the General Estates in 1789, it
actually meant the abdication of the ruling system. Or when
the King of Spain in 1931 allowed the republicans to gain

control of the communities in the country, he sealed the fate of the Spanish crown. Again when the German Republic after 1930 had to watch calmly while the National Socialists won one victory after another in the elections, the decisive victory of German counter-revolution had already been won.

Since Engels, on the basis of the events during the period of the Socialist Law and the one-sidedness of his entire judgment, considered German Social Democracy as an actively revolutionary party, he was compelled to draw the same conclusions from the election results of 1890 and 1893: it would be simply stupid for a revolutionary party not to employ so-called legality under such conditions, and to render its certain success doubtful by any premature putsch. The political leaders of the movement must only recognize the correct psychological moment for a transition from legality to revolutionary action. Consequently Engels was in complete accord with the apparently peaceful tactics of German Social Democracy after 1890. At the same time he permitted his opinion that the age of barricade revolts was past to be spread by the press, but the necessary supplementary statement that the German revolution would therefore have to assume the form of a military revolt could not be printed in Germany, because of the imperial public prosecutor. Externally, therefore, an agreement had again been obtained between the official policy of the German Social Democrats and Engels, since both rejected barricade fights and recommended legality.

If the Second International had actually been the heir of the First International, it would first of all have had to consider the existing revolutionary possibilities and to direct the tactics of the workers in all countries accordingly. Even after 1889 Engels considered Russian tsarism as the chief foe. However, since 1890 a Franco-Russian alliance had been concluded. This meant that the French capitalist class was ready to ally its fate to that of the Tsar. At the beginning of the nineties the Dual Alliance, of Russia and France, faced the Triple Alliance, Germany, Austria, and Italy. It was therefore believed that the coming European war would be a struggle between the Dual and the Triple Alliances. England still maintained its neutrality then. Consequently the International was concerned with the practical question regarding its attitude towards a war between the Dual and the Triple Alliances.

Engels answered this question with the frank realism which was characteristic of him: He did not believe that in Germany the Hohenzollern regime would survive the crisis and the strain of a world war. During the next great war the Social Democrats would obtain power in Germany, whereupon the German workers would strike against the Tsar and his allies in the manner of 1793. Engels was convinced that a German victory would simultaneously be a victory for the revolution. The entry of German troops into Russia would also assist the outbreak of the revolution there and lead to the overthrow of tsarism. If the later developments from 1914 to 1918 are considered, it becomes evident that Engels's predictions were by no means fantastic. In Germany as well as in Russia the World War actually swept away the monarchies, to replace them at first by Red republics. Furthermore the German and the Russian revolutions alike were military revolts, as Engels had predicted. The decisive difference, however, was that the German workers' revolution did not come at the beginning of the World War, as Engels had desired, but at the end, after the frightful struggle had consumed and paralysed all the forces of the German workers.

The policy which Engels recommended to the International for the future world war corresponded in its methods to the tactics pursued by Marx and himself during the war of 1870-1: no feeble policy of neutrality or formal peace declarations by the workers, but instead concentration of all proletarian and revolutionary forces against the chief foe. In 1870 until Sedan it had been Napoleon. Subsequently

Marx and Engels turned about, supported the new French Republic, and urged that pressure be put on the German Empire to prevent the annexation of Alsace-Lorraine. In a future war between the Dual and the Triple Alliances, Engels would have wanted the International to support Germany in the same manner; for in Germany the Social Democrats would soon replace the Hohenzollern regime, and a socialist Germany would return Lorraine to the French people in any case. Engels died in 1895 firmly convinced of the imminence of the great decisive struggle, which, in Germany as well as in Russia, could only terminate in a victory for the revolution. Nevertheless for the surviving leaders of the International the situation was by no means so simple. Ten years after the death of Engels, England and France had formed the Entente. In Germany in the meantime the Social Democrats had not yet obtained power, and Wilhelm II continued to reign. It was an exceedingly serious responsibility for the International to support either one side or the other in a future world war. If it favoured the Triple Entente, England, France, and Russia, it required the German workers to submit to the Tsar. In the opposite case, the French workers would have been required to recognize the rule of Wilhelm II. Neither was very well possible. Yet there would have been other ways of continuing a realistic international policy in line with the ideas of Engels. Thus the forces of the International could have been employed to isolate the Tsar. Around the turn of the century a situation developed in the internal politics of France where the French bourgeois republicans absolutely needed the help of the socialists. At that time the socialists would perhaps have been able to disrupt the Franco-Russian alliance. Simultaneously the German Social Democrats would have had to guarantee that they would not tolerate any attack by their government on France.

Several other methods could be imagined by means of which the socialist International could have followed a uniform political course during the period prior to the World War. Actually, however, it was incapable of such action. Realistic power politics, along the lines laid down by Engels, would have required the workers to judge every war according to the advantages or disadvantages which they would derive from it. Thus, for instance, the German working class would have had to approve a war against the Tsar, but to reject unconditionally a war with France, as soon as France should have dissolved the fateful alliance with tsarism. Nevertheless international strategy of this type, deciding each case individually, contradicted completely the basic pacifistic sentiment of the European workers. The majority of the socialist workers did not differentiate between useful and harmful wars; rather they wanted no war at all. Moreover the categories into which Marx and Engels divided wars have nothing to do with morality. It was rather unimportant for both men whether a state was the aggressor or the victim in a war; who was right or wrong in the current sense of the terms. Marx only inquired whether a definite war and the victory of a particular side would or would not aid the revolutionary and proletarian cause. Marx and Engels would have greeted every defeat of the Russian Tsar, no matter whether Russia was formally right or wrong in the particular war. Yet a conception of this type can only become popular in times when the masses are imbued with a genuine spirit of revolutionary solidarity. Thus in Europe prior to 1848 the democrats would have greeted every war against Metternich's Austria. On the other hand, the social-democratic workers of the generation prior to the World War wanted peace and expected the International to prevent the threatening war by means of a miracle.

Formal pacifism, which ruled the Second International, made it impossible for the workers to follow a realistic policy. Since the labour parties outside of Russia could neither carry out a revolution in their own country nor approve any policy which contained even the risk of war, they were actually powerless and defenceless. For this reason the discussions at the international socialist congresses prior to 1914 all exhibit the same characteristics of ambiguity and helplessness. The delegates discussed measures to be taken by the labour parties in case of any war danger and, understandingly enough, were unable to arrive at any practical plan. There was nothing else left but to utter dire threats against the capitalistic governments, which impressed no one and consequently were of no avail. It would have been even more expedient if the socialist parties had openly declared that they were only a minority in all countries and consequently incapable of preventing a war. Under such circumstances the International agrees that the working class in each country has a right to defend that country, on condition that the parties will employ all their forces to restore peace. A sober statement of this kind, based upon reality, would, however, have contradicted the formal radicalism which ruled the majority of the International. The International therefore maintained its formal gesture of protest against the capitalistic governments until the eve of the World War of 1914. Thus when the parties were later forced to vote war credits and to conclude a truce with their governments, the collapse of the International was all the worse.

In 1929 the leading Austrian Socialist Renner made a notable remark upon the role played by the simple desire for peace in the Second International. In a historical retrospect Renner relates how the International Socialist Congress at Copenhagen in 1910 had to take sides in a quarrel among the Austrian workers, over the separation of the majority of the Czech workers from the general Austrian trade-union organization. In this matter they were concerned with the important fundamental question whether the Czech workers had the right to support the struggle of their people for national liberation, and consequently to organize separately within the Czech nation. Renner writes:

" The relation of the Second International to the awaken-

ing nations was a divided one. It greeted their awakening
and liberation with sincere sympathy and moral support.
But the imperialist struggle of the major powers made use of
this movement and turned it into one of the most effective
instruments for war. Once in the history of every nation the
dilemma arises: liberty or peace? And just at that time this
dilemma began to split several socialist parties. Within the
Polish Social Democratic Party, as well as in the Czech party
and several others, certain groups became convinced of the
inevitability of war and began to pin their hopes for national
independence on the outcome of the war. Moreover the
most extreme Russian group at all times regarded a warlike
catastrophe not as an evil to be feared but as the awaited
opportunity for liberation. The Second International, however, fought with impassioned sincerity for the maintenance
of world peace. In this, too, lay a mighty intellectual advance over the youthful Marxian formula of martial revolutions and revolutionary wars, the two assumed chief levers
of history. That war, at a definite stage of development, is
no longer revolutionary but reactionary, and that peace becomes an absolute good, is a perception which first matured
after the World War and is by no means yet uncontested.
In Copenhagen the Second International confirmed the principle: world peace above all; national liberation only by
peaceful evolution; a final solution of the national problem
will be possible only in a socialist society! It did not express
these principles in any resolution, but it acted according to
them, by unconditionally condemning Czech separation."

In this passage Renner presented the pacifism of the Second International very clearly and strikingly and declared
just as frankly that this basic political principle was not in
agreement with the teaching of Marx. Renner regarded the
conception that peace is an absolute and ultimate good as an
advance over the view of Marx and Engels. It is no concern
of the historian to pass judgment on philosophic points of
view. Yet when the age of imperialism is considered, one is

led to the conclusion that such a theory of peace as an absolute and ultimate good did not blend very well with the period; for imperialism is the expression of the greatest concentration of violence at home and abroad. Whoever completely rejects violence as an instrument of political struggle during such a period is at a hopeless disadvantage when faced by opponents who rely only upon force. If it was known during the age of imperialism that a political movement would employ peaceful methods under any circumstances, it was no longer necessary to fear it. Because the socialist parties, at least in their official doctrines, always decided in favour of peaceful solutions, they were entirely incapable of pursuing a realistic course in foreign affairs and internal politics, and they actually abandoned the field to their imperialist opponents.

In addition, this pacifistic tendency of the Second International led to another important consequence. In every country the ruling class knew how to present itself and its imperialist policies as *the* national tendency. At the same time the socialists, by speaking only of peace and international understanding and opposing nationalistic power politics, isolated themselves even more from all the other groups of the nation. The unhappy contrast between the socialist minority and the so-called " bourgeois " majority of the nation appeared to have special significance, since the socialists were "anti-national," while the bourgeois groups were nationalists. Since the awakening of national feeling at the right moment is an enormously powerful weapon in a political struggle, the socialists were thus forced into a position where they might sustain the most serious defeats; for in a decisive crisis a nationalist movement sweeps along not only the middle classes but also the majority of the workers. Abstract pacifism has no power of resistance if the existence of the nation is really at stake. Revolutionary democracy during the period of 1848 was actually able to make use of nationalism for its own purpose; the Second International, on the other hand, allowed itself to be manœuvred into a position of isolation, where the " trade " ideology of the workers, together with pacifism, manned a forlorn hope. The events at the outbreak of the World War and the later victories of fascism in major European countries made this situation only too clear. In 1910 the Copenhagen congress of the International had indignantly condemned the Czech socialists, who had then decided in favour of a nationalist policy; yet history has shown that the Czech separatists were right, for with this step the Czech workers laid the foundation for a vital democratic movement in the later Czechoslovak Republic.

On the major questions of practical politics the Second International was in complete agreement with liberal bourgeois democracy. Both movements advocated peace abroad and legality at home, free trade, general suffrage, extension of parliamentary institutions, social legislation, and the protection of labour, and they opposed the excesses of trust and monopoly capitalism. What would have been more logical than a tactical alliance between the liberal democrats and the socialists against imperialism? After 1889 a group arose within the socialist labour movement which advocated such tactics. They were the revisionists. They demanded that the socialist International abandon its meaningless revolutionary phraseology, act on the basis of existing facts, strive for practical successes by extending bourgeois democracy and social legislation, and welcome every ally who was prepared to follow the same course. During his long stay in England, Bernstein, the most important theoretician of German revisionism had been vividly impressed by liberal democracy and tried to transfer its achievements to the Continent. In France Jaurès followed the same practical course. The chief mistake of the revisionists was that they failed to recognize the actual character of the imperialist period. They believed in the possibility of gradual peaceful progress, and they did not see that imperialism necessarily produces the most frightful wars, revolutions, and counter-revolutions.

Despite all that, the practical advantages of the revisionist theory for the labour movement were far greater than those of official radicalism. Had the socialist parties accepted the teaching of revisionism, they would have been freed from their isolation. They would have proposed practical solutions for all political questions and would have taken up the struggle against imperialism and militarism within a broad popular movement. In this way the labour parties in the major countries would have entered into an actual struggle for power, and the experience of the struggle would soon have enabled them to free themselves from the illusions of formal pacifism. Nevertheless the majority of the International refused to acknowledge the logical justification of revisionism and rejected it with impassioned vehemence.

For the majority of the workers the gesture of protest and isolation with respect to the bourgeois state and capitalist society had become a vital necessity. During great national crises this isolation collapsed, but in his daily life it was his class-consciousness that gave the worker the necessary support to bear all his worries and privations. To be sure, popular Marxism had lost all its revolutionary and practical political components, but it endowed the socialist worker with self-reliance, consolation, and hope for the future, almost reminding one of a religious movement. If they had accepted the proposals of the revisionists, however, by acting on the basis of the existing state and allying themselves with bourgeois parties, the socialist workers would have been compelled to renounce their Utopian belief in the future and their vitally necessary class sentiment. In order to justify their practical and peaceful policy, the revisionists were forced to turn upon the prevailing official, dogmatic Marxism of the Second International. On the other hand, the theoreticians, representing the majority, opposed

Bernstein and his friends in the name of Marx. Yet if content, and not external form, is considered, it must be admitted that the revisionists were actually much better Marxists than their " radical " opponents; for Marx always demanded that the workers make use of the actual political possibilities and rejected any isolation of his party.

Within the International revisionism was represented chiefly by a minority of the German party and by Jaurès and his French friends. On the side of official radicalism were the German and Italian majority as well as a French group led by Guesde. The Russian socialists likewise supported the radicals, because the official radical phraseology was easier to reconcile with their revolutionary tactics than the formulas of the revisionists. Finally, the Austrians leaned more towards the revisionist theories; but since they had no opportunity to practise revisionism in their own country, they generally assumed an intermediary position. As a rule the radical tendency triumphed at the international congresses, since it was supported by the influential authority of the executive committee of the German Social Democratic Party. Besides the so-called radical majority and the revisionist minority, there was still a third group in the International prior to the World War. It was numerically very weak, but its adherents were the only ones who actually comprehended the period of imperialism and who therefore advocated that the working class should prepare for the coming wars and revolutions. This revolutionary Left wing consisted of a group of Russian socialists, led by Lenin, a number of German socialists, under the leadership of Rosa Luxemburg, and finally a tiny group of Dutch Marxists. Within this actually revolutionary and Marxist Left wing great differences of opinion also existed over details. Outside of Russia, the Left wing had no influence on the broad masses.

The positive achievements of the Second International up to 1914 manifested themselves chiefly in the elevation of the standard of living and in the improvement of the working conditions of the European industrial workers. The untiring activity of the trade unions, which were influenced by the socialist parties, was able to better the social position of the workers in the important industrial countries. It is furthermore significant that all the organizations of the Second International rested upon self-government by the workers. On all controversial questions the ultimate decision lay in the hands of the members themselves. The leaders of the labour parties could only retain their positions as long as they obeyed the will of the membership. In this sense the Second International performed an important educational function for democracy, by making it possible for the workers to test practical self-government within their organizations. Even if these achievements of the Second International have been suppressed again in parts of Europe, still the history of the labour movement cannot be imagined without the period of the socialist International and its free organizations. Nevertheless, on the other hand, the Second International was incapable of reviving revolutionary democracy in Europe and effectively opposing imperialism.

PART III

FROM 1895 TO THE PRESENT [1937]

✍

FROM 1895 TO THE PRESENT [1937]

1. The Labour Parties prior to the World War

The Beginnings of Bolshevism

During the period of the Second International, from 1889 to 1914, the four major powers, Germany, Austria-Hungary, Italy, and France, together with Switzerland, Holland, Belgium, and the Scandinavian countries, formed a unit. In all these states the majority of the industrial workers supported a socialist party belonging to the Second International.

In Germany the Reichstag elections of 1903 brought new and greater successes for the Social Democrats, who polled one third of all the votes cast. Nevertheless the power of the German ruling class remained unshaken. If they were unable to carry out a violent revolution, the Social Democrats could at least have attempted to obtain constitutional reforms, by means of a coalition with the Liberals and the Centre Party. The great majority of the Centre voters were Christian workers, as well as west- and south-German peasants who were by no means in sympathy with the Prussian ruling class. Moreover the German bourgeoisie, including a good many great industrialists and imperialists, was embittered over the inadequate government of the bureaucrats and the arrogance and narrow-mindedness of the Prussian nobility. Just because in Germany the feudal state had never been changed into a bourgeois-capitalistic one, many causes for friction existed. If the Social Democrats had abandoned their isolation, they would have been able to carry the Left wing of the liberals and the popular section of the Centre with them. The immediate consequence would have been a constitutional conflict between the Reichstag majority and the imperial government. It can be imagined what the consequences of such a conflict might have been.

Aside from the weakness of the so-called bourgeois parties in Germany it was chiefly the desire of the radical majority of the socialist party for isolation that made a coalition of this type impossible. Except for a few election agreements, which remained without any further political consequences, there was no co-operation between the socialists and the bourgeois opposition in Germany until 1914. Only in Baden did the Social Democrats unite with the Liberals to form an active majority in the Diet. Nevertheless the example of Baden had no effect beyond its borders. Political initiative remained in the hands of the imperial government. In 1906 a conflict developed between Reichschancellor Bülow and the Centre. In consequence Bülow formed the Conservative-Liberal bloc. All the liberal groups followed Bülow's slogans in the hope that the government would grant concessions to the bourgeoisie and mitigate the excessive predominance of the Prussian nobility. Not only did the National Liberals support the government, but also all the Independent groups, whose resistance to imperialism had constantly diminished since the death of Eugen Richter.

Characteristically enough, the actual conflict between Bülow and the Centre was concerned with a question of colonial politics. Because of a native revolt in German Southwest Africa, greater funds were required than the Centre and the Social Democrats were willing to grant. Bülow dissolved the Reichstag. In the new elections of 1907 the Conservative-Liberal bloc opposed the Centre and the Social Democrats. The quarrel over Southwest Africa was really not a question concerning a vital interest of the German masses. Yet the government and the imperialists allied with it succeeded in organizing a large, popular, national movement for the defence of Germany's position in the world. In the elections the government parties won so many votes that the Social Democrats lost half their seats in the Reichstag. Thus an insignificant colonial conflict was enough to defeat the strongest socialist party in the world in an election. So slight was the power of attraction of peaceful and anti-imperialist ideas as soon as a question arose which, even slightly, went beyond the concerns of daily life. All the Liberals immediately went over to the government, millions of indifferent voters espoused the national cause, and the Social Democrats lost a series of their firmest strongholds. If all this happened because of South Africa, what would occur in Germany, Fránce, or Italy when the threat of a European war actually materialized and the existence of the nation was at stake?

The ruling groups of Germany certainly did not know how to exploit the favourable situation of 1907. The Emperor and the Prussian nobility destroyed their authority with new mistakes. In 1908 the notorious interview with Wilhelm II appeared in the *Daily Telegraph*. The result was a storm of indignation on the part of the entire German nation against the Emperor, which seriously injured the prestige of the monarchy. In 1909 the Prussian nobility disrupted the Conservative-Liberal bloc, because the junkers refused to make the slightest concessions to the bourgeoisie. The German bourgeoisie, including the manufacturers and the imperialists, felt profoundly disappointed and hurt. The subsequent Reichstag election of 1912 again resulted in a great victory for the Social Democrats, who won 110 seats out of a total of 397. In 1913 a local conflict between the military authorities and the civilian population in the Alsatian city of Zabern led to stormy debates in the Reichstag and to great agitation in the nation. Almost the entire nation protested unanimously against the methods of the Prus-

sian nobility and the officers. At the time of the outbreak
of the World War, order prevailed in Germany externally,
but the moral authority of the government was seriously
shaken and the overwhelming majority of the nation regarded the ruling system critically. Yet Social Democracy,
owing to the above cited causes, was incapable of leading the
masses and overthrowing the rule of feudalism.

The role played by the slogan of general suffrage in the
Habsburg monarchy before 1914 is extremely odd. As a result of experiences in other countries, no one any longer believed in the revolutionary effects of general suffrage. Consequently the Habsburg Empire used the slogan of general
suffrage for its own purposes. Whenever the Emperor Franz
Joseph quarrelled with the Hungarian oligarchy, the court
party threatened the Magyar nobility with the introduction
of general suffrage. Generally this was sufficient to force the
Hungarian politicians to yield. Thus until 1914 the introduction of general suffrage into Hungary proved superfluous. On the other hand, in the Austrian half of the Empire
general suffrage was actually introduced in 1906. Nevertheless it did not lead to any democratization of conditions in
Austria. The ruling Austrian bureaucrats hoped that under
general suffrage the bourgeois nationalist parties would lose
a number of seats to the Social Democrats. Acute social
struggles would thus be added to the old national quarrels
within Parliament; consequently Parliament would be split
into a number of warring factions, thus making it easier for
the bureaucrats to run things in their own way.

The result was just what the bureaucrats had expected.
From 1906 to 1914 the Austrian Parliament was generally
unable to act and the government dispatched current business in a dictatorial manner. If a state, because of internal
contradictions, loses its vitality, general suffrage cannot save
it. If the Viennese court party also wanted to introduce general suffrage in Hungary, it was only because it hoped to
disrupt the Budapest Parliament in this manner. Until now

Hungary had always had a stable working majority in Parliament, composed of representatives of the landowners and the wealthy bourgeoisie. General suffrage would have disrupted this majority and replaced it by a medley of Slavs, Rumanians, and groups representing the workers and the petty bourgeoisie. The Viennese government could have done as it pleased with a motley parliament of this sort. Apparently no one seriously considered the possibility that in a country such as Hungary a parliament based on general suffrage could also be the first step towards a social revolution.

Seven years after its introduction into Austria, Italy also received general suffrage. In both countries the practical consequences were very slight. When the Kingdom of Italy had been founded, only the wealthy upper class had had the franchise at first. In 1881 a partial electoral reform had been carried out, as a result of which the first socialist deputies appeared in the Parliament at Rome. Shortly before the World War, Giolitti introduced general suffrage. In 1913 the election results in the urban industrial districts were favourable for the socialists. The Parliament as a whole however, remained unchanged; for in the backward rural districts the elections were still predetermined by the landowners, officials, and other local powers. Before 1914 opposition to the ruling system was embodied in two movements. The socialists advocated improving the condition of the urban and rural workers. They protested against the violence of the ruling class and the spread of corruption. Owing to this attitude of protest the Socialist Party won considerable prestige and relatively many adherents, even among the educated classes. Yet during the decade prior to the outbreak of the World War the majority of the students supported Irredentism, the nationalist movement which had gradually travelled the path from Mazzini to modern imperialism.

The proletarian as well as the nationalist movements

gradually accustomed themselves to extra-parliamentary methods. Even though the official Socialist Party preferred the path of legality, still the wretched condition of the urban and rural masses repeatedly forced them into strikes and local revolts. On the other hand, the memory of Garibaldi's national voluntary corps remained alive among the Irredentist youth. The net of patriotic societies covering all of Italy furnished them with an organizational basis, and actually every university and every high school in Italy was a nucleus of nationalistic activism. After every real or imagined wrong suffered by the brothers in unredeemed Italy beyond the Austrian border, vociferous demonstrations were held in front of the allied country's consulates in Italian cities. Striking workers and demonstrating nationalists alternately disturbed the peace of the ruling bureaucrats. The Italian Socialists recognized the economic need of the masses, but they had no ready national program, since they wanted peace with Austria and rejected colonial adventures. Irredentism, on the other hand, which gradually united the modern capitalists and the students, who wanted action, certainly had no remedy for the social needs of the nation, but it had a fiery nationalistic program.

The ruling Italian group called itself liberal or even democratic, because Italy had a parliamentary form of government and since 1913 even manhood suffrage, freedom of the press, and freedom of association. Actually the majority of the Italian people still lived under mediæval conditions. In 1913, on the occasion of one of the frequent shootings in southern Italy, Mussolini, then a Left-wing Socialist leader, wrote in his newspaper, *Avanti:* " How is it possible that defenceless old men and pregnant women are shot down, even today, in Italy, a country which we picture as the great teacher of civilization? And how is it possible that the government, even if it has no millions left for such purposes, sends the people of Rocca Gorga, who ask for canalization projects, doctors, water, and light, nothing but carabinieri (police) , who drown the holy protest of the people in blood?

" We have already said that . . . more tolerable living-conditions must be created for rural Italy, in order to decrease the causes which repeatedly lead to what we in Italy already call ' classical excesses ' and which result in suffering for unarmed people who have no intention whatsoever of revolting against the government, but who only demand what for more than a century has been the common possession of all civilized nations."

Signora Sarfatti, Mussolini's biographer and likewise a former Socialist, describes the conditions in southern Italy at that time: " During the previously discussed years shameful but typical incidents had repeatedly occurred in the market-places of southern Italy. Down there a struggle still went on against starvation wages and an almost brutish standard of living. . . . The ruling class of the south, influenced by the Spaniards, did not defend itself with economic means, but appealed to ' Papa State ' and employed the latter's carabinieri and soldiers for its protection. It was a mediæval situation: stupidity and grasping arrogance on the one side, on the other stupidity and fanatical embitterment among the people, who desperately opposed the soldiers. Once a shot was fired in the general excitement, the square was soon reddened with blood."

Even though the ruling class in countries like Italy could introduce general suffrage without thereby endangering its dominant position, still the situation in a highly civilized industrial country like Belgium was very different. The wealthy bourgeoisie of Belgium feared that the introduction of a general and equal franchise would automatically result in a legal transfer of political power to the socialist workers. Until 1914 the Belgian Socialist Party, although constantly increasing in number and fighting spirit, attempted in vain, despite several general strikes, to force the concession of an equal franchise. After 1893 Belgium had a system of plural voting, which guaranteed a parliamentary majority for the wealthy class. As a result the Catholic Conservative Party remained in power. Until the World War the ruling class in Holland also refused to give the workers an equal franchise.

From 1889 to 1914 not even a consistent attempt was made in any of the previously mentioned countries to drive the ruling imperialists and the feudal or semi-feudal groups from power by means of an alliance between the workers and the middle classes. In France, on the other hand, as a result of the Dreyfus affair, the Left bloc undertook an experiment of this sort. The socialist workers and the peasant and petty-bourgeois radicals united to consolidate bourgeois democracy at least in France. During the early years of the twentieth century it appeared temporarily as if bourgeois democracy would actually triumph in France and would even open the road for social democracy. The offensive of the Left collapsed completely, however, and French political conditions returned to the unstable equilibrium which had already characterized the Third Republic until 1889.

During the period from 1889 to 1914 liberal democracy, as represented by the Second International, had only achieved successes along very definite lines. In the four major powers the capitalists, the colonial politicians, and the militaristic monarchists retained power, and in Belgium and Holland, with their great concentration of capital and their important colonial possessions, democracy also made no progress. In Switzerland, on the other hand, liberal democracy maintained its position, while it advanced victoriously in Scandinavia. All this meant that liberal democracy was unable to defeat imperialism anywhere. It found a favourable soil only in smaller countries that had no acquaintance with power politics and for whom national questions did not exist. Switzerland, too, had neither colonies nor any desires for conquest. It was composed of French, German, and Italian groups that had consciously separated themselves from the corresponding nations. Thus a " nationalities question" could not exist in Switzerland; or, rather, the rise of a nationalities problem would have brought about the destruction of Switzerland. If Swiss patriots wanted to protect their fatherland, they had to keep German or French nationalism at a distance. The desire for neutrality completely ruled Swiss foreign policy. The Swiss militia was trained solely for the purpose of protecting the soil of the fatherland from the encroachment of belligerent powers. Thus prior to 1914 Switzerland as well as Norway and Denmark was completely separated from the rival political groups of Europe. There was nothing in these countries which had even the remotest resemblance to the imperialistic policies of the major powers. Thus conditions were favourable for the development of liberal democracy.

England differs from the countries previously discussed in the circumstance that until 1914 the overwhelming majority of the industrial workers remained loyal to the bourgeois parties. Consequently the influence of the Second International on English internal affairs was insignificant. However, in England too, just as on the Continent, until 1914 the working class restricted itself to the methods of liberal democracy when it wanted to fight against imperialism. Approximately after 1900 it became evident that the confidence of the workers in the ruling Conservative Party had been shaken. The ruling party neglected social legislation, and certain judicial opinions which paralysed the trade unions were not superseded rapidly enough by new legislation. The embitterment of the workers over the Conservative government led to a new attempt to found an independent parliamentary labour party in England. The elections to the lower house in 1906 resulted in a great defeat for the Conservatives. They were left with only 167 out of a total of 670 seats in the lower house. The Labour Party won 43 seats, but the Liberals received 377. In addition there were 83 Irish. From this it is clear that the majority of the English workers simply returned to the Liberals as soon as they lost faith in the imperialists. Thus English liberalism once again experienced a strange resurrection, contradicting all objective conditions. In England from 1906 to 1914 liberal democracy, under the leadership of the courageous and determined Prime Minister Asquith, led a notable struggle for peace, free trade, and liberty against the imperialist party and the upper house. Nevertheless during these eight years of great political tension, which was intensified by mass strikes, the political Labour Party was unable to maintain an independent position in public life alongside of the imperialists and the liberal democrats. Within and outside of the lower house the Labour Party was nothing more than a minor appendix of the Liberal mass party. It was the World War, with its pitiless destruction of all untenable compromises, that finally delivered a death-blow to English liberalism and thus separated the British workers from liberal democracy.

From the above it is evident that during the period of the Second International, when the working class in England as well as on the Continent, west of Russia, wanted to influence the policies of the state, it employed the methods of liberal democracy. However, in the United States and in Russia the situation was different. On the Continent and in England the collapse of the Revolution of 1848 and the parallel decline of the Chartists destroyed the tradition of the older democratic movement, which opposed the " people " to the upper class. In America, on the other hand, there had been no counterpart to the unsuccessful Revolution of 1848. On the contrary, the popular tendency had triumphed anew in the great Civil War of the sixties, so that the tradition of Jefferson and Lincoln remained unbroken for the future. After 1890, with the disappearance of free land, the pressure of monopoly capitalism on the broad masses became increasingly noticeable in the United States. Popular resistance did not manifest itself, however, by founding a socialist labour party in the continental European manner or by strengthening a capitalistic-liberal group as in England between 1906 and 1914. In the United States the type of socialism represented by the Second International remained an insignificant fragmentary group. The mass of workers, farmers, and small business men, united by a feeling of unity as the " people," opposed the monopoly capitalists. Either they attempted to found new parties on a basis of social democracy, or the masses took possession of one of the two great historical parties. The Populists of the nineties and the later Farmer-Labour movements belong to the former category; the latter type of action is represented by the Democratic Party under the leadership of Bryan and Wilson, and for a short while by the Republican Party under Theodore Roosevelt. The struggle between monopoly capitalism and social democracy was in full swing in the United States at the outbreak of the World War.

In Russia, during the generation prior to the World War, the democratic mass movement of the Russian people was just as unbroken as in the United States. In Russia, however, unlike America, Marxist ideas had a decisive influence on the movement. Four tendencies fought for power in Russia. First of all there was feudal absolutism: the Tsar, the great landowners, the high officials, officers, and ecclesiastics — in short, the actual usufructuaries of the old absolutist system. In the second place there were the capitalists and the imperialists, who called themselves " liberal " in Russia. They wanted a more modern political order in place of the backward and inept bureaucratic government and endeavoured to obtain reforms of this sort. They were always ready, however, to unite with the Tsar and his officials against the onslaught of the labouring masses. The third force was the so-called " populist " movement, led by intellectuals, whose aims comprised a peasant revolution, the division of the large estates, and a democratic republic. Finally, corresponding to the growth of large-scale industry, a socialist labour party also developed gradually in Russia.

Besides several minor tendencies, two divergent main currents of thought manifested themselves among the Russian
socialist democrats. In 1903 the controversy led to a split in
the party. After that the majority faction, or Bolsheviki, opposed the minority group, or Mensheviki. The Mensheviki
were a radical socialist labour party, approximately corresponding to the labour parties of western Europe during the
same period. They sought to organize as many Russian workers as possible, in so far as the persecutions of the Tsarist police permitted it. The labour party was to be ruled by the
democratic self-government of the members. The Social
Democratic Party should promote the material interests of
the workers, and since the bourgeois revolution was still im-
pending in Russia, the party should also support this revolutionary struggle with all its strength. However, in the
opinion of the Mensheviki only the bourgeois parties could
lead the Russian bourgeois revolution: It is the duty of the
working class to follow the lead of the capitalistic or petty-
bourgeois revolutionaries. In an agrarian country like Russia, where the industrial working class is only a minority,
the Social Democrats cannot determine the tempo of development.

The conception of the Bolsheviki, which Lenin had already developed repeatedly during the period before 1914
in his books, articles, and speeches, was a very different one.
For the first time since the death of Marx and Engels a man
appeared who by studying the works of the masters and at
the same time by critically observing conditions in his own
country revived revolutionary democracy in the spirit of
1848. Lenin was the first Social Democrat who understood
the professional isolation of the labour movement and fought
it as the chief obstacle of a revolution. Lenin's remark that
the ideal of the Social Democrat should be the tribune of
the people and not the trade-union secretary actually un-
covered in a single sentence the fundamental difference between original Marxism and the theory and practice of the

Second International. At the same time Lenin always paid the greatest attention to the daily needs and worries of the factory workers and during his entire life he valued highly the practical activity of the trade unions. The same is just as true of Marx and Engels. However, what Lenin rejected was the pseudo-radical professional limitation of the labour party and of the proletarian organizations in general, which rendered socialism incapable of carrying out a revolution.

Lenin agreed with the Mensheviki that the coming Russian revolution could only be a bourgeois upheaval. However, it did not by any means follow that the leadership of the bourgeois revolution would have to belong to the capitalistic or petty-bourgeois parties. It was rather the task of the Russian Social Democrats to carry with it the millions of poor oppressed Russian peasants, as well as the workers. Its goal would have to be the establishment of a Russian republic in the form of a " democratic dictatorship of the workers and peasants," after the overthrow of the Tsar. A Russian republic of this type would still be a bourgeois state based on bourgeois private property. Yet the large landowners would be expropriated, the poor peasants would receive land, and the workers would be able to procure complete freedom of action and all modern social achievements. Russia was on the brink of a bourgeois revolution, but the capitalists and the so-called liberals, with their fear of the broad masses, would have no desire to complete their own bourgeois revolution. Eventually, therefore, the coalition of the labouring classes, the allied workers and peasants, would have to lead the bourgeois revolution to victory against the will of the bourgeoisie. In Lenin's propaganda, there again appears for the first time in Europe a vital conception of social democracy as a revolutionary alliance of all the labouring people for the purpose of overthrowing the privileged upper class.

Until 1914 Lenin not only had borne the name of Social Democrat with pride, but had also advocated the traditional form of a democratic republic at all times. For Lenin, too, it was self-evident that after the victory of the revolution an all-Russian national assembly, elected by the entire nation, would have to convene in order to decide the organization of the republic. The workers' councils, the Soviets, had already appeared in the Revolution of 1905. They were assemblies of the factory delegates of the fighting and striking workers. Thus the Soviets were important fighting organs of the revolution. However, before 1914 no one thought that one day the Soviets would take the place of a Russian parliament, and before 1917 Lenin, least of all, had any plans of this kind.

Nevertheless, before 1914 Lenin already manifested a certain anti-democratic tendency in the question of party organization. According to Lenin's view, the Social Democratic Party should not be a broad mass party, but rather a small group of professional revolutionaries, whose task it should be to direct the sympathetic masses. This party of professional revolutionaries should be firmly organized and disciplined, with supreme authority resting in the hands of the party leaders. Lenin did not think of a socialist party as a broad self-governing mass movement of the workers; he rather desired a carefully selected revolutionary general staff, absolutely capable of fighting, and obedient to its leaders. On the organization question Lenin's position was in sharp contrast to the other social democratic parties of his time. It can hardly be doubted, however, that Marx and Engels would have acted in a similar manner if they had ever been destined to direct a larger movement independently in a revolution. For in their own party and in the organization led by them Marx and Engels alone determined their course autocratically and never respected the votes of the members. Thus Lenin actually revived original Marxism together with all its contradictions. It was this remarkable internal contrast in his *Weltanschauung* which later made it possible for Lenin to develop the most radical form of popular demo-

cratic self-government in his Soviet system and then soon
thereafter to destroy his own new democracy by means of his
party dictatorship.

The Russian Revolution of 1905 seriously endangered the
existence of tsarism. Not only did the industrial workers
strike and fight, but large sections of the peasantry were also
carried along by the movement, and revolutionary risings
took place in the army and navy. However, since the majority of the troops remained loyal to their officers and to the
Tsar, the Revolution was suppressed. Several years elapsed
during which the revolutionary forces had to recover from
the defeat. After 1912 the rise of a new revolutionary wave
was apparent in Russia, and when the World War broke out,
the Russian Social Democrats prepared for a decisive battle
with tsarism.

2. The World War and the Third International

Of the four types of bourgeois democracy that had appeared
before 1914, two were locally restricted in their extension.
Colonial democracy belonged to the transoceanic countries
colonized by the white nations, while imperialist democracy
developed in a pure form only in the British Empire. On
the other hand, social democracy had a general European
significance during the period prior to 1848, and liberal democracy approximately from 1880 to the World War. Both
movements had the misfortune that their protests lagged behind the social and economic development of the period.
Until the Revolution of 1848 social democracy embodied the
resistance of the upright petty bourgeois against early capitalism. Liberal democracy before the World War was the
protest of the capitalists, who favoured free competition,
against the new form of concentrated monopoly capitalism.
Both movements were certainly able to present impressively
the moral shortcomings of the prevailing modern economic
system, but they were incapable of opposing either early

capitalism or imperialism by another social system, upon the same advanced technological and productive level.

In both cases the socialist allies of bourgeois democracy were theoretically capable of supplying this deficiency. Marx and Engels wanted to give the democratic movement of 1848 a practical social form but they were unable to make any headway in the face of the petty-bourgeois narrow-mindedness of the period. Somewhat different was the connexion between modern liberal democracy and the parties of the Second International. The socialist parties isolated themselves as trade movements of the industrial workers, and the connexion with the liberal democrats was the one narrow and difficult road by which the socialists could gain any influence at all on the politics of the period. In this manner the socialists did not intervene in the political struggle with their strong and modern weapon — namely, with plans for a new large-scale collective economy — but only with the weak and outmoded weapons derived from the arsenal of liberal democracy, the catchwords of free trade, peace, and progress. Consequently the World War was simultaneously a catastrophe for the Second International and liberal democracy.

Before 1848 social democracy had promised the labouring masses that a new age of human equality and happiness would be combined with the victory of the political revolution and the acquisition of general suffrage. The Revolution arrived in 1848, but none of the promises of the democrats were realized. The result was a general loss of confidence in democracy. The more recent liberal democracy before the World War had been much more modest in its promises. It promised neither a social upheaval nor a general revolution. It was so very cautious that it assured the nations no more than the maintenance of peace. Now not even this had been possible. Consequently the World War resulted in a moral and organizational collapse of the Second International, which had been the actual representative of liberal democracy on the Continent.

However, the revived social democratic movement in the United States also belonged to the victims of the war. President Wilson had the best intentions of promoting social progress in his own country and of securing the victory of democracy on an international scale through America's entry into the war. The founding of the League of Nations under American leadership was to inaugurate a new era of general democracy and social progress. Nevertheless Wilson's party was not strong and realistic enough internally to cope with the enormous difficulties of the World War crisis. In the United States the capitalists took possession of all public positions of power, including the war-time economic apparatus, and it was impossible for Wilson to effectuate the principles of social democracy at the peace negotiations. The peace treaties of 1919 meant the unrestricted success of the victorious imperialist group. At home Wilson's party had lost the confidence of the socially progressive elements; at the same time, however, despite all sacrifices, it had not regained the favour of trust capitalism. Consequently in the American presidential election of 1920 the capitalistic Republicans won a decisive victory and retained power until 1932. Social democracy, in the spirit of Bryan and Wilson, was no longer a strong factor in American politics. The complete international defeat of Wilson's ideas manifested itself in the refusal of the United States to join the League of Nations, inspired by Wilson.

The entry of England into the World War immediately led to the collapse of the unnatural Liberal position. In order to be able to conduct the war, Asquith was compelled to avail himself of the aid of the Conservative Party. The influence of the imperialists grew constantly within the various combinations and coalitions which ruled English political life after 1914, until they were finally able to force Asquith and his more intimate friends from power. The former Liberal Minister Lloyd George headed a new coalition government, whose nucleus was formed by the Conservative

Party. With his energy and oratorical talent, Lloyd George once again endowed the ideals of Great Britain's imperialist democracy with splendour and power. Imperialist democracy carried with it the masses of the mother country as well as the colonial democracies of the dominions and led England to victory.

The entry of all the eight major powers into the World War meant the triumph of imperialism and the prostration of its opponents. Nevertheless as the war continued to drag on and demanded ever increasing sacrifices and privations from the labouring masses, the opposing groups gained new strength. In Russia the February Revolution of 1917 had first replaced tsarism by a government of the bourgeois imperialists, but the first revolutionary wave was not permitted to subside. With the October Revolution the Bolsheviki under Lenin obtained power, and a democratic dictatorship of the workers and peasants was established. The new Russian social democracy, arising from the victorious Revolution, now challenged the imperialism of the seven other major powers to a struggle.

In the experiences of the Russian Revolution Lenin had found a new form for the democratic movement of the labouring masses, in contrast to traditional parliamentary democracy. The Revolution of 1917 had revived the councils of the workers, soldiers, and peasants. Lenin now discovered that the Soviets were the germs of an entirely new political type like the Paris Commune of 1871. The difference between the councils and the bourgeois parliaments does not lie in the external phenomena of electoral techniques, such as direct or indirect elections, or elections on the basis of residence or profession; the decisive point is rather that the councils overcome the traditional differences which until now had separated the legislative parliament from the executive apparatus of administrative and military officials in the larger European states. With the aid of the soldiers' councils the Revolution smashed the centralized power of the army

officers. Simultaneously it eliminated the power of the professional civil servants, of the police and the judiciary. In
every locality the workers' or peasants' council is the sole
agency of power. There is no other armed power except the
workers' militia, and administrative matters are dispatched
by simple commissars of the Soviets, who are subject to the
constant control of the labouring masses. In this manner the
councils are able to eliminate the great political shortcoming
of all the previous continental European constitutions, with
the exception of Switzerland and Norway—namely, the
erection of a wall, by the centralized apparatus of the state,
which blocks every advance of the labouring masses on the
road towards actual self-government.

The Soviet state as Lenin imagined it and as it actually
appeared to arise from the practical developments of the
Russian Revolution was actually a revival of the communal
type of democracy. The great practical difficulty was the
economic, military, and political co-ordination of the local
councils, which were particularly dispersed during the period
of revolution and civil war, for uniform action within the
framework of a great modern state. The Soviet Republic
in Russia maintained itself under enormous difficulties, and
when the military collapse of Germany and Austria-Hungary
took place in 1918, the militaristic monarchies of central
Europe were replaced by democratic republics, based upon
workers' councils. The radical wave emanating from Russia
also overflowed into the Balkans, appeared to carry Italy
with it, and even threatened France.

In England, too, the end of the war brought a turning-
point of great historical significance. For the first time since
the Chartist period millions of workers lost confidence in the
bourgeois leadership. While the disunited liberal groups
declined to political fragments, the Labour Party rapidly
grew to be the second greatest party of the country, a party
capable of carrying on a contest for power with the Conservatives. During their entire political life Marx and Engels

had waited for the introduction of general suffrage in England in the hope that the class party of the workers would then take up the struggle for power. After 1919 this hope finally seemed to be nearing fulfilment.

After the collapse of the Central Powers the World War was succeeded by a major struggle between the new social-democratic movement emanating from Russia and imperialism. In order to carry on the Revolution on an international scale, Lenin created the Third International. To emphasize the difference between the new parties which accepted Bolshevism and the outmoded Social Democrats, the former called themselves Communists, just as Marx and Engels themselves had done during the period of the Revolution of 1848. In their programs, at least, the Communist parties recognized and avoided all the mistakes which the Social Democrats had made during the period of the narrow proletarian "trade" parties and liberal democracy. To be sure, the Communists emphasized the leading role of the proletariat in the Revolution, but they went beyond the trade interests of the industrial workers. Everywhere they appealed to the peasants and the other toiling groups. They recognized the importance of the national question and they called upon the oppressed nations in all parts of the world to strike for freedom. They advocated realistic power politics. Their ultimate goal was international peace, but they recognized that the workers could not reject war and violence as a means towards this end. The brutal energy of imperialism, which did not shrink from any means in order to retain power, was to be opposed by the equally brutal energy of the working people. The working-class state would wrest economic power from the minority of trust capitalists. The centralized militaristic economy serving the interests of monopoly capitalism was to be transformed into a correspondingly centralized collective economy in the interest of the working people.

The struggle between international imperialism and the

renewed social democracy, emanating from Moscow, lasted approximately until 1923. The result was a complete defeat for democracy on all fronts, above all also in Russia itself. The close association of the revived revolutionary labour movement with the fate of the Russian state sealed its doom. As they were in extremely great straits from 1918 to 1920, the Russian Bolsheviki had to be helped rapidly by victorious revolutions abroad. Thus the new Communist parties outside of Russia did not arise organically on the basis of conditions in their own countries and the experiences of their working classes, but they were artificially organized and established from Russia, and in their unfinished state they prematurely threw themselves into struggles to which they were not yet equal. Around 1921 Lenin recognized that there was no longer any hope for a victorious workers' revolution in any country outside of Russia within the near future. Consequently the Bolsheviki beat a retreat. In Russia itself the Soviet Republic was degraded to an empty form. A centralized dictatorship of the Bolshevik Party replaced the self-government of the labouring masses. At the same time the Communist parties outside of Russia changed into propaganda societies for the Soviet government, in which all individual vitality was suppressed from above, and which were no longer of any use as independent forces for a democratic movement of the working people.

During the same period, as the Russian Revolution grew inert and Moscow became the capital of a bureaucratic system of state capitalism, monopoly capitalism strengthened its power in the United States. The nationalist Right bloc ruled France, and in Italy violent imperialism triumphed in the form of a Fascist dictatorship. It has already been emphasized repeatedly that the old self-styled liberal group had been a hindrance to social development in Italy for two generations. After the World War the only question was who would push aside the old so-called Liberals and modernize Italy — the socialists or the consistent imperialists.

However, the socialist workers' parties exhibited neither a desire for power nor the ability to organize the country. Consequently the victory went to the Fascists. Mussolini revived the Garibaldi tradition of the voluntary private army, composed of the nationalist youth. The red shirts became the black shirts. To be sure, their attacks were no longer aimed at Austria, the Pope, or the tyrant of Naples, but rather at the trade-union headquarters and the editorial offices of the socialist newspapers. It is a sad spectacle to see how in Italy, after the collapse of the older national and revolutionary democratic movements, enemies took possession of their tactics and methods and employed them for diametrically opposed purposes. In Italy Mussolini first presented the tactics of the Fascist storm-troops to wear down the democrats and the socialists by means of petty warfare, with the more or less open connivance of the official organs of the state, until the moment for the ultimate counter-revolution has arrived.

In Germany, too, the republicans and the socialists were not equal to the task of dealing with concrete questions of power. After 1919 the army was already an assured instrument of the counter-revolution. The situation in the administrative and judicial departments was not much better. Under the Republic the power of monopoly capitalism in economic life grew stronger from year to year. In addition there was a profound division among the German workers which was skilfully exploited by the counter-revolution. The determined, revolutionary, but numerically weak minority of the German workers was destroyed in hopeless minor struggles. Thus after a few years the German Republic was already completely undermined. At many points the German Revolution of 1918 shows an astonishing similarity to the French February Revolution of 1848. The German Majority Socialists played approximately the same part as the French Socialist Democrats of 1848. Immediately after the Revolution both parties undertook the work of carrying out very estimable and objectively valuable social reforms in the interest of the labouring masses. Yet both parties equally neglected the concrete instruments of power of political life. As a result their social policies lacked any real foundation. In both cases to the Left of the official Social Democrats were a number of discordant, partially rash, and extremist radical groups. The really serious revolutionaries, such as Blanqui in 1848 and Liebknecht and Rosa Luxemburg in 1918, were almost completely isolated and could not change the fate of the movement. In both cases the counter-revolution watched for the outbreak of struggles within the working class, and the January battles of 1919 actually broke the power of the German Republic just as the June days of 1848 destroyed the power of the French Republic. The only difference was that in 1848 after the moral and political collapse of the Republic the popular dictator was immediately present, while in Germany a corresponding dictator first became influential many years later, and the Republic, unable to live or to die, maintained a precarious and painfully spasmodic existence. In 1923 under Chancellor Cuno the government of the Reich fell into the hands of the capitalistic parties, who were no longer displaced from power. In Japan the old lords continued to rule. In the newly organized border states of the former Russian Empire, in the succession states of Austria-Hungary, and on the Balkan Peninsula, everywhere the anti-democratic forces gained the upper hand, with the sole exception of Czechoslovakia, where a successful social democracy was established. In the British Empire, however, imperialist democracy retained power. At the same time it had to fight against the social democratic movement as represented by the constantly growing Labour Party.

3. *The Rise of Fascism*

The decline and the weakening of the democratic forces on a world scale continued until 1933. In that year a long and irresistible development culminated in the abolition of the last democratic forms by Hitler's government in Germany. Yet in the same year, with the inauguration of President Franklin D. Roosevelt in the United States, a vital movement for social democracy was revived in the economically most important country of the world. Thus in 1933 a new period began in the history of democracy.

From 1918 to 1933 the moral crisis of liberal democracy had grown more and more acute. There was a repetition, to some extent in the same forms, of the phenomena that had followed the collapse of revolutionary democracy after 1848. At that time a large section of the disappointed popular masses turned their backs on liberty and self-government and cried out for a strong leader and just dictator, who would be better than all the unreliable party politicians. It has already been described how after the summer of 1848 the storm wave of Bonapartism in France carried with it the popular masses, which were embittered by the course of the Revolution. Bismarckism in Germany was a parallel phenomenon. After the battle of Königgrätz, Bismarck was supported by the majority of the German people, not only by the junkers and the capitalists, but also by the broad masses, who now laughed at the weakness and the phrases of the democratic and liberal politicians and were happy that one great man now achieved what had been the stumbling-block for the orating deputies of Paul's Church. At the same time, after 1848 proletarian anarchism developed on the extreme Left, as the movement representing those men who now no longer wanted to have any dealings with elections and party politics. It has likewise been described above how the entire movement for the formation of independent labour parties on the Continent, and the concurrent alienation of the English trade unions from Chartism, to a certain extent represent a reaction to the failure of revolutionary democracy. Similarly the recoil of the European masses from social democracy during the period following the Revolution of 1848 until 1870 may be described as a broad arc of which Bonapartism and Bakuninism were the extremes.

The crisis of liberal democracy after the World War proceeded along parallel lines. Liberal democracy had to sustain the onslaught of a violent imperialist movement, employing popular methods, from the Right, and the attack of a radical working class which no longer believed in traditional democratic forms, from the Left. In 1917 Lenin's Bolshevism had still been a very democratic movement. Yet even in the earliest polemics of the Bolsheviki against the Social Democrats the question was not always: "Genuine popular democracy of the Soviets against the spurious and inadequate democracy of the bourgeois parliaments," but the slogan was simply: "Democracy versus dictatorship." The masses had become accustomed to identify liberal democracy, with its peaceful and parliamentary methods, with the concept of democracy as such, corresponding to the prevalent usage among the intellectuals and the politicians.

Yet when the Communists opposed democracy and advocated dictatorship, it was more than a mere inaccurate use of language among the leaders and their followers. As Russia's position became more desperate, Lenin and his lieutenants abandoned the democracy of the toilers and relied more and more upon a party dictatorship. Similarly it was just the radical workers in all countries who, having been agitated by the experience of the war, lost all confidence in every type of democracy. For fifty years the workers had governed themselves in the socialist organizations and freely determined their own affairs. What had been the result? Until 1914 the number of socialistic and democratic deputies had constantly increased in the parliaments of all countries, and what was the result? On the eastern and western fronts men lost their belief in free self-government. If they themselves had not made any headway with the usual methods, perhaps the will of a strong leader would now help them to achieve socialism and a better world. Without a doubt in 1919 the

majority of the European workers were ready to obey the
commands of Lenin and Trotsky, in order to destroy capitalism and militarism. Even later, when Soviet Russia and
the Third International had long since ceased to be the
driving forces of the world revolution, they continued their
criticism of bourgeois democracy and parliamentary methods among their adherents.

Before 1914 imperialists everywhere, with the exception
of England, had already regarded democracy as their foe.
The French parties of the Right wanted a military or monarchist dictatorship and only accommodated themselves to
a republic based on general suffrage as a makeshift solution.
In the words of a famous junker, the German ruling class
would have preferred to fetch "a lieutenant and ten men"
to disperse the Reichstag. The American trust capitalists
endeavoured to buy the political parties. In Austria and
Italy no one had any respect for Parliament, and in Russia
and Japan the upper class also served the existing authorities.
After the World War the popular imperialist group began
very systematically to disparage democratic principles among
the masses, and to rival the Communists in their praise of dictatorship. In place of the Bolshevist dictatorship advocated
by Moscow, the imperialists recommended a fascist dictatorship as a remedy for all problems.

After the free self-determination by the members had been
completely suppressed in the Communist parties, the adherents of liberal democracy were the only defenders of the
democratic principle on the European continent. Their position was exceedingly weak and unfavourable. Owing to
the defection of the Communists, the socialist workers' parties were disorganized and weakened. The bourgeois Left,
such as the Democratic Party in Germany, the French Radicals, or the old group of politicians in Italy, led by Giolitti,
was even weaker than before the World War. Above all,
however, the ideological position of European liberal democracy was hopelessly unfavourable. The liberal democrats

considered it their duty to select the smallest of the multitudinous evils which threatened the masses. After the horror of the World War they wanted to spare the nations a new war and consequently advocated international understanding. In internal affairs they considered a social revolution impossible and endeavoured to restrain the masses from putsches and adventures. Finally, they wanted to protect at least the most important civil liberties, such as general suffrage and the rights of the trade unions.

As a result of their pessimistic and cautious Cassandra tactics the liberal democrats were forced into a disastrous buffer position under the hate-filled attack of the imperialists from the Right and the Communists from the Left. The patriots, particularly among the oppressed or wronged nations, wanted a new national upsurge. The bourgeois and socialist democrats opposed them and preached international reconciliation. The starving and suffering masses cursed capitalism and demanded a social upheaval. Again the democrats warned and exhorted the masses to retain peaceful methods. Particularly in central Europe, the crisis arising from the World War assumed the most horrible forms. The mass of workers and unemployed were compelled to deny themselves everything, while a small minority of speculators grew richer and richer. The victorious dominant nations disregarded the vital spirit of the defeated and backward nations. But if the youth and the active groups of the nation revolted against the shameful present and wanted to work for a better future, it now appeared as if democracy stood in their way: apparently democracy meant that the status quo ought to be maintained, that the ruling class should continue to grow rich, that the masses should continue to starve, and that the fatherland should be humbled for ever. This entire shameful and unnatural situation calls itself democracy, culture, and humanity!

Liberal democracy, which before the war had already been weak and incapable of any action on the European continent, after the World War allowed itself to be forced into the part of an ill-natured old meddler who was unacquainted with the world and forbade the youth to sacrifice themselves for a better future. Owing to a fantastic reversal of all concepts and a distortion of all standards, a point was reached where considerable sections of the nations, and certainly not the worst ones, were filled with an unreasoning hatred for everything that smacked of democracy or humanity. A political tendency which continued to advocate only peace and legality during a period of the most frightful world crisis and extreme violence was first manœuvred out of all ideological positions and finally became the victim of its stronger and more ruthless opponents.

Until 1933 fascism triumphed in one form or another in Italy, Germany, Poland and the border states, in Hungary and the Balkans, in Portugal, and also for some time in Spain. After 1924 the Left in France still won repeated victories in the elections to the Chamber, but it was just as incapable of governing as before 1914. In every serious situation the Right bloc gained the upper hand.

In their classic reflections on the "tyrants" Aristotle and Plato had already proved that during the crisis of a liberal constitution the dictatorship of a great man, or of one who is considered "great," can easily be established. History furnishes numerous examples from Pisistratus of Athens to Napoleon III of France. The new element in modern fascism is the union of the dictator with imperialism — that is, with the particularly violent, nationalistic faction of monopoly capitalism. The nationalists, the military, and capitalists of the smaller states imitated the example of the corresponding movements among the major powers. After 1918 fascism had the great advantage over its opponents of appearing to be the only political force actually able to speak in the name of the entire nation. The popular democratic front of 1848 was forgotten. The unity of liberal bourgeois society had been disrupted long ago. The so-called Marxists had become

a "trade" party of the industrial workers and had in turn
been split since the World War. In contrast to all the fragmentary groups of modern political life, the imperialists
and nationalists represented one powerful and fascinating
idea, the unity and the greatness of the nation.

4. Democratic and Socialist Positions at Present

On the European continent bourgeois democracy had maintained its position in Scandinavia and Switzerland. A new
bourgeois democratic state, of astounding stability, arose in
Czechoslovakia. Within the Czech nation two socialist workers' parties, a great democratic peasant party, as well as
smaller parties representing the artisans and the Catholic
petty bourgeoisie, united under the leadership of Masaryk.
It was a genuine coalition of working people and united the
most important economic groups on a nationalist basis. This
Czech government bloc eradicated the Habsburg traditions
within the country, created a reliable army and administrative apparatus, divided the large estates, and safeguarded the
trade-union rights of the industrial workers. Capitalistic
private property remained in existence, but the capitalists
were unable to seize political control in order to alter to
their advantage the compromise upon which Czech society
rests. The democratic Czech government bloc also endeavoured to attract the democratic forces among the national
minorities within the state. Up to the present it has proved
to be far superior to all fascist tendencies. The Communists,
who during the early years of the Czechoslovak Republic
vehemently opposed the idea of social compromise upon
which the new state was based, have also drawn closer to the
government coalition recently for the purpose of defeating
the fascist danger. The success of Czechoslovak democracy
is chiefly due to the circumstance that it has transplanted old-
fashioned but still vital political ideas into the present: a class
alliance in the spirit of the social democracy of 1848 could

be victorious because it was capable of satisfying the demands of modern power politics and public economic regulation.

From 1918 to 1934 the socialist municipality of Vienna was another island of social democracy in central Europe. However, isolated and dependent on its own modest forces, as it was, it succumbed to the superior power of the fascists and capitalists in 1934. Yet the outstanding accomplishments of the socialist community of Vienna in the fields of social welfare, cultural elevation of the masses, and planned communal economy show what democracy, based upon the masses, can achieve — even when it is confined within the boundaries of an anti-democratic petty state.

Since Hitler's seizure of power in 1933, the great defeats of liberal democracy initiated an important realignment of the toiling masses in Europe. The great majority of the workers recognize that outmoded political methods are useless and they seek new ones. This change is already most evident in the field of international politics and in the question of war. During the first period of its existence, while Russia and America kept aloof, the League of Nations had been chiefly an organ of the European powers who had been victorious in the World War. This situation changed during recent years, with Soviet Russia's entry into the League, while Japan, Italy, and Germany assumed attitudes of increasing opposition to the League. In 1935, when the League of Nations replied to Italy's attack upon Abyssinia with economic sanctions, it actually became the organ of an international democratic policy for a short while. Now the bourgeois democratic countries, such as England and its dominions, Czechoslovakia, and Scandinavia, and the state-capitalistic dictatorships in Russia and Turkey controlled the League of Nations. The pressure of the Left parties forced France to support the League policy, although in a very vacillating manner. Thus in 1935 the bourgeois and socialist democrats together with the state-capitalistic countries faced the fascist powers and their followers in the international arena. To be sure, the League was able to offer the Abyssinians but very little positive assistance in their struggle against Italy. Nevertheless the events of 1935 are historically significant as the first sign of serious international democratic solidarity since 1849.

The question of sanctions against Italy represented a turning-point for the parties of the socialist International. Should the policy of abstract pacifism and absolute non-violence be continued, or should one recognize that peace must be organized by means of concrete instruments? Only if the allied friends of peace can muster enough physical force to outmatch any possible combination of the peace-disturbers will peace actually be secured. The majority of the European socialist workers supported the sanctions policy of the League of Nations, no matter what the consequences might be. With that the most dangerous dogma of the older liberal democracy, the doctrine of absolute pacifism, was actually overcome. This important change in socialist foreign policy is paralleled by a corresponding re-education in internal political questions. The socialist parties begin to unite with the Communists and the still existent bourgeois democratic groups to form popular fronts. They endeavour to view problems, not only from the point of view of a particular trade, but rather on a national scale. They recognize the necessity of meeting fascist violence with force and of opposing modern monopoly capitalism with a planned economy in the interest of the labouring people.

The chief cause for the failure of the League's action against Italy was the reluctance of the English government to go to war with Italy because of Abyssinia. It is evident that the English Conservative Party is socially heterogeneous. On the one hand hundreds of thousands of industrial workers vote for the Conservatives and they are represented by a strong Tory-democratic absolutely anti-fascist wing of the party; on the other side, however, are the great English capitalists, who cannot see why they should sacrifice their wealth and their lives on the side of the workers in a world struggle between fascism and social democracy. The result is that the English government party follows a middle-of-the-road course and endeavours to remain neutral in the international struggle between the fascists and the anti-fascists. In recent years the foreign policy of the English government has been sharply assailed by the Labour Party. This too is a fact of great historical significance, for it is the first time that a socialist mass party in a major power pursues an independent active foreign policy which is not formally pacifistic. In the World War the socialists had no independent policy when they voted for war credits and supported a truce, but obediently followed the slogans of the government and public opinion. In recent years, however, the English Labour Party strongly opposed the tactics of the government and demanded active resistance to all fascist dictators, despite any consequences which might result. The great majority of English workers were also ready to approve England's rearmament, since a future British Labour government could not face the fascists in an unarmed state. Twice already the English Labour Party had formed shortlived minority governments. It is now preparing to transform the English Constitution, economy, and foreign policy in accordance with its ideas, in case it receives a majority in the lower house. A fascist party has also appeared in England recently; it is numerically weak, although several influential groups among the ultra-conservative bourgeoisie are in sympathy with it. Hitherto, however, the forces of the labour movement and of Tory democracy have shown themselves to be superior to fascism.

While the English Labour Party is developing a modern realistic policy, the French labour movement is still retarded by the paralysing traditions of the past. At first Blum's Popular Front government, composed of Socialists, Communists, and petty-bourgeois Radicals, was greeted with

great hopes, but it soon became evident that it only continued the tradition of the older Left-bloc governments. The
Popular Front government introduced very estimable social
and economic reforms, but it was unable to effect any changes
in basic constitutional questions (Senate), in the army, and
in the administrative apparatus, and despite its support of the
League of Nations, the foreign policy of the Popular Front
remained formally pacifistic. Thus Blum's government rapidly lost its prestige at home and abroad and was defeated
in its first serious conflict with the Senate. The resignation
of Prime Minister Blum was followed by the usual French
transitional government.

Spain has also been the scene of a Popular Front government in recent years. Here, however, great international
rivalries are so peculiarly intermingled with the local conflicts of Spanish society that even a brief sketch of Spanish
developments during the past decade would greatly exceed
the limits of this book. Attention may, however, be called
to one fact — the appearance of the International Brigade,
which saved Madrid from the attack of the Fascists, thus giving the Spanish Popular Front government time to organize
its own army. That thousands of men from all parts of Europe and America rushed to Spain as volunteers to sacrifice
their lives for democracy in its struggle against fascism was
a completely new phenomenon, which had no longer been
conceivable since the generation of 1848.

Since the World War, Belgium has general suffrage. Yet
the Belgian Socialist Labour Party was unable to assume
power alone, nor did it form a popular front, but recently it
entered into a coalition with the capitalistic Liberals and
with those Catholic Conservatives who still believe in parliamentary methods. It is clear that a coalition of this type
can only defend the status quo, but cannot carry out any
basic political or social reforms. As a result Belgium, a
country of workers, has a strong and active fascist movement,
which not only has determined the country's foreign policy,

but has also obtained threatening successes at home. Holland likewise has general suffrage since the World War, but the structure of the state has remained unchanged.

In the United States the great economic crisis shook the faith of the masses in the unhampered activity of private industry as advocated by large-scale capitalism. Ideas of social democracy were rife among the majority of the nation. The movement was headed by President Roosevelt, who was first elected in 1932 and then re-elected by an overwhelming majority in 1936. Roosevelt's New Deal belongs completely to the ideological sphere of social democracy. To be sure, the President wants to retain private property, but at the same time to curb the influence of monopoly capitalism in the interest of the urban and rural toilers, to elevate the workers' and farmers' standard of living by means of a comprehensive planned public economy, and to safeguard them against crises. Simultaneously, President Roosevelt enlarged America's army and navy, opposed the isolation of the United States, and advocated an active international policy to safeguard peace. The process of development in the United States is still in full swing, as the trade-union organizations and their struggles indicate. The opponents of the New Deal are to some extent still powerful in the judiciary and in local administrations. The President is supported by the majority of the Democratic Party. But he also has important Democratic foes and many friends in the Republican camp. In recent years new parties, intended to present more timely solutions of current social problems, were frequently formed in the United States. Most important among these experiments is the young American Labour Party which received almost half a million votes in the New York municipal elections of November 1937 and was an important factor in the election of Mayor La Guardia.

Within the British Empire a strong government, influenced by ideas of social democracy, exists in the Irish Free State, where President De Valera established his power on a coalition of petty farmers and workers and energetically suppressed all fascist tendencies. On the other side of the earth, New Zealand has a successful labour government, which gained the confidence of the farmers and considerably improved the standard of living of the population by means of planned economic measures. In Australia the Labour Party is fighting a bourgeois capitalist party for power, whereby a farmers' party is the decisive factor at present. In the federal Parliament this agrarian party co-operates with the bourgeoisie, while in Victoria it is allied with the workers. Several Australian states are governed by the Labour Party, and the high standard of living, the political and trade-union liberties of the Australian working people appear very secure. In India the National Congress Party, which contains important social-democratic elements, obtained power in most of the provinces as a result of the new Constitution. In South Africa, however, a small white upper class rules the labouring masses of the Negro population, who have no civil rights. The conditions in Canada are very complicated. Here the differences between the industrial capitalists and the workers, and between the financial capitalists and the farmers, have grown more acute. The old historical Liberal and Conservative parties are disintegrating, but as yet no new national parties have taken their place. At the moment groups in sympathy with fascism have appeared in the east and a radical anti-capitalistic farmer movement has arisen in the west. Yet these groupings cannot be regarded as definitive. The ultimate political and constitutional position of the Jewish working class in Palestine is also in doubt.

The Chinese National Revolutionary Party, the Kuomintang, as originally founded by Sun Yat-sen, had been a genuine social-democratic movement. During the last decade, however, the military dictatorship of General Chiang Kai-shek repressed the popular forces and the working class of China. The outbreak of the Sino-Japanese War in 1937 liberated the masses from this oppression and opened a new period in the history of democracy in eastern Asia. In Japan the elements of the various revolutionary, democratic, and socialist movements are also present and wait only for a suitable opportunity.

Mexico at present has a kind of workers' and peasants' government. Despite the cultural backwardness of the country, the social revolution in Mexico has liberated stupendous energies since the World War. The party which governs Mexico follows the tradition of Juárez in attempting to maintain the country's independence and to build a new social order, with division of the large estates and state regulation of industry.

The state-capitalistic dictatorship of Turkey is likewise the product of a social upheaval, which at the end of the World War under the leadership of Mustafa Kemal swept aside the historical Turkish ruling class. Mustafa Kemal is the only contemporary dictator who employed all his force to clear away the refuse of a thousand years of political, economic, and intellectual oppression which had burdened the Turkish peasants until then. Thus this dictatorship not only meant a technical advance over previous periods, but at the same time, an extraordinary elevation of the power of judgment, education, and social position of the masses.

It is worthy of note that at the present social democracy and the labour movement are particularly strong in countries which lacked an important socialist and Marxist tradition during the period of the Second International, such as England and Ireland, the United States, Australia, New Zealand, and Mexico. Marx himself would not feel very distressed over this circumstance, for he always considered a vital, advancing movement much more important, even though it did not cite him, than a nonentity which clung to his coat-tails.

5. General Critique of Democracy

Historically, democracy does not exist as a thing in itself, as a formal abstraction. On the contrary, democracy is always a definite political movement, borne by definite social forces and classes, fighting for particular aims. A democratic state is therefore a state in which the democratic movement rules. Democracy as a political movement is divided first of all into socialist and bourgeois democracy. Socialist democracy wants self-government by the masses, whereby the socially important means of production should be owned by the community. The socialist parties of the nineteenth and twentieth centuries are representatives of a movement of this kind. Nevertheless up to the present socialist democracy has not been capable of obtaining power in any state.

Bourgeois democracy likewise strives for self-government by the masses, while maintaining the principle of private property. In contrast to socialist democracy, bourgeois democracy has obtained power in a number of states in modern times. In itself bourgeois democracy is not uniform, but appears historically in four different forms. On the one hand we find social democracy. This movement also wants to maintain the principle of private property, but it endeavours to establish the political rule of the toiling masses, in a struggle against the feudal and the capitalistic upper class. Countries in which social democracy prevailed were France at the time of Robespierre and the United States during the presidency of Jefferson. In the recent past, between 1903 and 1914 Lenin presented a classic formulation of social democracy in his theory of a democratic dictatorship of the workers and peasants.

In contrast to social — and evidently enough also to socialist — democracy, the three other forms of bourgeois democracy reject the class struggle and endeavour to adjust the differences between the wealthy upper class and the labouring masses. This compromise assumes either an imperialist

or a liberal form. Imperialist democracy wants to procure
the means which will make possible a compromise between
the employers and the workers with the aid of imperial expansion and power politics. Since the time of Disraeli,
Great Britain has been the classic country of imperialist democracy. Liberal democracy, on the other hand, wants to
safeguard the economic and cultural progress of mankind by
eliminating force and power politics, and promoting peace
and free competition, thus obtaining the basis for class compromise. In modern times liberal democracy developed pre-
eminently among the smaller nations, such as Switzerland
and Norway.

Finally, colonial democracy is the special form of bourgeois democracy in the transoceanic countries where the
white immigrants find either immense unoccupied or only
thinly populated areas for colonization. In these countries a
class compromise is made possible by the presence of free
land. The United States until approximately 1890, and
Canada until the World War, are examples of colonial democracy.

The degree of variation in the democratic movement of
modern times is extraordinarily great. Lenin's Bolsheviki
as well as Theodore Roosevelt's Progressive Republicans
and Chamberlain's tariff-reformers belong to the history of
modern democracy. Democratic movements ruled in one
form or another in Swiss mountain cantons, in fishing villages on the Norwegian coast, and in the industrial regions
of Lancashire. This alone is enough to show the inadequacy
of any formulation of democracy as a uniform generality.
Only exact, detailed investigations of special types of democracy can advance historical and political understanding of it.

In modern times a democratic state is logically a commonwealth where one of the cited forms of modern bourgeois
democracy prevails. To judge the social content of a state
correctly, it is not enough to observe the existing written or
traditional constitution; the important thing is to determine

the manner in which the institutions of the state actually function, the relations of the various classes to each other, and the actual rulers of the state at any given moment. Aristotle presented the classic example of such an investigation of the state. He is never satisfied with simply declaring that a state is an oligarchy or a republic, but in every single case he analyses the actual social conditions in great detail and seeks the real wielders of power.

The mediæval feudal state was a clear unequivocal type, just as a socialist state would also be a definite form. In addition to the other manifestations of the bourgeois state, the decisive, important, basic fact of bourgeois private property is common to modern democratic states. Therefore within states based upon the same fundamental economic fact it is not very easy to determine the exact point where democracy ceases and oligarchy begins. Modern social evolution has produced such complicated transitional conditions and compromise products that any unequivocal judgment is not always immediately apparent. Social forces change incessantly even though the constitutions remain static. Thus, except for a few changes, the Constitution of the United States is still the same as in the days of Washington, and yet what immense changes have occurred in American society and consequently also in the real American constitution since then!

It is relatively simple to ascertain the states in which social democracy prevails. Robespierre's guillotine and Jefferson's economic measures against finance capital are definite enough. In the case of the three other types of bourgeois democracy, all of which rest upon or aim at a compromise between capital and labour, between rich and poor, the problem is much more difficult. What is the common factor underlying all three types, as well as social democracy, which differentiates them from the usual type of bourgeois parliamentary state? A tentative definition, based only upon the empirical conclusions derived from a study of historical development, would have the following approximate form:

Even in the bourgeois-democratic state capitalistic private property occupies a decisive economic position. Yet the capitalists conclude a compromise with the workers, and this compromise is maintained voluntarily by both parties, as a result of their conception of economic needs. Apart from their free will and opinion of economic needs, no decisive physical force is present which compels the masses to enter into the compromise. For if the capitalistic upper class brings the factor of an overwhelming military and police force into such a compromise, it is no longer a compromise. The preponderance of the upper class is then so powerful that the toiling masses can hardly hope to become an equal partner.

It is certainly not a coincidence that those countries that were able to develop stable forms of bourgeois democracy in modern times, such as the United States, Great Britain and its dominions, Switzerland, and Norway, all conform in certain points. Before 1914 all of them had only small standing armies in times of peace, as well as highly developed, decentralized forms of self-government. If the United States during the generation prior to the World War is compared with France during the same period, both republics exhibit a mixture of democratic and anti-democratic elements. If corruption in individual American cities and the events during some strikes in the United States are considered, the anti-democratic forces appear predominant. Nevertheless during this period the situation in the United States was very different from that in France. Corrupt professional politicians could obtain power in an American city only because the majority of the inhabitants were indifferent to public affairs. Yet as soon as the corruption and maladministration grew unbearable, the mass of workers, business men, and others organized. A reform movement developed. At the next election the corrupt politicans were swept away, and the city or state was cleansed of corruption. This continued until the energy of the citizens again subsided and the professional politicians dared to reappear. At any rate in America no one can resist the serious will of the majority of the citizens when they unite and attack their foes. The small army of the federal government plays no part in the situation.

On the other hand in France until 1914 the standing army was always the unknown quantity in every struggle for political power. All the crises of the Third Republic from its establishment until the World War are connected with the army: the MacMahon crisis, the Boulanger affair, the Dreyfus case, and finally the fight over the three-year period of military service. The maintenance of a strong standing army was a necessity for France, in view of her strong militaristic German neighbour. The United States, on the other hand, was in a more fortunate position, since it had no serious military opponent on its own continent. The different military and political situations of the United States and France necessarily produced a varying alignment of the social forces in the respective countries. There was also the additional difference between the loose federal system of government in the United States and the historical, traditional rigid centralization of the French state. Before 1914 American capitalism had already attained a much greater degree of concentration and was certainly much stronger than French capitalism. Yet outside of the economic sphere, in a narrow sense, French capitalism had allies which the American capitalists lacked. For this reason, despite the many negative individual characteristics of American public life, bourgeois democracy in the United States was always more firmly and securely established than in France.

Thus a certain elective affinity is evident between democracy and that type of political organization which can be characterized as " communal." During brief periods of open warfare or civil war a democratic movement also needs a strongly centralized power, like that of 1793, in order to triumph. Nevertheless, according to previous historical experience, a democratic commonwealth can achieve a stable existence for a longer period only if local self-government predominates. Considerable practical difficulties result, however, if the democratic principle of local autonomy must be combined on a large scale with the necessities of a great modern state and modern unified economic organization. Yet the development of the British Empire and the United States proves that these difficulties are not insurmountable.

Another much discussed question is the relation of democracy to so-called legality. Is democracy, as such, a form of political organization which more than any other guarantees peaceful evolution? Is it permissible to speak of a democratic method, where the ballot decides, in contrast to a method of political force? Here, too, the democratic state must be differentiated from the democratic movement. Every state, no matter what sort of constitution it possesses, asserts its own legality. It demands that its laws be respected by all the inhabitants, and it pursues as a traitor anyone who wants to change the laws forcibly. This is as true of a democratic state as of any other. An absolute monarchy or a capitalistic oligarchy can maintain orderly legality for just as long a period as a democracy. For a hundred and fifty years, from its establishment to the Revolution of 1848, the absolute Kingdom of Prussia, for instance, enjoyed a completely undisturbed, peaceful, and legal internal political development. Necessary reforms were carried out by the absolute monarch in the form of new laws. Similarly from 1688 to 1867 England experienced a period of completely undisturbed legal development under the rule of a capitalistic minority. Thus in the sphere of legality the democratic state can by no means raise any claim to pre-eminence over any other forms of political organization. The same is true with respect to the decision of controversial questions by the ballot and the will of the majority and not by force. It is as true of a democracy as of any other state having a representative ruling body. For centuries before it became a bourgeois democracy England had been ruled peacefully by the majority decisions of the upper and lower houses. Similarly Sweden enjoyed four centuries of peaceful development, thanks to the rule of a feudal Diet, which then evolved organically into a modern parliament. However, the opponents of an established political organization will always be inclined to doubt the legality of the existing state. If the state is attacked by force, it will also be compelled to defend itself by means of force: This holds true for a democratic state as well as for any other, and in this respect democracy occupies no special position.

The democratic movement, just like any other political tendency, has employed the most diverse means to realize its aims. The history of French democracy from 1789 to 1871 is literally written in blood. The American democrats conducted the greatest civil war of all times in order to maintain their form of political organization. Up to 1847 the Swiss democrats triumphed by the ruthless use of force in the cantons as well as in the entire confederation. Norwegian democracy owes its existence to the Revolution of 1905, which was able to take place without any bloodshed, but which nevertheless represented a complete break with constitutional legality. Finally, in Great Britain from 1912 to 1914 the Ulster Protestants were steadfastly resolved not to submit to a parliamentary decision which appeared intolerable to them, and they prepared to oppose the Irish Home Rule Bill with armed force. The workers, farmers, and business men of Ulster who united under Carson's leadership at that time, were proud of British democratic traditions. Nevertheless they knew of no other expedient than recourse to armed force, and half the English nation sympathized with them. Thus history proves that democracy, just like any other political movement, has employed either violent or non-violent methods, depending on conditions in a specific country at a particular time. The misinterpretation of democracy as the embodiment of non-violence only arose during recent times because democracy as a whole was confused with a special type of democracy, the liberal democracy of the last century.

It is impossible for the historical observer to speak of a catastrophe of "democracy" as such, because "democracy as such" does not exist. Only a particular form of democracy, which was weak from the beginning and which has been characterized as liberal democracy in this book, has collapsed. In order to avoid any misunderstanding, it should be emphasized again that this does not reflect upon the general estimate of the liberal idea. In so far as the latter—separated from any special party politics—expresses the right of the individual to develop freely, it belongs to the most valuable possessions of human culture. We are dealing rather with a very definite and circumscribed form of bourgeois democracy, which hoped to solve all the conflicts of the period by means of peace, free competition, free trade, and parliamentary legality. This specific form of democracy has finally collapsed. The history of the past hundred and fifty years has shown, however, that the decline of a democratic tendency is always followed by the revival of other forms of popular self-government. There is no cause for the assumption that it will be different in the future. In all countries the labouring masses—that is, the great majority of mankind—will gradually be compelled to recognize that their own self-government is a necessary prerequisite in order to achieve a worthy level of existence. It is only necessary to compare the condition of the urban and rural workers, for instance, in Switzerland and Australia with conditions in Italy and Poland to recognize the real value of democracy.

Finally our historical investigation had shown that not a single one of the democratic commonwealths already in existence prior to 1914 has succumbed during the present crisis.

Wherever democratic self-government has not been decreed mechanically by proclaiming a republic or general suffrage, but has developed historically out of the life of the working people, it exhibits a remarkable power of resistance. In modern times no real democracy has yet perished.

NOTES

〜

The following notes are in addition to the citations made in the text of the book itself and to the authors mentioned in the preface. No notes have been made on the known facts of modern political history. If the reader wants more details and a special bibliography of them, he will find them in the volumes of the *Cambridge Modern History* and in the corresponding articles of the *Encyclopædia of the Social Sciences* and the *Encyclopædia Britannica*.

There is a good bibliography on Marx and Marxism for English readers in G. D. H. Cole's *What Marx Really Meant* (New York: Alfred A. Knopf; 1934), pp. 305 ff. Another detailed bibliography is in the article " Marx " by Karl Korsch in the *Encyclopædia of the Social Sciences;* a shorter bibliography in Otto Rühle: *Karl Marx* (New York: Viking Press; 1935).

ABBREVIATIONS:

ME I–IV = Marx-Engels: *Gesamtausgabe, 3. Abteilung, Briefwechsel zwischen Marx und Engels,* Vols. I–IV.
ME VI = *Gesamtausgabe, 1. Abteilung,* Vol. VI.
Kugelmann = Karl Marx, *Briefe an Kugelmann* (Berlin, 1924).

〜

WHAT IS DEMOCRACY?

p. 3. Babeuf's letter: Mathiez: *Autour de Robespierre* (Paris, 1925), p. 256.
p. 4. Article of Engels: *ME VI,* p. 289.
p. 6. Philipp Stein: *Fürst Bismarck's Reden,* I, p. 129.
p. 7. Engels: *Politisches Vermächtnis* (Berlin, 1920), p. 18.

ROBESPIERRE AND JEFFERSON

pp. 10 ff. A. Mathiez: *La Révolution française,* Vols. I–III (Paris, 1932–3). — A. Mathiez: *Autour de Robespierre* (Paris, 1925). — Charles Beard: *Economic Origins of Jeffersonian Democracy* (New York: The Macmillan Company; 1915).

FROM NAPOLEON I TO LOUIS PHILIPPE

pp. 24 ff. France under Louis Philippe: *ME VI.*
p. 30. Article by Engels: *ME IV,* p. 348.
p. 31. On Blanqui see Kautsky: *Krieg und Demokratie,* I (Berlin, 1932), p. 326.

EARLY SOCIALISM

pp. 33 ff. *ME VI* and the remarkable book: *Geschichte des religiösen und atheistischen Frühsozialismus, nach der Darstellung August Beckers vom Jahre 1847* (Kiel: E. Barnikol; 1932). — L. Blanc: *Organisation du travail* (many editions).
p. 39. Letter of Engels: *ME I,* p. 42.

SOCIAL OR BOURGEOIS DEMOCRACY?

pp. 41 ff. *ME VI.*

THE ENGLISH CHARTISTS

pp. 48 ff. *ME VI.*
p. 52. Harney's speech: *ME VI,* p. 582.

MARX AND ENGELS ON THE EVE OF THE REVOLUTION OF 1848

pp. 58 ff. *ME VI.*

FRANCE, 1848

pp. 76 ff. Charles Seignobos in Lavisse: *Histoire de France contemporaine,* Vol. VI. — Lamartine: *Histoire de la Révolu-*

tion de 1848 (Brussels, 1849). — Émile Thomas: *Histoire des ateliers nationaux* (new edition, Oxford, 1913), a very important source.

THE DEFEAT OF THE REVOLUTION IN CENTRAL EUROPE, 1848-9

pp. 105 ff. *ME I.* L. Bergsträsser: *Geschichte der politischen Partein in Deutschland* (Mannheim, 1926), pp. 34 ff. — F. Sigel: *Denkwürdigkeiten* (Mannheim: W. Blos; 1902). — J. Mazzini: *Essays,* edited by Bolton King (London).

WHY DID DEMOCRACY FAIL IN 1848-9?

p. 125. Miss Goldsmith's picture is reproduced as the frontispiece of Lavisse, Vol. VI.

p. 125. Proclamation of the provisional government: Lamartine: *Histoire de la Révolution de 1848,* p. 396.

STRUGGLES AMONG THE ÉMIGRÉS 1848-59

pp. 133 ff. *ME I, II.*

THE BEGINNINGS OF SOCIAL DEMOCRACY

pp. 145 ff. France under Napoleon III: Seignobos in Lavisse, Vols. VI and VII. *ME III.*

THE FOUNDING OF THE FIRST INTERNATIONAL

pp. 170 ff. *ME III.* — *Kugelmann,* pp. 15 ff., 19, 21, 50, 62 ff.

NAPOLEON'S COLLAPSE

pp. 176 ff. *ME IV.* — Seignobos in Lavisse, Vol. VII. — *Kugelmann,* pp. 55, 77 ff.

THE PARIS COMMUNE AND THE END OF THE FIRST INTERNATIONAL

pp. 185 ff. *ME IV.* — Seignobos in Lavisse, Vol. VII. — *Kugelmann,* pp. 81 ff., 91, 93.

BOURGEOIS DEMOCRACY IN AMERICA, ENG-LAND, AND SWITZERLAND

pp. 208 ff. America: *ME IV*, p. 725 (Index). *Kugelmann,*
pp. 21, 93. — England: *ME IV*, p. 731. *Kugelmann,* pp.
58 ff., 69 ff., 93. — Switzerland: *ME IV*, p. 743.

SOCIALISTS AND ANARCHISTS AFTER 1871

pp. 222 ff. *ME IV*. — M. Nettlau: *Anarchisten und Sozialrevo-lutionäre* (Berlin, 1931), very important from the anarchist point of view.

REACTION IN EUROPE AFTER 1871

pp. 225 ff. *ME IV* (Russia after 1871). — H. Wendel: *Aus dem südslarwischen Risorgimento* (Gotha, 1921) (Balkans).

FRANCE AFTER THE COMMUNE, AND BOULANGER

pp. 240 ff. Seignobos in Lavisse, Vols. VII and VIII. – *ME IV*.

IMPERIALISM VERSUS LIBERALISM

pp. 262 ff. Lenin's famous book *Der Imperialismus als jüngste Etappe des Kaptalismus* was written in 1915 (German edition: Hamburg, 1921). — An important document of the Liberal fight against Imperialism is Eugen Richter: *Politisches A B C-Buch* (Berlin, 1896).

LIBERAL DEMOCRACY AND THE SECOND INTERNATIONAL

pp. 287 ff. The best history of the Second International from the Socialist point of view is K. Renner: *Karl Kautsky. Skizze zur Geschichte der geistigen und politischen Entwicklung der deutschen Arbeiterklasse* (Berlin, 1929). From the Bolshevist point of view: Zinoviev: *Der Krieg und die Krise des Sozialismus* (Vienna, 1924).

p. 289. Program of the People's Party: E. Richter: *A B C-Buch*, p. 445.

pp. 298 ff. Letters of Engels: *Politischen Vermächtnis*, pp. 15 ff.

FROM 1895 TO THE PRESENT

pp. 324 ff. Mussolini's article: M. G. Sarfatti: *Mussolini, Lebensgeschichte* (Leipzig, 1926), pp. 157 ff.

pp. 330 ff. Lenin's theory: A. Rosenberg: *History of Bolshevism* (Oxford University Press, 1934), pp. 20 ff. — Discussion on Democracy: Lenin: *Die Diktatur des Proletariats und der Renegat K. Kautsky* (Leipzig, 1919). — Trotsky: *Terrorismus und Kommunismus. Anti-Kautsky* (Hamburg, 1920). — Kautsky: *Krieg und Demokratie* (Berlin, 1932), and the above mentioned book by M. G. Sarfatti.

INDEX

i

DATE DUE

OCT 16 75			